Richard Chandler Alexander Prior

Ancient Danish Ballads

Volume I

Richard Chandler Alexander Prior

Ancient Danish Ballads
Volume I

ISBN/EAN: 9783744770071

Printed in Europe, USA, Canada, Australia, Japan

Cover: Foto ©Thomas Meinert / pixelio.de

More available books at **www.hansebooks.com**

ANCIENT DANISH BALLADS

TRANSLATED

FROM THE ORIGINALS

BY

R. C. ALEXANDER PRIOR M.D.

VOL. I.

WILLIAMS AND NORGATE
14, HENRIETTA STREET, COVENT GARDEN, LONDON;
AND
20, SOUTH FREDERICK STREET, EDINBURGH.
1860.

INTRODUCTION.

The fine ancient ballads of which a translation is here offered to the public, have hitherto been very little known in this country from the language being that of a small state, and one which few are at the trouble of studying. How much they deserve attention, may perhaps be conjectured by those who will be at the pains to look through these volumes; for to reproduce them exactly in another language is impossible. Translation of poetry is usually a very thankless task, nor can I flatter myself with having brought out the various scenes and figures pictured with such truthful colouring in the originals, more successfully than those who have attempted the same from other languages; yet as ballads are extremely simple in their construction, and free from idiomatical expressions, I have ventured to make this effort with the hope of at least drawing attention to some of the finest of their kind, and the most ancient, that any country possesses. Several of them were translated by Robert Jamieson for the "Northern Antiquities" Edinbro' 1814, but the language that he used, an extremely broad form of Scotch, has scarcely made them better known to the English reader. A few others have appeared in the sixth volume of the Foreign Quarterly Review, and several in the Howitt's "Literature of Northern Europe." There are two or three of them paraphrased from a German translation by M. G. Lewis in his "Tales of Wonder." Others by Jamieson are to be found among his "Popular Ballads," and two of them in the notes to Scott's Lady of the Lake. There were also twelve of them published by Geo. Borrow in 1826 in a work entitled "Romantic Ballads," now become very scarce.

These were all made from the editions of Vedel, and Syv, or from the Danske Viser published by Nyerup, Abrahamson, and Rahbek, which the careful researches of the younger Grundtvig, the son of the well known Revd. N. S. Grundtvig, have shown to be very much and very materially altered by their respective editors from the ancient originals.

Vedel published his book in 1591, and seems to have had no idea of the antiquarian interest attached to the songs of his country, but to have collected them, as he repeatedly says, for the innocent entertainment of his readers. All honour be due to him as the first in the North of Europe, who formed such a collection, and to Sophia, queen of Frederick II, at whose desire he printed them.

This Queen, as the story goes, was on a visit to the great astronomer, Tycho Brahe, and detained some days at his house by continued wet weather. To entertain her he introduced to her his friend and neighbour, the Pastor Vedel, who read her some ballads of his collection, with which her Majesty was so delighted, that she laid on him her express command to publish them. The present editor, Svend Grundtvig, has been fortunate enough in most cases to discover contemporary or more ancient manuscript copies of the same ballads, and in many to recognize Vedel's corrections of them in his own hand-writing. The great fault that pervades Vedel's edition is his desire to introduce something extravagant in place of the natural; so that where one ancient copy gave any thing more egregiously preposterous than another, that was the reading he was sure to adopt in his text. He seems to have considered too much what would please the peasantry, the order of people for whom he made his collection.

But injudicious as his alterations often were, we owe a deep obligation to the venerable pastor for having rescued from oblivion these very characteristic ancient pieces, that have not only given his readers the innocent entertainment he intended them, but been a fountain of fine poetry to Danish writers of succeeding generations. For what Percy's Reliques effected in this country, its ballad literature has done in at least an equal degree for Denmark.

Svend Grundtvig is publishing his new edition of them under commission from his government, and in the two first volumes, and the part of the third, which have already appeared, has given more correct copies of those which Vedel printed, and introduced a considerable number, that were previously quite unknown to the public, and in most cases many different readings of them. His several introductions to these ballads display a depth of research, that perhaps has never before been devoted to any edition of popular poems. But while the accomplished editor shows a most intimate acquaintance with the ancient literature, history, and mythology of the northern nations, and of England, he scarcely, I think, gives their due importance to the beautiful romances of the South, those namely of Spain and Portugal, the Italian novels, and the lays and fabliaux of the French trouveres, which embody so much of the floating fiction of the Middle ages, and which are shown in this work to be so closely connected with the Danish, and our northern ballads generally.

In 1695, a hundred and four years after Vedel's publication, P. Syv reprinted his work, and added a hundred ballads to it, that had never been published before. There have since that time been several other collections made, but these, as the best of them are incorporated into the 'Danske Viser' of Nyerup, Abrahamson and Rahbek, need not be more especially noticed. From this last work, the 'Danske Viser', are translated all such as will be found here, but not in Grundtvig's book.

To those who would study the valuable literary works which Denmark has produced during the last fifty years, a knowledge of these ballads is essential. Ingemann in his romances, and Oehlenschläger in his tragedies, have based their fables upon them, and some of the finest of the shorter poems of other authors make allusions to the superstitions and traditions embodied in them. Denmark has escaped the insipid epoch of classical mythology, and, trusting to these, her own resources, has produced a native literature, which, were the political power of the country greater, would be studied and admired by all who have any taste for true poetry.

These ballads were for many ages the ordinary dance-tunes in Denmark, as very similar ones are in the Faroe islands to this day. Lyngbye in the preface to his edition of the "Færoiske Quæder" says of these islanders what was once equally applicable to the Danes and all the other Scandinavians. And here it may be as well to remark, in passing, that under the term *Scandinavian* are included the people of Denmark, Sweden, Norway, Iceland, and the Faroe and Shetland Isles. Their languages are all derived from an ancient Norse, which is still preserved nearly pure in the Icelandic; and their religion, laws, and manners seem to have been very much alike; nearly related to the German, but essentially national. It is convenient therefore to have a common term to comprehend them all.

"Their greatest amusement is dancing. Old and young take part in it: their sedentary work and the damp weather make it in some degree necessary. From Christmas till Shrovetide is the proper dancing season, but beside this they dance also on holidays and all occasions of festivity. They use no instrumental music, but dance to songs. It is now the one and now the other, who leads the song, and all who can sing join in it, at least in the refrain. The dance consists in this, that the men and women mutually hold each other's hands, and make three steps forward or to the side, keeping time, and then balance a little, or remain standing still a moment. If there is any one who does not observe this, he disturbs the whole dance. The object of the song is not only like dance-music to regulate the steps, but at the same time to awaken certain feelings by its meaning. One may see by the dancers' behaviour that they are not indifferent to the matter of the song, but with their countenances and gestures take pains to express the various meaning of it. This gives the dance, notwithstanding its uniformity, so much interest, that both young and old remain the whole evening in place with scarcely any cessation. These songs in the Faroe dialect are so numerous, that the same is seldom sung a second time the same winter. Most of them are pretty long, yet are never written down, but retained in the memory."

The Spanish ballads, with which we shall see in these volumes so many unexpected points of resemblance, seem to have been used in the same manner for dance tunes. Thus in Cervantes's tale of La Gitanella in his Novelas exemplares Vol. I. p. 4 (Madrid 1784) occur the expressions 'quando la oyeron cantar, *por ser la danza cantada*.' when they heard her sing, as the dance was sung;' and again p. 13, 'Mas de doscientas personas estaban *mirando el baile y escuchando el canto* de las gitanas.' 'More than two hundred persons were watching the dance, and listening to the song of the gipsies.' Our own word *ballad* would imply a similar usage.

Such then having been the purpose for which they were originally intended, it is almost as unfair to the merits of the following compositions to give them divested of their natural accompaniments of music and dancing, as on the other hand it would be to give the music and the dances without the songs of whose meaning they are the expression. But I trust that, defective as they are in this respect, they yet have very strong claims upon our attention as pictures of medieval life. The tales they relate were most of them common to all the Western nations, but in each country were told in a way to convey the most curious information respecting the manners and customs of that to which they belonged.

The actions that they detail are in general purely imaginary, and even in the historical ballads are seldom strictly true. But what they convey to us with the greatest accuracy, and in colours most faithful to nature, are the feelings with which the doings of the great were regarded by the people at large, the feelings of an order of society, which historians busied with the affairs of courts and armies and ecclesiastical foundations, seldom condescended to notice. As mere tales I fear they may some of them appear childish, and disappoint the general reader. As pictures of society, not Danish only, but West European, during the 14th and 15th centuries, I am sanguine that they will all of them have great interest for the antiquarian. But even as compositions they are generally very beautiful and of great artistic merit. The careless ease and simplicity of the ballad is apt to deceive us into the belief that it is the unpremeditated spontaneous effusion of an illiterate peasantry. But the truth is, as Ticknor has very well observed in the words adopted for our motto, that "although there is nothing easier than to make a ballad, there is nothing more difficult than to make it what it ought to be." Excellence in ballad writing is the result not merely of genius but of much cultivation, and there cannot be a greater mistake than to suppose, from ballads being now sung about the streets by a set of vagabonds and low people, that these ancient ones too were intended for that class, and originated with it. Far from this,

> What to the kitchen now is bann'd,
> And alehouses and stalls,
> Was once with pleasure read and heard
> By dames in princely halls.*

Like tunes that become popular, they may descend to the vulgar, but they evince a high poetical tone of feeling that never could have arisen from that class. They date from a time when there was much uniformity of character, when the ranks of society had not developed and separated themselves, nor adopted that difference of language that is observable where there is a very highly refined upper class, and a low proletariat; a time when a whole nation sang as one man; and when the harper, who charmed the nobleman on the dais, was heard, and equally enjoyed and applauded by the humblest retainers who sat below, and the tastes of all were incessantly cultivated for a peculiar style of composition, the mediæval romance, that for a time was equally the favourite over all the North and West of Europe. The lays that were approved were sure to be carried by the wandering minstrel to other halls and other districts, and from these was formed the popular ballad. The great uniformity of expressions, that frame-work of commonplaces, in which we find not only the Scandinavian, but our own and the Scotch, the German and Flemish, and in a less degree even the Spanish ballads constructed, shows how great this intercourse must have

> 'Det der nu' — says Reenberg — 'er
> Fordömt til Borgestuer,
> Er fordum bleven liist og hört
> Med Lyst af ädle Fruer.'

been. At the present day people of cultivated minds may write in imitation of these old compositions, and a Percy, a Lady Wardlaw, a Goethe or Uhland, even surpass them, but the time is gone by, when any such could arise from among the people at large.

Who were the authors of the following ones, it is now impossible to discover. They are, many of them, found in manuscripts that are three hundred years old. One thing only is pretty clear, that in great part they are the composition of ladies. The manuscripts, in which they are preserved, are almost every one of them in female hand-writing, which alone might lead us to expect that females had composed them. But it is also remarkable that wives invariably give their husbands the best possible advice, and that men, who are pictured as fine characters, follow their advice. Now as gallantry towards the fair was not a prominent characteristic of the Danes or any other Scandinavians in former times, we cannot suppose that any thing so flattering to them was composed by men, but feel justified in admitting the conclusion to which Oehlenschläger, N. M. Peterson and other Danish critics have arrived, that we are indebted for most of them to the ladies.

There is almost as conclusive internal evidence that they are in great part also the work of persons of education and refinement. Some, it is true, like 'Swain Felding and Queen Judith,' No. 31, are very coarse, interesting as they are, considered as pictures of society; but in the touching narratives of 'Axel and Walborg,' No. 78, 'Fair Anna,' No. 148, 'The Buried Mother,' No. 35, 'Folker Lowmanson,' No. 65, 'Hillelille,' No. 94 E, 'Mar Stig's daughters,' No. 73 and in the beautiful tales of faery, 'Elfin Hill,' No. 136, 'Sir Tonne,' No. 102, and many others, there is a delicacy of feeling far remote from the tone of the vulgar, and which leads us to the same conclusion respecting the Danish, as that to which Robert Chambers has arrived respecting the Scotch ballads, that the best of them have originated with persons moving in good society, who have adopted a language and mode of expression familiar to the humble as well as the higher classes. What W. Grimm means in saying that a ballad *composes itself*, 'ein Volkslied dichtet sich selbst,' p. 546, I do not know. He probably would merely say that a tale falls naturally into certain set forms; but it is strange that a man so distinguished by his deep research should adopt such a mode of explaining things. We should wonder, if we heard as eminent a geologist account for the origin of a fossil by saying that it came of itself.

Ballads seem in most countries to have come into vogue about the same period, the fourteenth and fifteenth centuries. Many of them, as will be pointed out in the introductions to the following translations, are clearly a popular representation of an older tale, and, as Sir Walter Scott has remarked, "the farther our researches are extended, the more we shall see ground to believe that the romantic ballads of later times are, for the most part, abridgements of ancient metrical romances, narrated in a smoother stanza and more modern language." Bord. Min. III. 36.

In most parts of Europe they have been superseded by a higher class of literature, or stifled in the excitement of politics. Many, especially in the Netherlands and North-Germany, were totally lost in the general wreck of every thing during the religious and civil wars of the 16th century. In Spain the old romances, which are the counterparts of our ballads, had from mere change of fashion been thrown aside and forgotten, till the Germans began to collect them, as the Spaniards say, for their weight in gold. But in some countries, as Scandinavia and Scotland, they seem to be still almost as great favourites with the people, as ever they were, and in the distant and solitary Faroe islands, as we have seen above, they are still flourishing in all their pristine vigour.

Most persons upon first opening a volume of Danish ballads are struck with their originality. But upon comparing them with those of other countries, we shall see that the Danes shared with the rest of Western Europe in the fictions as well as other fashions of the middle ages, and have only retained more of them, because they have been more isolated and stationary.

It is remarkable that in France and Italy, where so many of these fictions originated, they seem to have never become popular with the humbler classes, but to have been in vogue for a time as a recreation for the wealthy, and then to have passed out of fashion. As far as I am aware, we have not a single ancient narrative ballad extant in French, Provençal, or Italian.

Several of the Danish are so singularly like Scotch and English ones, as to have led some very eminent writers in this country and on the continent to a theory of their origin, to which I am unable to subscribe. They have assumed the surely untenable position, that we could not have derived them from any common centre, or from each other, in modern times, and have maintained that we must therefore, both of us, the Danes and ourselves, have received them by tradition from that remote period, when we formed one nation together before the immigration of our ancestors to this island. This very startling opinion was first enounced by Robert Jamieson in his Popular Ballads Vol. II. p. 87. It has since been maintained by the great Swedish historian Geijer in the introduction to his edition of 'Svenska Folkvisor' p. XXVI and in his Samlade Skrifter Vol. III. p. 359, where he says "There is such a close agreement between many English, Scotch, and Scandinavian ballads, as cannot be explained by the similarity of national character, but must arise from the closer community of the people (från folkens närmere gemenskap) in old times." In a note he refers to Nyerup's remarks in the Danske Viser, who in Vol. V. p. 12, adopts Jamieson's opinion, and quotes his words. The editor of the Knaben Wunderhorn in the Heidelberg Jahrbuch for 1809 supports the same theory in respect of several German ballads, and endeavours to show that in the course of many successive centuries they have not lost their identity. But of more importance than all these authors' opinion is the accession of William Grimm to the same theory at page XXXI of the Preface to his fine translation of 'Altdänische Heldenlieder,' where he says —

"It is remarkable how similar they are to the English both in their depth and views of society, (Weltansicht) and in external form. Only that it seems as though the English from being collected later, were more finished, but also more diffuse (breiter).

"This agreement may be easily explained from history, inasmuch as already in the fifth century Jutes and Anglosaxons peopled England, and later in the ninth century whole hordes of Northmen went and settled there; indeed Danish kings, Canute the Great for instance, ruled over the island, so that their similar mode of living, and the intercourse of the two nations between each other scarcely need be taken into account. Herder has translated an English ballad in which riddles are proposed as in 'Hero Vonved,' (the Childe Norman of this work) and in Percy's Ancient Reliques there is recourse had to the same stratagem as in 'Ingeborg's disguise.' Both nations also have the Refrain in common, a thing that is not to be regarded as indifferent."

The same opinion is expressed by Talvj, now Mrs. Robinson, in her 'Characteristik der Volkslieder Germanischer Nationen,' p. 216, and by the Howitts in their 'Literature of Northern Europe' Vol. I. p. 244, and Lord Ellesmere, and other writers.

Landstad alone takes a view of the matter that seems agreeable to reason, namely, that ballads may have been communicated from one nation to another, and become popular in those which had a kindred feeling, in the 14th and 15th centuries. He says in his Norske Viser p. XVII.

"The comparison of these ancient songs among the different northern nations is very instructive, and shows better perhaps than any thing else, how a kindred character of mind, *det aandelige Slægtskab*, in spite of subsequent bodily separation, preserves union among races. Such comparison will present us with a lively picture of the remarkable community in culture, language, and literature among all the Northern races about the Baltic and German ocean at that period. For not only was the poetry and its forms the same every where, but one and the same ballad was adopted by the dwellers in each country, and is still found localised in these different regions."

With every feeling of deference and respect for the eminent writers who have suggested and supported the hypothesis of their extraordinary antiquity, I venture to think that it is quite visionary, and that none of our own or of the Danish ballads are older than the thirteenth century, and very few older than the fifteenth. As Robert Jamieson was the first who stated it, it will be best to transcribe his words.

"I am fully persuaded that many of the traditionary ballads, still current in our own country, have been *virûm volitantes per ora* in the north of England, and the Lowlands of Scotland, ever since the first arrival of the Cimbri in Britain. They have no doubt often changed their dress, and assumed some peculiar shades of complexion from the manners and habits of the different ages through which they have been handed down; but in their general *stamina*, and the leading features by which they are distinguished, seem not to have undergone any material alteration. This is evidently the case with the Danish ballads, particularly those in the latter part of the volume, which have been given by the editor [Syv] from popular recitation; and having passed through the same alembic with the

Scottish ballads have come out of it, of nearly the same form and quality." He says a good deal more about the Cimbrians, and the state of society among them "when they possessed themselves of a great part of England soon after the departure of the Romans."

It is not worth while to cavil about the term, *Cimbrians*. He clearly means the people whom we usually call Angles and Saxons, and these, he maintains, brought to the island many of the ballads which are still sung among our peasantry, more especially those which have their parallels in Denmark: and it is this opinion which is supported by the high authority of William Grimm, and Geijer, and others.

Before entering into the arguments against it, I cannot refrain from expressing my strong suspicion, I might almost say, my conviction, that in the collection of Peter Buchan there are some which he composed himself in imitation of Danish ones, and which of course bear the stamp of their origin. There are sufficient however to make Jamieson's opinion plausible without having recourse to Buchan's work, which, it is but justice to him to say, was published after his death. But let us consider the difficulties that lie in the way of our acceding to it.

1st. The *language* at that time spoken by the Angles and Saxons was extremely different from our modern English. Our words may, it is true, be in great part derived from their's, but they have been reduced in the number of their syllables; their inflexions have been replaced by prepositions and auxiliaries; and their syntax and arrangement altered to such a degree, that had any poem been written a thousand years ago in the rhiming metres now used in ballads, it could not possibly have passed gradually with the change of the language into a modern Scotch or English ballad.

2dly. The Anglo-Saxon poets used *neither metre, nor rhime, nor stanza.* Their verses were all alliterative. In other words, instead of being rhimed, they usually contained in every two lines three words beginning with the same letter, two in the first line and one in the second. But these lines, although they had a certain modulation and two decided accents in each, were free from the shackles of accurate *rhythm*, that fixed recurrence of accented syllables which constitutes metre. Nor were they ever arranged into either stanzas or couplets, as in all ballads of modern times, but unlimited in the number of verses required to express the poet's thought. So differently constructed is an Anglo-Saxon poem from any that moderns write, that there is scarcely any kind more difficult to translate into metrical verse. One might as easily make a ballad of an ode of Pindar, or a Greek chorus. That there were no metres used by the Anglo-Saxons at the time when they settled in England we have the authority of Bede, who in defining rhythm says, "It is a modulated composition of words, not according to the laws of metre, but adapted in the number of its syllables to the judgement of the ear, *as are the verses of our vulgar* (native) *poets.* Rhythm may exist without metre, but there cannot be metre without rhythm. Metre is an artificial rule with modulation; rhythm is the modulation without the rule. Yet for the most part you may find by a sort of chance some rule in rhythm; but this is not from an artificial government of the syllables. It arises because the sound and the modulation lead to it. The vulgar poets effect this rustically; the skilful obtain it by their skill." He then explains his meaning by quotations from Latin hymns.

This passage settles the question as to the impossibility of any thing in ballad metre, which we have in common with the Danes, having been brought over in that form by the Angles and Saxons at their conquest of the island in the 6th and 7th centuries.

A rather more rational theory has been maintained by some other writers, that it was not the Angles and Saxons, but the Danes in the 9th and 10th centuries, who brought them. To this there is the same objection, that the Danes and other Scandinavians then, and for a long time afterwards, used the same alliterative irregular verses as the Anglo-Saxons. It may be urged that the song ascribed to Canute is in rhimed stanza; but the lines in question are most certainly of a much later period than his reign, and not earlier than some part of the 12th century.

They are

> Merie sungen ðe muneches binnen Ely
> Tha Knut ching reu ðærby;
> Roweð, Knites, noer ðe land,
> And here we ðes muneches sæng.

> Merry the monks at Ely sang,
> As steer'd along Canute the king;
> "Row, men, row me near the bank,
> "To hear how sweetly the monks can sing."

They are given by the writer of the Historia Eliensis as sung in the street in his own time, 1166—1169, and there is no authority whatever for their being King Canute's composition.

That the Danes and Anglo-Saxons were acquainted with rhime before the Conquest there is no doubt, for they used the hymns of the Roman Catholic church. We have also in the Exeter Book p. 352 a whole poem in rhime, but this is evidently the work of a recluse, and not a specimen of *popular* poetry, for every word in it rhimes, the lines rhime with each other, and they are alliterative too. For instance

<blockquote>
Bald ald þwiteð
Wræc fæc wriþað
Wraþ að smiteþ.
</blockquote>

In the Battle of Brunanburh, and all other songs which appear to have been popular, the usual alliterative verse is employed without rhime.

It is possible certainly that some of their subjects may be derived from a remote antiquity, and thus be common to England and Denmark, but it is not possible that they have come down to us embodied in the ballads that we have now. The changes which have taken place in the various Scandinavian dialects are not so great, but still are such as to require an entire remodelling of a poem to present it in the modern language; as may be seen in the versified translations of the ancient Eddas.

3dly. If we admit the correspondence of Danish and English ballads to be a proof of their having come down to us from our ancient common home on the continent, we must admit the same in regard to those of many other nations, with whom we have ballads in common; Bretons, Poles, Spaniards, Lithuanians

&c. and go back still farther to the cradle of our race in Asia to find their origin: and this Prof. P. A. Munch seems inclined to do. See Introd. to 'Habor and Signild' No. 21. (Vol. I p. 205.)

But every archæologist knows that fashions belong to particular epochs, and that, let the subject of enquiry be a building, a dress, a manuscript, a piece of furniture, a piece of music, or a picture, there are certain peculiarities that mark the epoch to which it belongs, and decide unequivocally, to which it should be referred. The characteristics of their age are equally marked upon literary productions, and all these refer the Danish ballads to a period from the 13th to the 15th or 16th centuries. As it is upon 'Fair Anna' that Jamieson founded his theory, I have taken pains to follow out that ballad to its original source in a lay imitated by Marie de France from a Breton original in the 13th century, the so called 'Lay of the Ash,' and traced it through the variations it assumed in Spain, Italy, Germany, Flanders, England and Denmark. This the reader will find in Appendix II. It would have extended the limits of this work too far to have done the same by the other ballads that have been adduced in support of Jamieson's theory; but I believe it might be proved that there is not one which is exclusively the property of ourselves and the Scandinavians, or of an earlier date than that one. Some readers may think that it detracts greatly from the interest of these ballads to divest them of the vague mystery with which their origin has been shrouded. I trust to attach a much greater interest to them by showing them to be illustrative of the manners of a great part of Europe at the period to which they really belong.

The correspondence of many of them with those of Spanish and other alien races, as will be shown in these volumes, will prove that they were merely a portion of the fictions common to all West-European countries during the Middle Ages. I believe them to have been for the most part formed upon French romances. It may be remarked that at a particular period of civilization the songs of most nations are narrative, and that at a later period this style is abandoned for the sentimental. All the old Scandinavian ballads are narrative, and such are nearly all the cotemporary lays and romances of France and England, Spain and the Netherlands. It may be considered as a proof that the Welsh popular poetry is not of very ancient date, whatever may be its merit otherwise, that it contains no narrative ballads.

Whatever may have been the period at which the Danish Ballads first came into vogue, it is evident from the language, that it was not till the 15th and 16th centuries that they assumed the form in which we now have them. It is probable that the Swedish and Norwegian and Faroese ballads originated at the same time, for they all treat of the same subjects. In regard to several of them, the source is obvious enough. It was about the year 1226 that the Romance of Tristram was translated into Norse by Brother Robert at the command of King Hakon Hakonson, and so became generally known to the Scandinavians,—and, as we shall have occasion to see, has furnished many situations and incidents to the ballad singers. The poems of Marie de France were also translated into Norse by command of that monarch, and became a second fertile source of incident. This work under the name of 'Streng-leikar eḑa lioḑabok' has been lately published by Prof. Keyser and Prof. Unger at Christiania. But beside these works, and several others, which were translated by order of the king, there were numerous lays and romances floating about in every part of Europe, the common property of all nations, and it cannot be doubted that these found their way to Denmark too, and furnished the material for ballads of a more popular character. See Wright on the Middle Ages, Vol. II. ch. xii.

All Europe seems at that time to have had the same literary taste, as it had the same taste in chivalrous usages, in architecture, and even in hand-writing. It is not only the tales themselves that are so widely spread. The same forms of expression, the same conventional phrases were common to all the ballad poetry of Europe. The metre too, the common stanza, was the same. Indeed the more we study the ballad literature of Europe, the more we shall see that, like the plants that cover its soil, the several distinct groups into which it falls, are nevertheless only parts of a great whole, more luxuriantly spread over some districts than over others, developing itself in richer and more varied colours here than there, every where presenting some characteristic forms, but harmonizing, all of them, with the tone that pervades the whole. What Herder in his Volkslieder says of the English and German ballads, is of general application to them all.

"These nations in point of rhyme, turn of expression, metre and picturing are very much alike, as every one must acknowledge who is acquainted with their Romances, Tales, and Ballads. The whole tone of this poetry is so uniform, that one may often translate word for word, turn for turn, inversion for inversion. In all these countries of Europe the spirit of chivalry has only one vocabulary, and therefore one mode of relating things. Ballads and Romances have every where the same nouns and adjectives, the same kind of terminations (Fallendungen) the same freedom of metre, even the same favourite tunes, the same romantic plants, beasts and birds."

If the translations now presented to the public were merely an expression of Danish thought in the Middle Ages, it could scarcely be hoped that the English reader would bestow more than a casual glance upon them, so entirely does the present generation seem to be weaned from all admiration of homely and simple productions, and so little do the smaller political powers occupy of the world's attention. But they present us with much more than the tales that amused an obscure people. They place before us a view of society, as it existed not in Denmark only, but in all the West of Europe, till about the end of the 16th century, when the invention of printing, the reformation, and the discovery of America gave a shattering blow to the ancient system of society, and mediæval habits of thought, and introduced new and severe studies to occupy the leisure hours that were once abandoned to the song of the minstrel.

It is especially for their antiquarian value that they are now presented to the public, as an invitation to the reader to step aside from the cathedral and the castle to the humble cottage of the cotemporary peasant. The severest critic who may peruse these pages can hardly be more conscious than the translator himself, how much they fail in giving the simplicity, the rough country life, that belongs to the originals. But to copy this in the English of literature would be absolutely impossible. It could only be done in some provincial or antiquated dialect, or, as R. Jamieson has shown us, in Broad Scotch. A peasant poet must talk as a peasant, he must even represent kings and queens talking peasant language, and acting like peasants. Such a transcript of the Danish might have the merit of fidelity, but would find only a very limited circle of readers, and the object in view, that of making these interesting compositions better known to the English public, be entirely frustrated. A writer in the Edinburgh Review, Vol. XXXIX p. 419, says of the Spanish ballads, what equally applies to the Danish, that "To feel their true value and power we must read large numbers of them, and read them too in their native language; for there is a winning freshness in the originals, as they lie imbedded in the old Romanceros, that escapes in translations, however free, or however strict."

The Danish originals of the following pieces have long been highly valued in Germany. Herder introduced several of them into his Essay on Popular Songs, and a translation of ninety-one of them was published in 1813 by W. Grimm; his well known 'Altdänische Heldenlieder.' But this was unfortunately made from the garbled copies printed by Vedel and

Syv, and gives a very inadequate idea of the originals. Others from the same source are introduced by Talvj in her Charakteristik der Volkslieder. A new translation of thirty-seven of those now in the course of publication by Svend Grundtvig has been lately published at Hamburg by Miss Rosa Warrens. It is much less literal than that of W. Grimm, but at the same time very much more readable, as being free from that singular uncouthness of metre which renders Grimm's otherwise excellent translation so wearisome to read continuously. The notes which she has added are short; but interesting, abridged the most of them from those of Grundtvig.

The only French translation with which I am acquainted, is the prose version of some of them by X. Marmier, and two quoted in the Barzas Breiz of Villemarqué.

A large proportion of these ballads exist, as might be expected, in the cognate Scandinavian dialects, the Swedish, Norwegian, Faroese, and Icelandic. Several of the Swedish have been translated into English and have appeared from time to time in the Reviews, in the Howitt's 'Northern Literature,' and in Keightley's 'Fairy Mythology,' and will be found to correspond as closely with the Danish, as different Danish copies do with one another. Indeed there can scarcely be a doubt that some of those which have been picked up in Sweden of late years are derived from printed copies of the Danish ones, and as little that some of the Danish are versions of Swedish originals.

It has been stated above that the narrative romance seems to have originated in the 13th century. This was one of those periods at which the human mind has made a sudden advance. There seems in that century to have been a craving for novelty, a desire for mental enjoyment, a demand for the gratification of taste. This awakening of intellect may have been in a great measure due to the establishment of rich monastic institutions, and of great families; to there being a class which had leisure and wealth; and also in some degree perhaps to the Crusades; but chiefly to the foundation of Universities in the twelfth century, and the struggle to obtain political and religious liberty in the thirteenth. The dark age was passed. The dawn of a new era broke upon society with a purer and clearer light. Among other developments of the awakened spirit of men was the rhimed romance, and this held a nearly parallel course with the fine style of architecture that originated in the same country and at the same period, the so called Early Gothic. This too had its birth in Normandy and the Isle of France, and spread over the rest of that kingdom, England, Germany and Spain, and all the West of Europe. It is from these rhimed romances, or from the beautiful Fabliaux abridged from them, that the Ballad has sprung. We have no evidence of its existence earlier than this century. Some attempts have been made to show that Normandy was indebted to other countries for its materials, and so, no doubt, it was in a great measure. Gisli Brynjulfsen has tried to prove that Iceland supplied this new style of fiction: others have traced it to the East, others to Brittany and Wales. The early date assigned to the fictions of these countries is so extremely doubtful, that no argument can be based upon their assumed priority. That many of the heroes and scenes have been adopted from foreign nations is obvious enough; but it was the habit of the old romancers to place their action as far off as possible, in order to allow themselves free scope for their imagination. So king Arthur became a favourite hero, not because all the stories about him are Welsh, but because he was a foreigner, of whom nothing definite was known, and the minstrel was free to sing of him what he pleased. There can be no question that it was from the court of France, and that of our Norman kings, that a taste for these fictions spread over the rest of Europe. That they should have originated at these rather than at any of the other courts, may have been owing to this, that Paris and London were at that time the only capitals in Europe in which a king and nobility resided, and where the poet was repaid with honours and emoluments.

Let me now beg the reader to endeavour to carry himself back to about the fourteenth century, the period when songs were the expression of the public mind and of daily life, a national era, a condition of popular ranks, and a tone of feeling, which will never return to us. I cannot do better than quote the words of Professor G. Stephens, the learned author of an article on Swedish ballads in the For. Quart. Rev. Vol. XXV. for what he says of them applies equally to the Danish.

"Ballad literature has this great value: it hands down to us features of bygone centuries, and practical illustrations of bygone systems, such as we can find in no other quarter. Like the old Bayeux tapestry with its bizarre Viking ships, and mailed warriors, and quaint accoutrements, and particoloured sails, and perpetually changing figures, through which we become in the simplest manner acquainted with the habits and dress, and armour and navigation of the Gallo-Scandinavian adventurers, who, 800 years ago, made conquest of our island, does the popular song reveal facts and feelings, customs and costumes, which are in the highest degree important and interesting: "The king is sitting by his broad board, and is served by knights and swains, who bear round wine and mead. Instead of chairs we find benches covered with cushions, or, as they are called in the ballads, mattresses, "bolstrar," bolsters, long pillows, whence comes the expression 'sitta på bolstrarna blaa' on the blue cushions seated. Princesses and noble virgins bear crowns of gold and silver; gold rings, precious belts, and gold or silver-clasped shoes, are also named as their ornaments. They dwell in the highest rooms, separate from the men, and their maidens share their chambers and their beds. From the high-bower-stair, Hög-lofts bro, they see the coming of the stranger knight, and how he in the castle yard taketh upon him his fine cloak, may be of precious skins — or discover out at sea the approaching vessel, and recognize by the flags, which their own hands have broidered, that a lover draweth nigh. The dress of the higher class is adorned with furs of the sable and martin, and they are distinguished by wearing scarlet, a general name for any finer or more precious cloth (for the ballads call it sometimes red and sometimes green or blue) as opposed to 'vadmel' (serge, coarse woollens) the clothing of the poorer sort. Both men and women play upon the harp, and affect dice and tables. Song and adventure are a pastime loved by all in common, and occasionally the men amuse themselves at their leisure with knightly exercises in the castle-yard. Betrothals are first decided between the families, if every thing follows its usual course; but love often destroys this order, and the knight takes his beloved upon his saddle-bow, and gallops off with her to his bridal home. Cars are spoken of as the vehicles of ladies, and from an old Danish ballad, in which a Danish princess who has arrived in Sweden laments that she must pursue her journey on horseback, we see that their use did not reach Sweden so early. The Danish princess who was to be the spouse of the Swedish king says

> Were I in my father's land,
> A car I'd have and driver grand;
> The Swedish ladies answer'd thus;
> 'No Jutland manners bring to us.'

Violent courtships, club-law, and the revenge of blood, which however could often be atoned by fines to the avenger, are common." Geijer Sven. Folk v. I. p. XIX.

"We cannot help remarking also that the popular ballads almost constantly relate to high and noble persons. If kings and knights are not always mentioned, still we perpetually hear of Sirs, ladies, and fair damsels—titles which, according to old usage, could only be properly employed of the gentry. We will not, it is true, assert that the old songs have preserved any distinction of rank; but in the meantime this will prove that their subjects are taken from the higher and more illustrious classes. Their manners are there chiefly represented, and the liveliness of the colouring necessarily excites the supposition that they spring from thence. On the other side again, they have been and remain as native among the common people, as if they had been born among them. All this leads us back to times, when as yet the classes of society had not assumed any mutually inimical contrast to each other, when nobility was yet the living lustre from bright deeds rather than from remote ancestry, and when therefore it as yet belonged to the people, and was regarded as the national flower and glory. Such a time we have had; and he only cannot discover it, who begins by transplanting into history all the aristocratical and democratical party ideas of a later time." "Further we find in the old ballads that there is not only no hate of class but also no national hate, among the northern peoples. This explains how it is that they are so much in common to the whole north, and this community of sentiment extends itself even to the ancient historical songs." Ibid. p. 20.

The old ballad literature also gains materially by nothing in it being forced. Composed in times when there was neither press nor criticism, affectation nor effect-seeking, premature feeling nor pretended taste, it was the instinctive and gradually moulded speech of heart to heart, relating many a peril dire by land and sea, or the real accident of a past age transformed into the rhymed legend of the next—

> "While eager groups were gathered round
> The wide hearth's blazing light."

or the poetry of love interpreted in some affecting story to the passionate stripling, or to melancholy age; or the national superstitions clothing with unreal forms the laughing wave and the everlasting wood. In all these cases the object was simply one — to *move*. This one point gained, the bard received the well-earned plaudit. The song was eagerly retained by many a listener; and now that age upon age has rolled by, thousands of these fine old ballads live, while the authors of every one of them have long since been forgotten.

But though the charms of shepherd song are, we doubt not, dear unto many a noble heart among us, the popular songs of the north have an especial interest for the British reader. The little glimpses into the Danish fields of poesy afforded in the volumes of the gifted Jamieson, were truly characterised as an event in the annals of our ballad literature. Since then no one has endeavoured to pry into and map out for us this unknown land of Scandinavian lore, and the labours of our most illustrious investigators lose not a little of their value from not being properly supported and illustrated by parallels and fillings up from purer sources. It is now admitted* on all hands that a thousand years ago the literature like the lan-

---

* Upon this point the Professor expresses himself rather inaccurately, for it is certainly not so generally *admitted* that the language of the North was a thousand years ago common to all its parts. Almost all philologists, except himself and Thorkelin, have considered Anglo-Saxon, or as he would prefer to call it, *Old English*, to belong to the Low German type.

guage, of the whole Teutonic North (including Britain) was almost common to all its parts. This result from similarity of origin, belief, Viking expeditions, and clanship, was only gradually broken in upon by an unequally proceeding civilization, the creation of isolated monarchies jealous of each other, and the growth of the dialect up to the language. Therefore it is that those parts of the great Gothic circle where the alterations have been most extensive must recover much of what is dear to them from regions far from the din of rapid change, and from tribes inhabiting a land where the stillness of the forest and the scantiness of population and communication are most likely to ensure simplicity of manners and purity of song and legend. But just this land par excellence is the Northern peninsula. Denmark, which lies so near the heart of the continent, has suffered much more change in the strife of centuries than either Norway or Sweden.

In Britain we have unfortunately and unpardonably lost most of our ancient ballad melodies; in the north a very large number are happily rescued. To judge of the collections before us without also adding specimens of the music in which they are enshrined, is almost unjust; indeed in many cases, it leaves us the body, when the soul has fled. The prevailing tone of these old Scandinavian melodies is simple and melancholy. Many of them have a certain family likeness with the ancient songs of Ireland and Scotland; and a considerable number are eminently beautiful." For. Quart. Vol. XXV.

If the following translations are what they ought

C*

to be, the reader, who condescends to peruse them, will find himself the spectator of a moving panorama, while the varied and interesting scenes so finely grouped by the master hand of the great historian of Sweden are passing before him. Some of the customs alluded to above, and others pictured in the following ballads, are still kept up in Norway and those other parts of Scandinavia which have been less affected by the progress of society, and a visit to these districts throws the same light upon the mediæval customs of our own country, and of all the West of Europe, as a visit to Pompeii upon those of the ancient Greeks and Romans. In turning over the French Fabliaux collected by Le Grand d'Aussy, and reading his very instructive and amusing notes to them, we shall see to our surprize a number of usages to have then prevailed in France and Spain and Italy, and indeed in all the most civilized parts of the West, which late travellers to the North have noticed as peculiarly Scandinavian. Such is the habit of all the members of a family and their servants, male and female alike, sharing the same dormitory. Allusion to this usage occurs again and again in the old romances. In Spanish for instance, in one of those on Montesinos, Duran Vol. IV, p. 84 we read

> Una noche estando así
> gritos da Rosaflorida:
> oyera la un camarero,
> que en su cámara dormia.
> — Que es aquesto, mi señora?

> One night, as Rosaflorida
> Thus wail'd aloud and wept,

>   Her sorrows heard a chamber swain,
>   That in her chamber slept:
>   "But what is this then, lady mine?" —

And not only did they share the same chamber, but shocking as it may seem to the delicacy of modern times, they stripped to the skin and slept naked. This is noted by Parker in his Domestic Architecture of the 14th century p. 75, and in that of the 15th century p. 102, as having been equally the case in England too. It is to this day the ordinary practice in Norway. That it was general in ancient times, is obvious, from several passages in the following Danish ballads, and in the French and other romances. In one of them, that of Gerard de Nevers, an old woman, who assists in undressing a damsel, expresses the utmost astonishment at seeing her get into bed in her shift; and in the miniatures, which adorn the manuscripts, the persons who are represented in bed, are always naked.

Throughout this work the reader will do well to bear in mind a remark that Parker makes in one of the passages referred to, that "it has been too much and too long the custom to view the manners and habits of remote times through a medium highly tinged with the results and conveniences of modern life, and therefore they have been seen under a false aspect. It is only by looking carefully into the dry schedule of the household effects of our remote ancestors, and taking the number of their pots and pans, their beds and tables, and other domestic goods, that we can judge how meanly they were lodged, and how far from luxurious their daily mode of life must have been."

What was the arrangement of the dwellings of men of rank in Denmark at this period, it is not very easy to ascertain, or what our ballad-singers supposed it to be. Professor Vedel Simonsen has published a very elaborate memoir on the subject in the Nordisk Tiidskrift for 1829, and in this has endeavoured to trace out the habits of his ancestors from the scattered notices of them that are found in the four volumes of the 'Danske Viser,' but has vitiated all his conclusions by mixing up indiscriminately the ballads of the heroic age with those of a later period, and confounding the description of the fortified castle of the king with that of the manor-house of the country-gentleman.

In the following translations the Borgeled is assumed to be the entrance gate to the premises, and here the visitor usually found one of the family waiting to receive him, and announce him. Through this he entered the 'Borgegaard' or courtyard, around which were the several detached buildings of which the dwelling consisted. The manor house, or Borg, stood in front, and rooms for the ladies, and for the retainers at the side of it, and the stables, kitchen, and Sten-stue, or stone-room for lying-in women, in other parts of the yard. Such a detached mode of building is general in all countries where wood is the material, from the danger of total destruction, if a fire broke out, and all were connected together. It is so in Norway and Jamaica, in Switzerland and Japan. This yard was the playground of the pages, and the exercise place of the troopers, and the scene of many scuffles and scoldings. From this 'Borgegaard' or courtyard the visitor approaches the door, drawing on his scarlet cloak as he crosses it. The master receives him cup in hand, or sometimes one of the ladies, but the first words they address to him are always, whether he will drink of mead or wine. He usually goes up the stairs, the 'Höieloft̃s bro,' to the ladies' chamber, the 'Höieloft,' on the first floor. The banquet hall or mess-room, 'Stue,' where the master sat with his troopers 'over breden Bord' over the broad table, seems to have been underneath.

Where the sleeping place of the family was, is not clear. From several passages where a young man wakes up and tells his dream to his mother, it seems, as stated above, that they generally slept in one room. There are others however where the chambers are described as separate, and in a detached building. The bridal chamber certainly was so, and is often called 'Brude-huset,' the Bridal house. Much will have depended on the rank of the family, the fashion of the district, the number of the persons, and the period described. From the ballad of 'Swain Felding and Queen Judith' No. 31, we see that even the Queen's palace was of wood. The 'Svale,' where the family is often represented as collected together, I take to be the same as the 'Stoep' of the Dutch at the Cape of Good Hope, a terrace elevated half a yard from the ground, and running round the house, with a penthouse over it. The 'Rosenlund,' which is the scene of so many adventures, is supposed by Professor Vedel Simonsen to be a small park, 'en lille Dyrehave,' between the entrance gate and the house, and to have had its name from the rosebuds, the

young ladies, who frequented it. But it is impossible
to think that any such little cockney park is meant,
as he describes, — a pleasure ground where the ladies
sat to listen to the birds singing, and to play the harp,
with brooks and little mills in it. It is very plain
that by 'Rosenlund' was understood exactly the same
thing as by the 'green-wood' of our own ballads, a
coppice of small trees and bushes, through which a
horseman could ride, as distinguished from a dense
forest of timber trees. For instance

> Herr Tönne rider i Rosenlund
>   At bede den wilde Hind;
> Der mödte han Dvergens Datter,
>   Hun hviler sig under en Lind.
>
> Sir Tonnè rides in the wood of rose
>   To hunt the forest hind,
> And sees beneath a linden-tree
>   An Elfin maid reclined.

A little park between the entrance gate and the house
was not the place to ride hunting in, or where he
was likely to meet an Elfin maiden, or a forest hind.

With regard to the ranks of society, it is not quite
clear that the Danes adopted the habits of the South,
or that they had among them a system of knight-
hood, such as it existed there. Perhaps it might be
more correct to say that those who composed the
ballads were not well acquainted with matters of
chivalry. We certainly do not find in them the re-
motest trace of the southern devotion of knights to
their ladies, or of knights sallying out to redress
grievances, or pledging their knightly word, or in short
doing any thing to indicate a pride of class, or claim

to respect *as knights*. They would seem to have been, many of them, men of great wealth and local power, and it is probable that in Denmark, as elsewhere in the middle ages, youths of gentle lineage were brought up at their courts, and there received their first instructions, to enter afterwards their patron's service as valets or pages. This was the only resource in those turbulent ages, when the power and the wealth of the crown, circumscribed within narrow bounds, could not offer nobler or more advantageous employment to those who wished to devote themselves to the service of the state. It was not then considered a degradation for a young gentleman to enter the service of a baron, it was but an exchange of personal services for past care and patronage. The households of the great lords were composed like those of kings, having corresponding officers.

The duty of the page, the 'Lille Smaadreng' of these ballads, seems to have been chiefly to wait upon the ladies by day and by night, to run on errands for them, and to pick up news for them. We do not find a trace of the education, which Ferrario in his Analisi degli antichi Romanzi Vol. I. p. 155 describes as having been bestowed upon them by their mistresses in the South of Europe, that of a love of God, and the art of making love to the Ladies, &c. They seem in Denmark to have been merely servants.

Who and what the 'Svend' or swain was, is not very clear; but he appears to have been the personal attendant upon a knight, and of a lower rank in life; not like the squire of the South, who was often of much higher rank than his temporary master, as at our own public schools, where that part of the Institution of Chivalry is to our great benefit as a nation preserved to the present day.

By 'Ung' seems to have been meant a young man of family, not old enough to be a knight, or not rich enough, but under no subjection to any other. It is here rendered 'Young.'

'Herr' seems to have denoted the possession of a home and property, and perhaps corresponds to the Scotch 'laird,' but is here translated merely 'Sir.'

It is to be remarked that throughout all the numerous Scandinavian ballads there is no reference to the admission of a young man to the rank of a Ridder or knight, and that we may conclude from their general tone, that they were not composed till after the observances of chivalry were out of fashion and forgotten.

There is of course in these ballads, as in those of most other nations, a great deal that turns upon the loves of young people. It appears that in those days an engagement was equivalent to a civil marriage. When a young man had "plighted his troth" to the maiden, he might live with her on the terms of husband and wife; as is to this day customary in Norway and in Wales, and to judge from numerous passages in the Scotch ballads, it was once, and that not very long ago, in Scotland also: for instance in 'William and Marjorie' Motherwell p. 186: and in that most pathetic and beautiful one of 'Fair Annie of Lochroyan' Gilchrist. I. p. 149. It is still customary also with the Boers at the Cape of Good Hope, who often come from the interior with a large family to baptize the children, and to be married themselves, and to have their wives churched the same day. Several of these ballads will scarcely be intelligible without our bearing this usage in mind.

The golden crown to which such frequent reference is made, is the maiden coronet, the 'virgin crant' of Shakespeare's Ophelia. Hamlet Act. V. sc. I. As the best account of it that I can find, I copy the following from Jamieson's notes to his translation of 'Axel-wold' in the Northern Antiquities.

"The Maiden Coronet, or tire for the head, although of various forms and qualities, according to the taste or condition of the wearer, was uniformly open at the top; and no one covered her head, till she had forfeited her right to wear the coronet, chaplet, garland or bandeau. This was the case in many parts of Scotland, till within the last twenty or thirty years. The ballads and songs of the northern nations, as will be seen by the specimens we have produced, abound with allusions to this very ancient usage, and every body in Scotland knows

"The lassie lost her silken snood
A-puing o' the bracken."

The ceremony of putting on the curtsh or close cap, on the morning after the marriage, when the young wife is no longer entitled to wear the *snood*, or maiden tyre, is still observed in the north of Scotland, and gives the matrons an opportunity of enjoying a scene of jollity and gossiping.

Some of the coronets worn by the peasant girls of Livonia, Courland, Esthonia and Lithuania are very picturesque and elegant. Some are simple bandeaus of dyed horsehair, curiously plaited, diversified, and figured. Others are of cloth, silk, velvet &c. tastefully ornamented with beads, spangles, gold and silver embroidery, precious stones, artificial emblematic flowers &c. and some raised before in form of a retroverted crescent, and tied with a ribbon behind. One, which seemed of very antique workmanship, I have seen upon a Lithuanian damsel, which was a solid, radiated, open crown of gilt brass, lined with royal purple velvet, perfectly orbicular, resting upon the top of the head (where the Scottish maidens used to wear the *cockernonie*) and held on by a fillet tied under the hair, which was plaited down the back and adorned with a bunch of different-coloured ribbons at the end. No entreaty could induce her to part with it.

This metal crown seems to be a humble relative of the golden one worn by Axelwold's mother, (See No. 52 st. 16) which was probably substituted, in a more ostentatious age, by the richer Asiatics and their descendants for the more simple, significant, and elegant garland of flowers, which the Greeks borrowed from them, or retained after their separation from them. This ornament the Greeks called Μίτρη. The bride upon her marriage dedicated it to Venus

Τῇ Παφίῃ στεφάνους, τῇ Παλλάδι τὴν πλοκαμίδα,
Ἀρτέμιδι ζώνην ἄνθετο Καλλιρόη·
Εὕρετο γὰρ μνηστῆρα, τὸν ἤθελε, καὶ λάχεν ἥβην
Σώφρονα, καὶ τεκέων ἄρσεν ἔτικτε γένος.

Agath. apud Sched. syngn. l. c. 4.

"Callirhoe dedicated her coronet to Venus, her hair to Minerva, and her girdle to Diana, for she had found a suitor, whom she loved; she had obtained the prudent youth; and becoming pregnant, she had brought forth a man-child."

The Jews still retain the usage of the nuptial coronet "A mulieribus quoque et virginibus in peculiare cubiculum sponsa non velato capite, passis capillis deducitur; festivæ cantilenæ nuptiales coram illa canuntur; illam in pulchro sedili collocant; crinem illi pectunt; capillosque in elegantes cirrhos et concinnos distribuunt; magnificam vittam imponunt &c. Singularis est mulierum in hoc capillorum comtu lætitia, quam elegantibus cantilenis, saltatione, ludisque testantur, ut sponsam exhilarent: magno id enim habent loco, Deoque gratissimum et acceptissimum opus esse censent." Buxtorfi Synagoga Judaica 12mo Basil 1680. p. 629."

Jamieson goes into other particulars of the marriage ceremony, which, as they have no connexion with the ballads before us, it is unnecessary to copy.

It is singular that while this use of the maiden coronet is still preserved in our own island, the commentators on Shakspeare, even Scotchmen like Chalmers, should have been so ignorant of it, as entirely to misunderstand the passage in Hamlet, where the priest speaking of Ophelia's equivocal character says Act. V. sc. 1.

> "She should in ground unsanctified have lodged
> Till the last trumpet; for charitable prayers
> Shards, flints, and pebbles should be thrown on her.
> Yet here she is allow'd her *virgin crants*,
> Her *maiden* strowments, and the bringing home
> Of bell and burial."

After the betrothal the bridegroom elect was called 'Fæstemand' and the maiden 'Fæstemö,' the French 'fiancé' and 'fiancée', but for which we have only the one word *trulove*, the proper meaning of which Geo. Hickes was the first to point out in his Thesaurus. See Gramm. Island. p. 4. Jamieson in the North. Ant. p. 384, shows that it has nothing to do with *true love*, but is derived from the Danish 'trolovet' *troth-plighted* or *promised*. It means *affianced*, and is applied to a false lover as well as to a faithful one. So in the song 'O wala, wala, up the bank' Gilchr. II. 297

"I leant my back unto an aik,
I thought it was a trusty tree,
But first it bow'd, and syne it brake,
And so did my *true-love* to me."

and

"O whareto should I busk my head?
Or whareto should I kemb my hair?
For my *true-love* 's forsaken me,
And says he 'll never lo'e me mair!"

and

"Saint Anton's well sall be my drink
Since my *true-love* 's forsaken me."

The word seems to have been first introduced into England through the North-country ballads, and I believe that many of these came down through Scotland from the Scandinavian islands. In accordance with this etymology, and to avoid the ridiculous contradiction of false *true* love, I have ventured to spell the word 'trulove.' Shakspeare uses 'trothplight' in the same sense, e. g. in Winter's Tale A. V. sc. 3.

— This your son-in-law
Is *troth-plight* to your daughter —

and in Henry V. Act II. sc. 1.

You were *trothplight* to her.

This betrothal seems to have been regarded as a very

serious ceremony, and all the kindred of the lady to have been present at it, and probably bound to avenge her for any infidelity on the part of her lover. It was also called 'Fæsten' *fasten, secure*. The word is used in Early English in Layamon's Brut l. 2251

| He heo hæfde i hond fæst | He had her in hand-fast |
| At foren his hired monnen. | before his household men. |

Upon this occasion there was usually a ring given by the lover to his mistress, and one given by her to him, to imply that a bargain had been made. That which Brynild gave to Sigurd or Siward, proved the source of the murders and wars so celebrated in ancient poetry. It is probable that a custom still kept up in many parts of Europe, that of exchanging a piece of money, or breaking a sixpence between two lovers, may date from a period when rings were coin, and the exchange of them regarded as a money transaction; and similarly our wedding ring may be but the money payment for the bride. In the Canton of Lucern in Switzerland a farmer's wife told me that a gold chain round the neck was as good as a ring. Such chains we know to have been used for money. In these ballads the lover proposes to purchase his lady's favour with as little delicacy as he would offer a price for a horse or a sword, and parents seem to have been satisfied if sufficient was given for it. The present made was often of great value, not only handsome dresses, and brooches, and gold crowns, and silver shoes, but castles and even towns.

It is not easy to distinguish between this, the 'Fästegave,' at the betrothal, and the 'Morgengave' given on the morrow of the marriage. Perhaps these ceremonies were not always separate.

The Fæstegave, tho' in later times given to the bride, was originally paid to the parents of the lady as her money value, or perhaps as the value of being her guardian, and she was sold to her suitor, and became his property and part of his chattels, as she is in several Oriental countries, and almost all barbarous nations at this day; and as it is evident from the 10th commandment of Moses, she was among the Israelites. If the father was dead, it was her eldest brother who sold her, or in some cases the mother. The expression used was unambiguous, kaupa quân, *buying* a wife. This, as in the case of the patriarch Jacob, was often so arranged with a needy suitor, as that he had to give so many years' labour for her instead of money or property. For instance in the Eyrbyggia Saga c. 28 Vigstyr tells the Berserk, Halli, who has demanded his daughter, that, as he is poor, he shall earn the marriage with hard work.

This Fæstegave seems in the course of time to have become the wife's dowry. But in different parts of Scandinavia there were different laws and customs, and, in our ignorance of the date and birthplace of much of the ancient poetry, it is impossible to distinguish the local custom from the general usage. The lady herself often bargained with her lover, what it should be, and seems to have treasured it up as her most precious possession, even when living with her lover as his Slegfred or mistress. See 'Fair Anna' No. 148, st. 18. It was evidence to the world that he admitted her personal rights.

The 'Morgengave' was some present which the bride was entitled to demand the day after her wedding. This too seems to have been arranged beforehand, as it could not be refused by the husband. We have the solitary case in No. 31 to the contrary, but that not in the oldest copy of the ballad. In general he was obliged to give it, no matter what the value, or what the consequences might be. The hoard of the dwarf Alberich, which Chriemhild had demanded and obtained for her morning-gift, was the cause of so many troubles to the house of the Nibelungs. The same custom of a Morning-gift prevailed in England in the Anglo-Saxon times, and it often consisted of a landed estate. In fact it was a marriage settlement.

It may not be improper to remark here, that in the Danish originals of these ballads, as well as our own and the German, and those of all Germanic nations, many things are said in an honest and straightforward way, which in poems of the present age would be rather insinuated than told. In editing originals it is necessary to give them, as we find them, and even Sir Walter Scott to whom, more perhaps than to any other author, we owe the purity that distinguishes the romances of this century from those of the last, has been obliged in his Border Minstrelsy to admit passages which he would not have written. A translator is allowed greater freedom, and in some of these ballads a few lines or a few stanzas have been omitted or altered, so that it is hoped that nothing will be found in them that can possibly offend even female readers.

In alluding to this I should be doing injustice to

these Northern nations, if I did not add that in the whole vast collection of Danish, Swedish, and other Scandinavian ballads there is not to my knowledge one of a demoralizing tendency. We shall estimate them and their popular literature the more highly, if we contrast their ballads with the Provençal romances, of which it has been truly said that "'The mixture of licentiousness and elegance, of ingenuousness even in guilt, of simplicity and sincerity united to the grossest corruption of morals, which those manners present, is striking and appalling;" and of their courts of Love that "their morality was a code of licentiousness and adultery, mixed with an affected display of refined sentimentality." No such charge can be made against our honest Northmen. Ungallant towards the ladies they certainly often were, and impetuous and sanguinary, but there is nothing of Southern depravity in them. Crimes were committed, great crimes, but not applauded, nor held up as examples for imitation; far from it, the parties in a case of adultery were subjected to the most rigorous punishment, the lady burnt on a faggot pile, and her paramour hanged. In respect to incontinence on the part of unmarried persons, it is extremely difficult to come to any distinct conclusion. In numerous places, as remarked above, the betrothal is regarded as equivalent to marriage, in others the parties are subjected to the same punishment as in a case of adultery; see for instance 'Buris and Christine,' No. 57, 'Medelwold and Sidselille,' No. 101, 'Samson' No. 6. Nay, in a Swedish ballad, 'Pehr Wattenman,' a son puts his own mother on the pyre, and in a Scotch one

'Lady Maisry,' a brother his own sister. It is probable that in these cases, although we are not told so, the lady was engaged to another man, or that from her superior rank, or from party feud the connexion was disagreeable to her family.

In regard to the Metre, that of the original has been followed as nearly as the difference of the two languages allowed. The Danish having many rhiming dissyllables allows of the so-called *female* rhime. In English this has a rather burlesque effect, and therefore has not been used. The rhythm is nearly the same as that of our English ballads, and it is the universal practice in the Danish, as well as our own, to end the sentence with the rhime, at the end of the stanza, or of the couplet, as it may be. This in the latter case often occasions a disagreeable breaking up of the story, but was necessary to allow place for the so-called *omquäd*, the chorus, refrain, or burden, which usually accompanied the song.

With regard to this *omquäd* there are two disputed points; first whether it was an essential part of the ballad, and secondly whether it was sung in chorus. As to the first question, Geijer who is a little apt to give the rein to his imagination, maintains that it was actually the most important part of all, in that it kept before the audience the feeling which the ballad was meant to express; that in fact the ballad was a mere example to illustrate the refrain. Others taking a more common sense view of the matter, look upon it as necessary to give the singer a little time to think what came next, and also as a symphony to complete the time of the dance. It seems in ge-

D*

neral to be quite irrelevant to the subject of the ballad, so much so that we find the same refrain used with several different ballads, and the same ballad with a great number of different refrains. For instance the one called 'The Power of the Harp,' No. 89, has in the different copies of it no less than ten various refrains. In short it seems to have been a matter of as perfect indifference to the company what the refrain was about, so long as it went to the tune, as it is to ourselves whether it shall be 'hey derry down,' or 'hey ninny nonny.'

As to the second question, that of its being sung in chorus or not, Geijer in this too takes his own view of the matter, and declares that if the company did sing it in chorus, it would disturb and disarrange every thing. But there is a fact that at once overthrows his theoretical notions, that in the Faroe islands, where these ancient ballads and songs are still kept up in the full spirit of former days, the refrain is always sung in full chorus, as in England and Scotland; and we know that so far from having any disturbing effect, it keeps the attention to the piece.

Where the refrain seemed to add any completeness to the ballad, it has been translated, but in other cases omitted altogether. It seems to have originated with church music, in which the responses were chaunted by the people, as Ferd. Wolf has shown in his work 'Ueber die Lais, Sequenzen und Leiche.'

The following 173 pieces are far from exhausting the whole stock of Danish ballads. The editors of the Danske Viser have published 222, and allude to several others which from various motives they omitted;

and Grundtvig in his still unfinished publication has added many more to these. Considering their unquestionable antiquity, their variety, and their beauty, they form the most valuable ballad literature in the world. Our own are very few of them so old, or so illustrative of the middle ages, and the Spanish contain few of any great merit, none that will bear a comparison with the best of these. But numerous as are the Danish, they form scarcely more than a third of the ballad literature of Scandinavia. Sweden possesses a great many excellent pieces which have been published in the 'Svenska Folkvisor' of Afzelius and Geijer, the 'Svenska Fornsånger' of Arwidsson, and the 'Sveriges historiska Visor' of Cavallius and G. Stephens. They are not so numerous as the Danish, nor, generally speaking, so perfect. The Swedes began to collect their national songs much later than the Danes, and have probably lost many of them. German translations of them have been published by Studach in his 'Schwedische Volksharfe,' and by Mohnike in his 'Volkslieder der Schweden,' and in his 'Altschwedische Balladen,' and by Talvj in her 'Charakteristik der Volkslieder'; and English ones by the Howitts, Keightley, and writers in the Foreign Quarterly Review.

There is still a third group which as yet is scarcely known in this country at all, comprising the Norwegian, Faroese and Icelandic, which from similarity of language may be classed together. A hundred and thirty-three of the Norwegian have been published by Landstad in his 'Norske Folkviser,' a work that has one great merit over all other collections of Scandinavian ballads, explanatory footnotes, and it is certain that there are many more of them known to the peasantry, and as yet unprinted. They have none of them appeared in English yet, and have not generally so high a poetical merit as from the Danish ballads of Norwegian origin might have been expected. Faroese ballads have been published by Lyngbye in his 'Færoiske Kwæder' and by Hammershaimb. The first of these gentlemen visited the islands upon a botanical excursion and having unexpectedly made the discovery of these fine remains, brought home copies of several of them and published them with a Danish translation. Hammershaimb is proceeding very slowly with the publication of others. These too are as yet unknown to the English reader. An eminent Scandinavian scholar, Dr. Charlton of Newcastle, tells me that they are many of them remarkably fine, and it is to be hoped that he will find leisure from his professional engagements to make a translation of them. The language is a peculiar form of Norse or Icelandic, which it requires much patient study to understand. Of the Icelandic ballads even less is known. A publication of them was commenced in 1854 under the name of 'Islensk Fornkwædi' by Sv. Grundtvig and Sigurdson, but is still incomplete. Some of the Faroese will be found translated into German in Raszman's work 'Die Deutsche Heldensage.' Considering how large a part of the Scotch population is of Norse origin, and how much of their ancient language they still retain, it is rather surprizing that hitherto no attention should have been paid by them to these collections. So late as the year 1834 Dr. Charlton found in the Shetlands an old man named

Hendrik Hendriksen and his daughter, a middle-aged woman, who could sing a long Norse song. In the Orkneys the language appears to be quite extinct, and none of their ancient songs to have been preserved.

The following pieces have been distributed into four groups.

I. Heroic, II. Legendary, III. Historical, and IV. Romantic.

It is to the first group, the Hero ballads, that the Danish editors and the German antiquarian, William Grimm, whose excellent translation has made them known to his own country, attach the highest importance. For the natives of the North they have a peculiar interest as portraying the manners of their ancestors, those heroes of old, whose fleets terrified all the coasts of Europe, whose gravehills are still pointed out to the traveller, whose very weapons are preserved in their Museums. To the English reader they may perhaps seem to be but a faint and imperfect echo of grand ancient Sagas or German romances. But there is a rude vigour in them, and a total absence of all sentimentality and affectation, to which we turn with pleasure from some of the fashionable writings of the present day. Several of them are remarkably fine. 'Siward and Brynhild,' No. 3, as restored by Grundtvig from an ancient manuscript, is a composition of a high order. Simple, grand, terrific, it breathes the very spirit of its stern era. 'Sir Lonmor' No. 4 is another poem of a similar gloomy and thrilling but more horrible character. 'The Sword of Vengeance' No. 26 carries impersonation, that soul of poetry, to its utmost limit. It is among these too that we find in Grundtvig's publication, and rather unexpectedly, for it seems to belong much more to the romantic group, the far-famed 'Habor and Signild,' No. 21, of which the Reviewer above quoted very truly remarks that it is one of the finest in the whole world. There are several others, which, as being derived from ancient Sagas, might have claimed a place here, such as 'Swennendal,' No. 84, "The Archer's vengeance,' No. 109, 'Hylleland and his bride' No. 133, and perhaps 'Signild and her brother,' No. 145 and 'Hogen's dance,' No. 163, but, as they seemed from their subjects to belong more to the period of romance than to that of the gigantic heroes of an earlier time, they are placed in the fourth group.

The second, that of the Legendary ballads, has only one of the grand character that belongs to the first, and that one is in a very imperfect state, the fine allegory of 'St. Gertrude,' No. 41. Of a more tender and domestic character the 'Buried Mother' cannot fail to be admired for its simple pathos by all who can for a moment forget that a belief in ghosts is exploded, and sympathize with the simple and credulous peasantry, to whom it was an example of the protection which Heaven extends to their orphan children. 'Little Katey,' No. 32, is also a great favourite with all the Scandinavian nations. Some of the Scriptural ones are very singular as exhibiting the ignorance prevalent until a late period in a nation, where Protestantism was so universally accepted, that we might have expected the peasantry to be more enlightened.

The third group, that of the Historical ballads,

contains the fine dramatic series of 'Marshal Stig,' upon which W. Grimm has bestowed his especial praise. The cruel tale of 'Sir Buris and the fair Christine,' No. 57 and 58, and that of 'Ebbe's daughters,' No. 67, exhibit the stern unrelenting character of the epoch: and there are few ballads in any language more affecting than that of 'Folker Lowmanson,' No. 65, and that of 'Marshal Stig's daughters,' No. 74. In 'Sir John Rimordson,' No. 77, we have a remarkably spirited sea piece.

It is in the fourth group, the Romantic ballads, that the general reader will probably find the greatest pleasure. Foremost among them is the exquisite tale of 'Axel and Walborg,' No. 78, and from its popularity over all the Scandinavian countries, its pathetic tenderness, and the curious insight it gives us into ancient manners and customs, it deserves the reader's especial attention. Geijer tells us that there is scarcely a cottage in Sweden, in which there is not a picture of the two unfortunate lovers. Under the title of the 'Fatal Appeal,' No. 94, is grouped a series of fine ballads, which seem to be the fragments of some very ancient romance or epic poem that is now no longer in existence. Among the more imaginative ones and fairy tales there are several of great merit. 'Sir Tonne,' No. 102, 'Elfin Hill,' No. 136, 'The Nightingale,' No. 116, 'The Elf and the Farmer's wife,' No. 124, 'Agnes and the Merman,' No. 153, 'Sir Olave,' No. 81, and 'The Raven,' No. 88. Several of these have long been popular in Germany, and not unknown in England. As tales of domestic suffering and heartfelt unaffected distress nothing can surpass the beautiful ballads of

'Fair Anna,' No. 148, and its near of kin 'Sir Peter and Christine,' No. 160, the thrilling simple tale of 'Medelwold and Sidselille,' No. 101, and 'Lady Bodild,' No. 144. Among those of a more stern and savage character 'Childe Engel,' No. 164, 'Young William,' No. 170, 'Ebbe Skammelson,' No. 92, and 'Proud Eline,' No. 139 deserve most notice, the latter perhaps especially. As specimens of more ordinary romance we have 'Fair Elsey,' No. 114, 'Malfred and Mogens,' No. 82, 'Esbern and Sidselille,' No. 165, 'Sir Sallemand,' No. 106, and 'Torkild Trundeson,' No. 100. As examples of the sportive and lively kind, not very common in the older Scandinavian literature, are the 'Little Horseboy,' No. 121, 'Gundelille and Sir Palle,' No. 147, the 'Ready Reply,' No. 91, 'Cloisterbreaking,' No. 166, and the genial humourous quaint 'Sir John,' No. 143.

It grieves me to see that, owing to my inexperience in correcting for the press, several misprints have escaped my notice, but I trust that they are not such as to obscure the meaning of the passages where they occur; and asking indulgence for these and all its other faults, I submit to a generous public the result of my humble labours, as not what I could wish it to be, but as the best that I have been able to effect.

R. C. A. P.

Halse House near Taunton
28th March, 1860.

COLLECTIONS OF ROMANCES AND BALLADS REFERRED TO.

Arwidsson, Svenska Folksånger, utgifne af A. J. Arwidsson. 3 V. 8vo Stockh. 1834.
Aytoun, Ballads of Scotland. 2 V. 12mo Edin. 1858.
Bell (Rob), Early Ballads. 12mo Lond. 1856.
Buchan, Ancient Ballads of Scotland. 2 V. 8vo Edinb. 1828.
Danske Viser fra Middelalderen udgivne af **Abrahamson, Nyerup og Rahbek**. 5 V. 12mo Copenh. 1812.
Depping, Romancero Castellano por G. B. Depping. 3 V. 12mo Leipz. 1844.
Duran, A. Romancero. 5 V. 12mo Madrid 1828.
Erlach, Die Volkslieder der Deutschen. 5 V. 8vo Mannheim 1834—6.
Evans, Old Ballads. 4 V. sm. 8vo Lond. 1777.
Faber, (Boehl de) Floresta de rimas. 8vo Hamb. 1827.
Fallersleben, Niederländische Volkslieder 8vo Hanover 1856.
Fosterländskt Album, Helsingfors 1845—7. 3 V. 8vo
Gilchrist, Ancient and modern Scottish ballads. 2 V. 12mo Edinb. 1815.
Grimm, (J.) Silva de Romances viejos. 12mo Vienna 1831.
Grimm (W.), Altdänische Heldenlieder. 8vo Heidel. 1811—13.
Grundtvig, Danmark's Gamle Folkvisor udgivne af Svend G. 3 V. large 8vo Cop. 1853—56—59.
Gutch (J. M.) Robin Hood. 2 V. 8vo Lond. 1847.
Hagen (F. H.) Helden-Buch. 8vo Berlin 1811.
Jamieson (Rob.), Popular Ballads. 2 V. 8vo Lond. 1806.
Jeune (Le), Proeven van die Nederlandsche Volkzangen. 8vo Hague 1828.
Kinloch (G. R.) Ancient Scottish ballads. 8vo Edinb. 1827.
Knaben (des) Wunderhorn. 4 V. 8vo Berl. 1845.
Landstad, Norske Folkviser. 8vo Christiana 1853.
Lewis (M. G.), Tales of Wonder. 2 V. large 8vo Lond. 1811.
Lyngbye, Færoiske Kvæder. 8vo Randers 1822.
Marie de France, Poésies. 2 V. 8vo Paris 1820.

Meinert, Volkslieder aus dem Kuhländchen. 8vo Vienna 1817.
Mohnike (Gottl.), Volkslieder der Schweden. 8vo Berl. 1830.
— Altschwedische Balladen. 8ro Stuttg. 1836.
Moore (J. S.), Pictorial Book of Antient Ballad Poetry. 8vo Lond. 1853.
Motherwell (W.), Minstrelsy Ancient and Modern. 4to Glasg. 1827.
Müller, Saga-Bibliothek. 12mo Copenhagen 1817.
Niebelung Lay, 'Der Niebelungen Lied' or 'Nòt.' The lay (or the fall) of the Niebelungs. Ed. F. H. von der Hagen, Breslau, 1816.
  The same translated by W. N. Lettsom, Lond. 1850, under the title of 'The Fall of the Niebelungers.'
Northern Antiquities, by **Weber**, **Jamieson** and **Scott**. 4to Edinb. 1814.
Oehlenschläger, Gamle Danske Folkeviser. 8vo Copenh. 1841.
Percy, Antient Reliques. 3 V. sm. 8vo Lond. 1812.
Pinkerton's Scottish Ballads. 2 V. sm. 8vo Lond. 1783.
Ritson (J.), Antient English Songs. sm. 8vo Lond. 1790.
Rodd (T.), Spanish Ballads. 2 V. 8vo Lond. 1812.
Scott, Minstrelsy of the Scottish border. 3 V. 8vo Edinb. 1810.
— Sir Tristrem. 8vo Edinb. 1811.
Schröter, Finnische Runen. 1 V. 8vo Stuttg. 1834.
Sheldon, Minstrelsy of the Scottish border. 4to Lond. 1847.
Simrock, Die Edda. 8vo Stuttg. 1855.
Svenska Folkvisor, **Geijer** and **Afzelius**. 3 V. 8vo Stockh. 1814.
Talvj, Charakteristik der Volkslieder Germanischer Nationen. 8vo Leipz. 1840.
Thijm, Gedichten uit de Noord- en Zuid- Nederlandsche Literatuur. 2 V. 8vo Amst. 1850—52.
Uhland, Alte hoch und niederdeutsche Volkslieder. 8vo Stuttg. 1844.
Villemarqué, Barzas Breiz. (Breton songs) 2 V. 12mo Paris.
Warrens (Rosa), Dänische Volkslieder der Vorzeit. Hamburg 1858.
Willems, Oude Vlæmsche Liederen. 8vo Gent, 1848.
Wolf y Hofmann, Primavera y Flor de Romances. 2 V. 8vo Berl. 1856.

CONTENTS OF VOL. I.

NO.   PAGE

INTRODUCTION III

PART I. HERO BALLADS.

1. Thor of Asgard 3
   How Thor recovers his stolen hammer.
2. Siward the Hasty swain 11
   How he rides a furious horse called Skimling.
3. Siward and Brynild 16
   How Hogen is induced by his bride Brynhild to murder his comrade Siward.
4. Sir Loumor 26
   How he murders his wife's brothers, and is himself and his brothers murdered by her.
5. Grimild's Revenge 38
   How she revenges upon her two brothers the death of her husband.
6. Samson 63
   How he elopes with the king's daughter.
7. Vidrick Verland's son and the Giant Langbane . 69
   How he destroys the giant and robs his hoard.
8. The Tournament 87
   How Childe Hummer fights a duel with his uncle Siward.
9. King Diderick in Birtingsland 106
   How three of the king's champions attack and destroy king Isak and all his court.
10. King Diderick and the Dragon 111
    How the king rescues a lion from a dragon and destroys the monster.
11. Wolf of Yern 121

NO.		PAGE
	How Vidrick Verlandson avenges Wolf on the king of Brattens Vendel.	
12.	Childe Orm and the Berm Giant	132
	How Orm obtains from his mother's tomb the sword Birting, and destroys the giant with it.	
13.	Rodengard and the Eagle	141
	How with a rune he fixes the eagle on a bough.	
14.	Ravngard and Memering	145
	How Memering destroys the gigantic slanderer of his lord's wife.	
15.	Memering	161
	How he sallies out in quest of adventures and meets Vidrick Verlandson.	
16.	The bald-head Monk	164
	How he defends his cloister and becomes its Abbot.	
17.	Sir Gensolin	173
	How his giantess bride comports herself at the wedding.	
18.	Stout Diderick and Olger the Dane	179
	How Diderick invades Denmark and is repulsed by Olger.	
19.	Childe Norman's riddle rimes	185
	How he sallies out to avenge his father's death, and how he contends with a shepherd at riddling.	
20.	Angelfyr and Helmer Kamp	193
	How these two brothers fall in a duel for the king of Sweden's daughter.	
21.	Habor and Signild	205
	How the Prince Habor disguises himself as a maiden and gains access to the daughter of Siward.	
22.	The Lombards	241
	How in time of famine every third man in Denmark emigrated to Lombardy and settled there.	
23.	Regnar and Kragelille	246
	How Regnar rides in search of king Sigurd's	

NO.		PAGE
	stolen daughter, and discovers her in the garb of a peasant girl.	
24.	Karl and Krageliile	257
	How he sends confidential servants to obtain a worthy wife for him, and how they discover the daughter of Brynhilde, and bring her back.	
25.	The Fight with the Worm	263
	How a little snake grows up under the Princess's care, and becomes a monstrous lindworm, which is destroyed by Rimboldson.	
26.	The Sword of vengeance	269
	How the sword of Sir Peter is eager to avenge him on his father's murderer.	
27.	Grimmer and Helmer Kamp	276
	How Grimmer gains his lord's daughter by destroying a giant.	
28.	Childe Ranild	286
	How at the advice of his lord's daughter he enters his service, and destroys a Trold, and plunders his cavern.	
29.	Olger the Dane	294
	How Olger is taken from jail, and fights a duel with a Trold in defence of the king's daughter, and kills him.	
30.	Swain Felding	304
	How he destroys a cannibal Trold, and founds a house of refuge.	
31.	Swain Felding and Queen Judith	317
	How he is sent as envoy to bring home his king's bride.	

Appendix.

A.	The Elder Hildebrand and the Younger. From the Flemish	325
B.	Riddle Rimes. From the Faroese	331

PART II. LEGENDARY BALLADS.

32.	Little Katey	345

NO.		PAGE
	How she resists the Prince's solicitations and threats.	
33.	Saint Olave's Voyage	356
	How he sails to Tronheim over mountains.	
34.	Saint Olave at Hornelen	362
	How he destroys the Trolds there.	
35.	The buried mother	367
	How she rises from her grave to visit her orphan children.	
36.	Sabbath breaking	372
	How two knights go hunting on the sabbath day, quarrel, and kill each other.	
37.	The cruel Sister	378
	How a maiden was drowned by her sister, and how a fiddle string made from her hair betrayed the murderess.	
38.	Sir Morten of Fogelsong	387
	How he rises from the grave to restore to two orphans the land he had unjustly taken from them.	
39.	Maribo Well	391
	How its waters restore to life the mangled limbs of a dead man.	
40.	Saint Stephen and Herod	395
	How a roasted cock crowed on his table to announce the birth of Jesus.	

PART I.

HERO BALLADS.

I.

THOR OF ASGARD.

This ballad is remarkable as being the only one in which an Edda poem has been preserved whole and sound in the memory of the peasantry. There are other tales in the Edda, from which popular ballads have been formed, but in these the heroes have usually been changed into Christian saints, or other alterations made in them, that have destroyed their original character. Vedel's edition of it seems to have been composed from two ancient Manuscripts with additions of his own, as usual, and these not very judicious ones. For instance after the 19th stanza he represents the Thusser king as driven by despair to surrender the mace; when it is evident that the delivery of it was merely the fulfilment of a bargain. It was to be the nuptial gift. The original poem in the Edda has been very finely translated into English by W. Herbert, and into German by Simrock. The present ballad has the appearance of being a burlesque upon it, but was probably meant to be serious. His astounding powers of eating and drinking were among the attributes of the God Thor.

As an instance of the occurrence of the same ideas to semibarbarous nations, we may remember that Homer too represents his greatest heroes as being the greatest eaters. See in B. IX the visit of Ajax and other chiefs to the tent of Achilles, where the backs of a sheep, a goat, and a fat hog are dressed for six people. The term 'aged father' in the 13th stanza was the proper title of the God Thor, not only in the Scandinavian, but in all the other northern nations. It is scarcely necessary to say that Thor was the son of Odin, and the god of thunder, and that it is from him that we still name the fifth day of the week 'Thursday'.

This ballad is also the oldest of those preserved in Sweden. Arwidson gives two forms of it.

It is not improbable that under this myth may be recorded a contest with some alien race. The Thusser are supposed to be Turks. By the loss and recovery of the hammer, the emblem of power, may be figured the temporary subjection of the Asæ, and their retaliation. But a more mystical interpretation of it has been suggested; namely, that the hammer is the emblem of thunder, which is lost during the winter months, but by the aid of 'Loki' *flame*, *heat*, is again recovered from the genii of cold and darkness habiting in the North, at the return of spring.

Thor of Asgard.

Grundtv. I. p. 3. Grimm p. 141. Arw. I. p. 3 & 7.

1 There rode the mighty of Asgard, Thor,
    His journey across the plain,
  And there his hammer of gold he lost,
    And sought so long in vain.

2 'Twas then the mighty of Asgard, Thor,
    His brother his bidding told;
  "Up thou and off to the Northland Fell,
    "And seek my hammer of gold."

3 He spake, and Loki, the serving man,
    His feathers upon him drew,
  And launching over the salty sea
    Away to the Northland flew.

4 He stopp'd, as he cross'd the castle yard,
    To cloak him in scarlet pall,
  And greeted the hideous Thusser king,
    And enter'd his lofty hall.

5 "Welcome, Loki, thou serving man!
    "Right heartily welcome here!
  "Now tell me how matters at Asgard stand,
    "And how in the country near."

6 "In castle at Asgard all is well,
    "And eke in the country near,
  "But Thor has his golden hammer miss'd,
    "And therefore am I come here."

7   "Hark thou my words! No more shall Thor
      "His hammer again behold;
      "For fifteen fathoms and forty deep
      "It 's buried beneath the mould.

8   "His hammer no more gets Thor again
      "From under the solid earth,
      "Till mine is the maiden Fredensborg,
      "And all that ye all are worth."

9   He spake, and Loki, the serving man,
      His feathers upon him drew,
      And back again over the salty sea
      To Thor with his answer flew.

10 He stopp'd, as he cross'd the castle-yard,
      To wrap him in scarlet cloak,
      And up to the castle chamber went,
      And thus to his brother spoke.

11 "Thy hammer thou gettest again no more
      "From under the solid earth,
      "Unless thou givest him Fredensborg
      "And all that we all are worth."

12 "Nay!" answer'd the haughty Fredensborg,
      And spake from her bench so bold;
      "Nay, give me even a Christian man,
      "But not that lothely Trold."

13 "Then let us our aged father take,
      "And comb him and dress him well,
      "And bear him in guise of a maiden fair
      "Away to the Northland Fell."

14 They brought her to court, the blooming bride,
    And into the banquet hall,
  And largess there with an open hand
    Was dealt to the minstrels all.

15 They took her, the young and bashful bride,
    To sit on her bridal chair,
  And forward stepp'd the Thusser king
    Himself to serve the fair.

16 A whole ox-carcase the maid ate up,
    And thirty sides of swine,
  And took to her meat seven hundred loaves,
    Before she would taste of wine.

17 A whole ox-carcase the maid ate up,
    Her loaves and her bacon first,
  And then twelve barrels of ale she drank,
    Before she could quench her thirst.

18 The Thusser king, as he paced the floor,
    His hands on his bosom beat;
  "Who then, and whence is the youthful bride,
    "So monstrous a meal can eat?"

19 And smiling beneath his scarlet cloak,
    Thus Loki, the page, replied;
  "Seven days it is since she tasted food
    "For longing to be thy bride."

20 Then brought eight champions, stout and strong,
    The hammer upon a tree,
  And heav'd it up for the youthful bride,
    And laid it across her knee.

21 Uprose from her seat that tender bride,
     Her hammer she took in hand,
   And, only the sober truth to tell,
     She brandish'd it like a wand.

22 The first she slew was the Thusser king,
     So lothely and fierce and tall;
   She came indeed to the wedding feast!
     She slaughter'd them great and small.

23 "And now" said Loki the wily page,
   "'Tis time that we all retire,
   "And home to our country bend our steps,
   "And comfort our widow sire."

NOTES.

St. 1. l. 1. **Thor of Asgard.** In the original he is called "Thor of Haffsgaard' i. e. 'of the sea-home', a name evidently corrupted from Asgard, the home of the Asir, the race of Gods from whom the early Scandinavian kings claimed to be descended.

Ib. l. 3. The hammer of gold is Thor's peculiar emblem. It was with this that he destroyed his enemies, the Jotuns. Like other weapons in early times it had its proper name, and was called 'Miölner', crusher. It never failed to strike the object at which it was aimed, and it always returned back to Thor's hand. It seems to have typified a thunderbolt. See for further information about Thor, P. A. Munch's Normændenes Gudelære i Hedenold, a compendious and excellent work.

St. 2. **His brother.** This is a mistake of the ballad-maker. Loki was of Jotun race, and although admitted among the twelve Gods called Asir, was rather their enemy than colleague. He is represented as handsome in person, but full of malice and craft, ever plotting against the Asir, whom he was obliged to serve. He was the father of the three monsters who at the end of the world should wreak their vengeance upon the Asir; namely the wolf Fenris, the snake Yormungand, and the goddess Hell, who received into Niflheim the souls of all who died of age or sickness. See Munch ib. p. 18.

St. 3. **His feathers**, the fieder-hamm or feather dress so frequently alluded to in these ballads. In the original Edda tale Thor borrows it from the goddess Freya. It occurs in the Old-Saxon poem, the Heliand, as applied to the wings of angels. Schmeller's Ed. p. 171. l. 22 'thuo thar suogan quam engil thes alowaldon obana fan radure faran an *Fetherhamon.*' 'Then there came rushing an angel of the Almighty from above from heaven, moving on *feather-ham.*' In another passage p. 50 l. 11 it is applied to the wings of birds. In Layamon's 'Brut' the wings that Bladud made himself are called Feðerhome. l. 2874.

St. 8. In the Edda it is the goddess Freya whom he claims, the Venus of Northern Mythology.

St. 10. This cloaking in the castle-yard was etiquette even among the Gods.

St. 12. Trold means any supernatural being, a sorcerer, a heathen, a Mahometan, a giant, any thing which is not like other Christian men. The word is properly pronounced *Trole,* but as this might perplex the English reader, it is used in these translations with the sound of *bold.*

St. 16. In the Edda her meal is only a little more moderate, one ox, eight salmon, all the sweetmeats, and three boatfuls of mead. Vedel with his usual taste for exaggeration allots her fifteen oxen, thirty swine, six hundred loaves, and twelve lasts of ale of two tons each.

St. 19. In the Edda Loki disguises himself as the bridesmaid.

St. 20. In the Edda Thrym, the Thusser king, is frightened at Thor's great glaring eyes, as he raises the veil to kiss his bride, but nevertheless orders in the hammer agreeably to the bargain made.

St. 22 l. 3.
 *saa slog hun ihiell di andre smaa trolde,
 at bröllupen monne hun gang.*
The meaning of the last line is obscure 'She must go to the wedding'. Vedel replaces it with *at dörren den giordis trang.* 'that the door became narrow to them'.

II.

SIWARD THE HASTY SWAIN.

This is one of those ballads in which Vedel by his injudicious tampering has caused the greatest confusion. In his edition Siward is represented without any cause whatever as leaping back again out of the castle-yard and breaking his horse's back and his own, contrary to the history of that hero in all other poems, Scandinavian and German. W. Grimm, to get over the difficulty, supposed the ballad to have been written upon some other person, and Siward's name to have been substituted for the right one. Now that Grundtvig has published the original manuscripts we see that the conclusion was Vedel's own composition.

This ballad is founded upon one of a great cycle of poems on the Welsing family, a subject that is the common property of all the German and Scandinavian races, and to which among others the fine epic poem "The Niebelunger's Fall" belongs. This cycle has been linked together into a continuous romance by A. Raszmann under the title of "Die Deutsche Heldensage", and is regarded by him as consisting of the disjointed fragments of an ancient epic, the outline of which he has tried to restore. His work is one of very high interest and full of information, and his account of Sivard or Sigurd very complete. The nonsense that has been written on the subject by some other German authors is almost incredible. Grundtvig sums up a few of these essays. "Some take Sivard to be Sigbert king of the Franks in the 6th Century, some hold that he was Arminius the Cheruscan, some that he was Claudius Civilis, some the Roman emperor Victorinus. Some have given his history an allegorical meaning, and supposed it to denote the change of the seasons, some the action of chemical substances on one another, and make Sivard muriatic acid, and his death its evaporation — some take him for the God Odin, or Thor, or Balder or Freyr, some take the romance for identical with the Iliad, and make Sivard Achilles and Menelaus both in one, some see in it the rape of Proserpine, and Sivard is then the god Bacchus &c. &c."

According to the Icelandic Sagas, Sæmund's Edda, and the Völsung saga, Sivard was brought up in the court of his father-in-law, King Hialprek, received from him his horse Grane, and made his first journey to the court of his mother's brother, Griper. This journey is described in the Gripi-spá, and it is on this that the ballad is founded. His horse Grani, *the grey*, is a descendant of Odin's horse, the eight-footed Sleipner, and plays a distinguished part in the Scandinavian poems. This is the horse upon which Siward carries off Fafner's treasure, and rides through the fire to obtain Brunhild, and which mourns over his death. Of this horse there is no mention in the German poems, an evidence that our ballad is of Scandinavian origin.

The following translation is made from Grundtvig's ms. A, but the 5th stanza is from his ms. B, to replace a rather insipid one that corresponds to it in A.

The statement with which it begins, that he killed his stepfather, is contrary to all the Sagas. It is probable that the peasantry have confused his fosterfather Regin, whom he did slay, with his stepfather, king Hialprek.

Siward the Hasty swain.

Grundtv. I. 9. Dan. Vis. I. 96 Oehl. p. 40. Grimm p. 37. Raszm. I. p. 295.

1 Siward had stricken his stepsire dead,
   And all for his mother's best,
   And now a journey was fain to ride,
   His manhood at court to test.

2 Before his mother he went to stand,
   His sword-blade slung at his side;
   "Dear mother, I'm longing to go to court;
   "To court that I could but ride!"

3 "I'll give thee, my son, a gallant horse,
   "To carry thee o'er the ground;
   "I'll give thee my horse, so far and wide
   "As Skimling the Gram renown'd."

4 Siward his gauntlets toss'd aside,
   And fine were his hands and white,
   And girded himself the noble horse,
   He trusted no menial wight.

5   Himself he girded the gallant steed,
      And rein'd him with golden wire;
    His eye was bright as the morning star,
      And flashing his bit with fire.

6   He vaulted and sat upon Skimling's back,
      And well he was skill'd to ride;
    To Skimling it seem'd a wondrous thing,
      That spurs drove into his side.

7   His mother, she follow'd him forth from town
      Far over the heath and mead;
    "Beware, my Siward, of Skimling's wrath;
    "O prithee, my son take heed."

8   "Nay, hear me, my mother, and grieve no more,
      "But lay your terror aside;
    "'Tis long that I lived and serv'd at court;
    "My horse I have learnt to ride."

9   So answered Siward, the Hasty Swain,
      Set spurs to his gallant steed,
    And off in three wide bounds he sprang
      Away to the field at speed.

10 Away so fiercely in three wide bounds
      He sprang over field and flood,
    That, only the sober truth to tell,
      He sweated with tears of blood.

11 Forth, forth he gallop'd three days and nights,
      He sprang over hill and dale,
    And rested before a lofty house,
      The castle of Berner Quale.

12 The king was standing in lofty bower,
    And gazing around so wide;
    "See hither is coming a hairbrain man;
    "How well he a horse can ride!"

13 "'Tis surely," replied the Danish Queen,
    And utter'd the words with grace,
    " 'Tis surely Siward, my sister's son,
    "But whence at so fleet a pace?

14 "And hark ye hither, my gallant men,
    "With courtesy treat our guest;
    "If yonder is Siward, the Hasty swain,
    "He bears not a word of jest."

15 And up rode Siward, the Hasty swain,
    And spurr'd his horse to the spring,
    And leap'd at a bound the castle wall,
    And stood before the king.

16 Fifteen the sentries on battlement,
    Were keeping their watch and ward,
    But none were aware, till horse and man
    Were both in the castle yard.

NOTE

St. 3. Gram means *furious*, but the horse is often called graa *gray*.

III.

SIWARD AND BRYNILD.

This fine ballad is one of those which Vedel altered to the confusion of commentators. Thanks to Grundtvig's researches we have now the original form of it, and find it agree much more closely with other Scandinavian and German poems upon the subject. For instance it is Signild who wears the ring, and not Brynild, as Vedel chose to give it. The tale has been treated in the Icelandic poems called the Völsunga and Wilkina Sagas, in the ancient German epic 'The Fall of the Niebelungers, of which there is a translation by Lettsom, and in 'The Horn-skinned Sigfrid', and, what is very remarkable, there is still retained in the memory of the Faroe islanders, and commonly sung to their dances, a whole cycle of poems detailing the history of Sigurd, who is the same as the Sigfrid and Siward of the Germans and Danes. There is an allusion to this cycle of tales in the Anglosaxon poem of Beowulf l. 1753, from which it has been argued that it was equally known in this island as among the Germans and Scandinavians. This conclusion is scarcely authorized by the passage in question, for in the first place the poem itself bears internal evidence of having been composed on the continent, and it is at a foreign court, and not in England, that the gleeman is represented as singing. In later times it has been mixed up with the story of Regnar Lodbrok in the North, and with that of Attila and Dietrich in Germany. It is rather curious that as the great epic poem of the ancients is based on the quarrel of two chieftains about a fair lady, so the great epic of the Northerns in the Middle ages is based on the quarrel of two ladies about a chieftain.

In the particulars there is a great difference among the many tales on the subject. The reader will find an excellent digest of them in Raszmann's admirable work, 'Die Deutsche Heldensage'. In the German tale the ladies quarrel at the portal of the great church at Worms. The poet could hardly have found a finer scene for it than this beautiful building, and it adds much to the traveller's interest in viewing it to fancy that he sees the very portal where an event occurred that led to such important consequences. The portal is in truth however by some hundred years more recent than the event and many of the poems that celebrate it. The Signild of the ballad is the Chriemhild of the Niebelung Lay. The German tale differs from the Scandinavian in regard to the murderer of Siward. The Sagas attribute the deed to Gunnar, or to his younger brother, the German poem to Hogen, as does our ballad also. In the main the story is every where nearly the same, that he was treacherously murdered at or near his own home. The Scandinavian version of the event will be found in Hagen's Heldensagen.

Brynild appears to have been a woman of great

vigour and violent temper, a female Achilles. To
bring her husband Gunnar to proper obedience and
deference to her will, she bound him hand and foot,
and hitched him up to a peg the three first nights of
their marriage. In this extremity the poor husband
applied to his friend Siward, who personated him, and
mastered the bride, and, before he left her, drew from
her hand the ring which he afterwards gave to his
wife Signild or Chriemhild, and which on Brynild's
recognizing it, led to the tragical consequences here
described. Sagas and ballads of a later date represent her as having previously borne a child to Siward,
namely the beautiful Aslauga, the wife of Regnar Lodbrok, whose romantic fate is the subject of the ballad
"Regnar and Kragelille" No. 23 below. This is inconsistent with the older sagas.

The stern necessity under which Hogen finds himself of obeying his bride against the dictates of honour,
friendship, and interest, and its dismal consequences,
could hardly be told with more dramatic and gloomy
effect than in this ballad. Hogen's suicide is contrary
to all other versions of the tale, German or Scandinavian. In the Niebelung Lay he is the hero of the
war to which this murder led.

Conybeare in his Anglo-Saxon poetry p. XLII gives
a translation of a fine passage from an Icelandic Saga
describing the affliction of Siward's widow, the Gudrun of the Icelandic, but the same as the Grimild,
Chriemhild, Sinild and Signild of other poems.

Brynhild had been put to sleep by Odin, and was
destined to remain asleep upon her hill surrounded by
flames, the mythic Waberlohe, until a man who had

never known fear, should come to wake her. She had been many years there when Siward arrived and found her tightly cased in armour, which he removed with the assistance of his horse Grani, and woke her. After enquiring who he was, she offered him a Minnetrank, or Love-potion, and being a Valkyrie, or goddess, she sung him runes for the guidance of his life. In the ancient Saga we have a very superior being to the lady who washed her clothes at the river-side described in the following ballad.

Siward and Brynild.

Grundt. I. 16. Dan. Vis. I. 132. Grimm p. 31. R. Warr. p. 224. Raszm. I. p. 208.

1 Siward had tamed and gently train'd
   His fiery steed,*
   And Brynild in the light of day
   From durance freed.

2 Proud Brynild from her tower of glass
   Did Siward take,
   And then to Hero Hogen give
   For friendship's sake.

3 Brynild and Sinild both so proud,
   Two maids of rank,
   Went down to wash their silken robes
   At river bank.

* See the preceding ballad.

4 "Hark now, fair Simild, prythee say,
    "Dear sister mine,
"How came those glittering rings of gold
    "On hand of thine?"

5 "How on my finger came these rings,
    "That gleam so bright?
"Siward the Hasty gave me these
    "His troth to plight.

6 "Siward the Hasty gave me these,
    "As troth he sware,
"And thee to Hero Hogen gave
    "As comrade's share."

7 So soon as this proud Brynelille
    Had heard her say,
In grief up to her bower she went,
    And sick she lay.

8 Up to her bower went Brynelille,
    And lay so low,
And Hero Hogen to see the maid
    Went to and fro.

9 "O tell me, maiden Brynelille,
    "My bride so dear,
"What in this wide world thinkest thou,
    "Thy heart would cheer?

10 "If in this world there were but aught
    "Could ease thy pain,
"Pay would I gladly all my gold
    "That same to gain."

11 "Nothing is there in all this world
    "My pain will ease,
  "Till in these hands false Siward's head
    "Once I can seize."

12 "But how then canst thou Siward's head
    "Or seize or take?
  "His, through whose flesh no sword on earth
    "Its way can make?"

13 "So hard his flesh, no sword on earth
    "Can give him pain,
  "None but his own, nor know I how
    "That sword to gain."

14 "Then seek him where in th'upper room,
    "He sits at board;
  "And beg him for his honour's sake
    "Lend you his sword.

15 "Beg him all for his honour's sake
    "Lend you the blade;
  "Tell him you must in joust defend
    "Your own dear maid.

16 "So soon as safely in your hand
    "That sword shall be,
  "I beg you by the mighty God,
    "Forget not me."

17 His head the Hero Hogen wrapp'd
    In purple hood,
  And where in chamber Siward sat,
    Before him stood.

18 "My comrade Siward, Hasty swain,
    "Here at thy board!
"Say, wilt thou for thine honour's sake
    "Lend me thy sword?

19 "Trust to me for thine honour's sake
    "That famous blade;
"I must in field to day defend
    "My own dear maid."

20 "Mine own good sword, mine Adelring,
    "Should I lend thee,
"'Twill give thee on every battlefield
    "The victory.

21 "Surely to thee, my friend, I trust
    "That sword so good;
"But guard thee well — beneath its hilt
    "Are tears of blood.'

22 "Guard' thee against those tears of blood,
    "That glow so red,
"If they should on thy finger run,
    "Thou'rt quickly dead."

23 The sword the Hero Hogen took,
    From scabbard drew,
And on the spot his dearest friend,
    His comrade slew.

24 In mantle fold the head he wrapp'd
    Dripping with gore,
And to the lady's bower aloft
    To Brynild bore.

25 "See here, and take the bleeding head,
      "And still thy pain;
   "I've, to my sorrow, for thy sake
      "My comrade slain."

26 "O take away the bleeding head,
      "Spare me the sight;
   "And now, to your great joy, to you
      "My troth I plight."

27 "Mine will I never give to thee,
      "Nor love thee more;
   "For thy sake I've my comrade slain,
      "And rue it sore."

28 His sword the Hero Hogen took,
      From scabbard drew,
   And the proud Brynild at a blow
      He cut in two.

29 And then against a jutting stone
      His sword-hilt stay'd,
   And through his heart the royal prince
      Drove the sharp blade.

30 Firm in the dingy mould stood fix'd
      His trusty sword,
   While from that noble prince's heart
      The life-blood pour'd.

31 Alas! That maid so fair and proud
      Had e'er drawn breath!
   Or two so nobly born should find
      So sad a death!

NOTES.

St. 1. This tower which Siward stormed may in the first place have been an allegory, and afterwards understood in a literal sense. In ancient German poetry a lady's virtue is often called a high tower. As

>Ic weet noch een so hoghen berch
>boven alle berghen is hi hoghe,
>die sal ic noch in dale brengen,
>daer om ist dat ic poghe.
> Der Ritter und die Maid, Fallersleben. p. 62.

>'I know a hill, a lofty hill,
>Above all others high;
>And that I'll yet bring down to dale;
>'Tis after that I try!'

St. 3 l. 1. The Sinild of this ballad is the Chriemhild of the Niebelung Lay, the Gudrun of the Icelandic. l. 3. Young ladies washing their clothes at the river's bank may remind us of the Phæacian king's daughter in the Odyssee B. VI. l. 85.

St. 7. Brynelille is merely 'little Brynhild'.

St. 12. Siward had a skin of horn, whence he was called Hörnen Siegfrid, from having bathed in the blood of the serpent Fafni.

St. 14. **For his honour's sake.** 'for erre siynn.' How it could be for Siward's honour to lend the sword is not at all clear. Comrades, 'Stall-brödre', may have been bound in honour to give each other every possible aid.

St. 20. **Adelring.** This was the famous sword forged for him by Regin, the one with which he slew Fafni, the serpent, from whom he took his title of Fafnisbane, Fafni's slayer.

St. 21. The tears of blood are drops of the serpent Fafni's blood. This famous sword, Adelring, Dietrich afterwards finds in the Dragon's cave. See No. X.

St. 25. **My comrade slain.** We shall estimate the greatness of the sacrifice which he made to his lady by considering how great was the attachment of comrades. It is related of one of these men that, unable to survive his deceased friend, he had himself let down alive into the same cavern with the dead body. See Herbert's Works Vol. I. p. 127.

St. 29. This ascribing royal birth to Hogen is contrary to the German tale which represents him as a mercenary soldier.

IV.

SIR LOUMOR OR THE VENGEANCE OF BLOOD.

This horrible tragedy belongs to the same cycle as the two foregoing ballads. The Signild of this is the Sinild, Grimild, Gudrun or Chriemhild of other poems, the widow of Sigfried, Siward or Sigurd. This tale, like the preceding ones, exhibits great difference in the particulars, but in its main points is nearly the same, whereever it has extended over Germany and Scandinavia.

According to the northern Sagas King Atle or Attila, represented in the ballad by Sir Loumor, invites his brothers-in-law Gunnar and Högne (Hogen) to his court and murders them. His wife Gudrun, their sister, avenges herself first by killing Attila's two children and giving him their flesh to eat, and their blood to drink, and then killing him in his bed. In the German poems Krimhild (Gudrun) invites her brothers, and incites her husband to kill them.

It seems to be also mixed up with the older saga of Siggeir and his wife Signy. Völs. Saga ch. 2—8.

For a German translation of the Northern Sagas, the Atla-kwitha and the Atla-mal see Simrock's Edda p. 246 and 253.

Nothing can show more strongly how much the northern nations were impressed with the duty of revenging the blood of their relatives, than the ascribing to parents the murder of their own children, and to husbands and wives that of each other and their dearest kin to gratify this savage instinct. It is not a little curious that such a fearful drama should be made a dance tune, but there can be no doubt that this among the rest was sung to the merry steps of the ancient peasantry of the north.

The arrangement by which the last words of the first line and the whole of the second one are repeated, occurs in many of the other ballads that are composed in couplets. In this one it adds to the gloomy effect, and is given as an example; but others, in which it is found in the Danish, are here printed without it, to save space, and avoid causing weariness to the reader.

Sir Loumor or the Vengeance of Blood.

Dan. Vis. III. 172. Grundt. I. p. 29. Grimm p. 253. R. Warr. p. 233. Raszm. I. p. 303.

1 Fair Signild's brothers took her hand,
And married her into a foreign land.
    Took her hand,
And married her into a foreign land.

2 Afar from home they made her wed
The man her father's blood had shed.
    They made her wed
The man her father's blood had shed.

3 Eight weary years her thrall she bore,
  Eight years saw not her brothers more.
              Her thrall she bore,
  Eight years saw not her brothers more.

4 She brew'd the mead and sparkling wine,
  And bade her brothers come and dine.
              The sparkling wine
  And bade her brothers come and dine.

5 Sir Loumor laugh'd with hearty glee,
  For eight years never laugh'd had he.
              With hearty glee,
  For eight years never laugh'd had he.

6 Fair Signild went to her lofty tower,
  And gazed around from hour to hour.
              On lofty tower
  She gazed around from hour to hour.

7 She saw along the mountain side
  Her seven long-wish'd-for brothers ride.
              On mountain side
  Her seven long-wish'd-for brothers ride.

8 Nearer they drew, and still more near,
  And now their voices she could hear.
              And still more near,
  And now their voices she could hear.

9 In scarlet cloak she wrapp'd her head,
  And up to Loumor's chamber sped.
              She wrapp'd her head,
  And up to Loumor's chamber sped.

10 "My lord, what welcome will you show
   "To these my brothers down below?"
            "Will you show
   "To these my brothers down below?"

11 "I'll welcome them with best of cheer,
   "As though they were my own come here."
            "With best of cheer,
   "As though they were my own come here."

12 And then into a laugh he brake,
   That made the very walls to shake.
            A laugh he brake
   That made the very walls to shake.

13 Spake then the babe, in cradle lay,
   It never spake before that day.
            In cradle lay,
   It never spake before that day.

14 "Ha! Ha! My father's laugh I hear,
   "That bodes my mother evil near."
            "Laugh I hear,
   "That bodes my mother evil near."

15 He rose and kick'd the cradle o'er;
   The babe left lifeless on the floor,
            The cradle o'er,
   The babe left lifeless on the floor.

16 The setting sun began to show,
   'Twas time they should to supper go.
            Began to show,
   'Twas time they should to supper go.

17 Her lord she placed at table-head,
   To chairs her several brothers led.
               At table-head,
   To chairs her several brothers led.

18 With wine she charged Sir Loumor's cup,
   With milk she fill'd her brothers' up.
               Sir Loumor's cup,
   With milk she fill'd her brothers' up.

19 But oft as she his goblet fill'd,
   The wine upon the floor he spill'd.
               His goblet fill'd,
   The wine upon the floor he spill'd.

20 She then to the sleeping room repair'd,
   And all her brothers' beds prepar'd.
               She then repair'd,
   And all her brothers' beds prepar'd.

21 Their beds on hard sharp stones she laid,
   Lest they should be to sleep betray'd.
               On stones she laid,
   Lest they should be to sleep betray'd.

22 She placed beside them, every one,
   A knife, they could rely upon.
               Gave every one
   A knife, he could rely upon.

23 She laid along the bedstead rail
   A naked sword and coat of mail.
               Bedstead rail
   A naked sword and coat of mail.

SIR LOUMOR OR THE VENGEANCE OF BLOOD.

24 And now the hour of night came on,
And time they should to bed be gone.
   Night came on,
And time they should to bed be gone.

25 Signild had scarce begun to doze,
Ere from her arms Sir Loumor rose.
   Begun to doze,
Ere from her arms Sir Loumor rose.

26 Softly he stole to the outer hall,
And murder'd there her brothers all.
   In the outer hall
He murder'd there her brothers all.

27 He took in turn each several bed,
And left those gallant brothers dead.
   Each several bed,
And left those gallant brothers dead.

28 He drew from each his sword and knife,
And took therewith the sleeper's life.
   His sword and knife,
And took therewith the sleeper's life.

29 He fill'd a cup with brother's gore,
And that to his wife, fair Signild, bore.
   With brother's gore,
And that to his wife, fair Signild, bore.

30 As soon as he approach'd her room,
Grew pale fair Signild's rosy bloom.
   Approach'd her room,
Grew pale fair Signild's rosy bloom.

31 "Tell me, Sir Loumor, gallant knight,
"Where went you then at dead of night?"
"Gallant knight,
"Where went you then at dead of night?"

32 "Outside, my dear, out on the hill,
"I heard, I thought, my falcon's yell."
"Out on the hill,
"I heard, I thought, my falcon's yell."

33 "Your falcons? — Why these sorry jests?
"God guard from harm our sleeping guests."
"Why these sorry jests?
"God guard from harm our sleeping guests."

34 He set her down the cup he bore,
A cup brim full of recking gore.
The cup he bore,
A cup brim full of recking gore.

35 "Now drink, fair Signild, prithee drink,
"From brothers' blood thou wilt not shrink."
"Prithee drink,
"From brothers' blood thou wilt not shrink."

36 "My thirst indeed must urge me sore,
"To taste your filthy cup of gore.
"Urge me sore,
"To taste your filthy cup of gore.

37 "Go back, my lord, to bed again,
"I little care, for those you've slain."
"To bed again,
"I little care for those you've slain."

38 "I reck not, though of all bereft,
 "So long as you, my lord, are left."
  "Though of all bereft,
 "So long as you, my lord, are left."

39 And now full eight years more were past,
 Since Loumor saw his brothers last.
  Eight years were past,
 Since Loumor saw his brothers last.

40 Sir Loumor bade brew mead and wine,
 And ask'd his brothers all to dine.
  Mead and wine,
 And ask'd his brothers all to dine.

41 Fair Signild laughs, as that she hears,
 She had not laugh'd for eight whole years.
  As that she hears,
 She had not laugh'd for eight whole years.

42 She placed Sir Loumor's guests at board,
 With honied words their wine she pour'd.
  Guests at board,
 With honied words their wine she pour'd.

43 Sir Loumor drain'd his cup with glee,
 So little fear of death had he.
  His cup with glee,
 So little fear of death had he.

44 She gave them down, whereon to sleep,
 To yield them slumbers long and deep.
  Whereon to sleep,
 To yield them slumbers long and deep.

45 She pillow'd them with cushions blue,
   And sleep-runes on them all she drew.
              On cushions blue,
   And sleep-runes on them all she drew.

46 Soon as her lord began to doze,
   Up from his arms fair Signild rose.
              Began to doze,
   Up from his arms fair Signild rose.

47 Nor slow was she his sword to take,
   And go their sleeping guests to wake.
              His sword to take
   And go their sleeping guests to wake.

48 Out to the courtyard Signild sped,
   And left Sir Loumor's brothers dead.
              To courtyard sped
   And left Sir Loumor's brothers dead,

49 Her heart was with such anger fill'd,
   All his three sisters too she kill'd.
              With such anger fill'd,
   All his three sisters too she kill'd.

50 A goblet then she charged with gore,
   And that to her lord Sir Loumor bore.
              Charged with gore,
   And that to her lord Sir Loumor bore.

51 But first a cord of silk she found,
   And foot and thigh Sir Loumor bound.
              Silk she found,
   And foot and thigh Sir Loumor bound.

52 And then with plaited braid for bands,
   She bound Sir Loumor's murderous hands.
         With plaited bands
   She bound Sir Loumor's murderous hands.

53 "Wake up, Sir Loumor, talk with me,
   "In sleep I will not murder thee.
         "Talk with me,
   "In sleep I will not murder thee.

54 "Drink now, my lord Sir Loumor, drink,
   "Nor thou from blood of brothers shrink."
         "Sir Loumor drink,
   "Nor thou from blood of brothers shrink."

55 "My thirst indeed must urge me sore,
   To drink thy filthy cup of gore.
         "Urge me sore,
   "To drink thy filthy cup of gore.

56 "Go back, sweet wife, to bed again,
   " I little care for kinsmen slain."
         "To bed again,
   "I little care for kinsmen slain."

57 He thought to grasp his trusty brand,
   But felt she had bound him foot and hand.
         His trusty brand,
   But felt she had bound him foot and hand.

58 "O spare me, Signild, slay not me,
   "I've never wish'd to murder thee."
         "Slay not me,
   "I've never wish'd to murder thee."

59 "It was by a murder foully plann'd,
   "My father sank beneath thy hand.
            "Foully plann'd,
   "My father sank beneath thy hand.

60 "None else than thou my father slew,
   "And all my seven dear brothers too.
            "My father slew,
   "And all my seven dear brothers too.

61 "And now I'll e'en avenge on thee
   "The many lives, thou 'st robb'd from me."
            "Avenge on thee
   "The many lives thou 'st robb'd from me."

62 From out her sleeve a knife she drew,
   And straight therewith Sir Loumor slew.
            A knife she drew,
   And straight therewith Sir Loumor slew.

63 Then spake the babe, in cradle lay,
   "I'll venge that deed some future day."
            In cradle lay
   "I'll venge that deed some future day."

64 "Thou'rt sprung, I know, from the same blood,
   "To me thou never wilt be good."
            "From the same blood
   "To me thou never wilt be good."

65 She seiz'd the brat, "I'll stop thy boast,"
   And dash'd its brains against a post.
            "I'll stop thy boast"
   And dash'd its brains against a post.

66 "And now that man for man I've slain
"I'll to my native land again."
"Man I've slain
"I'll to my native land again."

NOTES.

c. 53. In these ballads the second person is used in the plural, *you*, where respect is shown, as to a husband or father, and *thou* to a wife, an intimate friend, a child or an inferior. Signild, having got the mastery of her husband, now addresses him with *thee* and *thou*.

c. 63. This idea of the infant in the cradle resolving to avenge its father's death occurs again and again in these ballads, and we find it in a passage of a German one, Hammen von Reistett, Knab. Wun: II. p. 171.

> Ihr Herrn wissen was das bedeut:
> Das Kindlein in der Wiegen leit,
> Das noch kein Wort kann sprechen,
> Sein Vater den muss es rächen.

> Ye know the laugh is not in vain,
> That laughs a child in cradle lain;
> A child that yet no word can speak;
> His father's death that child shall wreak.

V.

GRIMILD'S REVENGE.

In a preceding ballad No. III we have had an account of the murder of Siward or Siegfrid by his brother-in-law Hogen. The three following describe how his death was avenged by his widow Grimild, the Signild of No. III, the Chriemhilt of the Niebelunger's Fall, the Gudrun of other ancient poems. They are clearly all derived from a German source, and have no great claim to poetical merit, but paint in very vivid colours the sanguinary and ferocious temper of the times, and are interesting as examples of how a tale is altered in passing from an Epic poem to a popular ballad.

Grimild's Revenge. A.
Grundt: I. 44. Dan: Vis: I. 124. Grimm p. 10. Raszm: II. p. 109.

1   It was the stately Dame Grimild,
    The mead she bade to brew,
    And many a hero stout and bold
    To banquet hall she drew.

2   She bade them come to deeds of war,
    She bade them come to strife,
    Where many a hero young and brave
    Was doom'd to lose his life.

3   A champion, such as Hogen was,
        Or Folker Spilleman, —
    Find one such as those brothers were,
        We surely never can.

4   But forward Hogen's mother stepp'd,
        "It seem'd," Dame Bodil said,
    "As in a midnight trance I lay,
        "That all the birds were dead.

5   "And this is what the dream will say,
        "If dreams ye understand,
    "'Twill cost you many a hero's life
        "To tread that heathen land."

6   But forward rode those gentlemen
        To where the torrent swept,
    And there they found a Merwoman,
        As under a hill she slept.

7   "Wake up! wake up! thou Merwoman,
        "Thou fair and lovely wife,
    "And say if in the heathen land
        "I'm doom'd to lose my life."

8   "O turn thee, Hero Hogen, turn,
        "Thou gallant knight so bold,
    "Thou hast at home on thine own land
        "So many a fort and hold.

9   "Wend homeward to thy grassy lands,
        "Avoid the fray and strife;
    "If to thy sister thou shalt come,
        "That visit costs thy life."

10   Then wax'd the Hero Hogen wroth,
       His sword in haste he drew,
     And struck the wretched Merwoman,
       And cut her neck in two.

11   "Nay! rather thou it is shalt die
     "Here on the glittering sand,
     "And I so hale and hearty ride
     "On to the heathen land."

12   Forward they rode, those gentlemen,
       To where the torrents sweep,
     And found th'unhappy Ferryman
       Beside his wife asleep.

13   "Wake up! wake up! good Ferryman,
     "And row me across the strait,
     "And thee I'll give my ring of gold
     "Full fifteen pounds in weight."

14   "Thyself retain thy ring of gold,
     "For that I little care;
     "To row and land thee at that place
     "For three I should not dare.

15   "I never on that shore will land,
     "Where waits me only woe;
     "Against Dame Grimild's stern command
     "Across I will not row."

16   So wroth the Hero Hogen wax'd,
       So fierce was he of mood,
     He lopp'd the honest boatman's head,
       And round him reek'd the blood.

17 The gory head he cast afar
    Into the roaring Sound,
    And after it the body threw
    To join upon the ground.

18 Gunter and Gernot, gallant knights,
    Steer'd off the boat from shore,
    But, ere they half across were come,
    A storm began to roar.

19 The oars with Folker's mighty stroke
    Were broken both in twain,
    But with his buckler Hogen steer'd
    Across the boisterous main.

20 And as the knights their anchor cast
    Out on the glittering sand,
    'Twas he, the Hero Hogen's self,
    The first debark'd on land.

21 It was the Hero Hogen's self
    The first debark'd on shore,
    And then came Folker Spilleman,
    And many heroes more.

22 High on the tower the watchman stood,
    Was pacing to and fro;
    "Two highborn youths are hither come,
    "And waiting stand below.

23 "Two warlike men are come to land,
    "And bright their weapons glance,
    "From head to foot in iron clad,
    "And gay their horses prance.

21 "The one bears on his shield a hawk,
      "All glittering bright with gold;
    "The other one a fiddle bears,
      "A Duke's son he so bold."

25 Out stepp'd the stately dame, Grimild,
      Could use the choicest word;
    "His fiddle bears not he forsooth
      "To serve a master's board.

26 "Two Duke's sons are those heroes both,
      "That glance in bright array,
    "And well they both are known to me,
      "My father's sons are they."

27. There waiting stood the Dame Grimild
      Array'd in verdant pall;
    "Now saving Hogen, him alone,
      "Be welcome hither all!

28 "Welcome, my friends, and take your seats
      "Within the festive ring;
    "But ne'er till death shall I forget
      "Sigfrid the murder'd king."

29 Uprose the count, Sir Guncelin,
      And thus to his men he cried;
    "To day the Hero Hogen comes,
      "Now let his strength be tried.

30 "We'll meet him hand to hand to day,
      "We'll smite him till he's dead,
    "And so his pleasant greenwoods gain,
      "And all his gold so red."

31   But answer Hero Hogen made,
        Where near the door he stood;
    "Ready am I to try the chance,
    "If ye but have the mood."

32   Out rush'd the band of faithful swains,
        And up to battle sprung,
    But ill they fared at Hogen's hand,
        The old and eke the young.

33   Asunder broke in Folker's hand
        His trusty blade of war,
    But from the castle door he wrench'd
        A heavy iron bar.

34   He heav'd a stroke, and on the ground
        Seven gallant men were strown;
    "Now God be prais'd" said Spilleman
    "I've made my fiddle known.

35   "My fiddle I so hard have play'd
    "To make you dance and spring;
    "From heavy work I am bathed in sweat
    "Within my mailcoat ring."

36   Then stepp'd the count, Sir Guncelin,
        Up to the proud Grimild;
    "Help us against these doughty foes,
    "Or let the strife be still'd."

37   "Heave on, heave on, my gallant men,
    "Who daily share my bread;
    "Heave on, nor from the combat cease,
    "Till Folker is lying dead."

38   "Hark thee, Grimild, hark, sister mine;
     "Deep driven is my wound:
  "That true thou never wast to me,
     "Too well I now have found.

39   "Seven long and weary days I've watch'd
     "Alike by night and day;
  "Before I yield me up, and die,
     "My death-wound I'll repay.

40   "My good and precious sword is gone,
     "And snapp'd my bar of steel,
  "But could I any weapon find,
     "My pain I should not feel."

41   Then answer'd him young Obbe Yern,
     Who stood thereby so near;
  "I'll lend thee a sword, the well tried blade,
     "My brother held so dear.

42   "Methinks a gallant knight thou art
     "And strong of limb and stark;
  "How well thou wieldest fiddelbow,
     "We've cause enough to mark."

43   "I thank thee much, thou man of worth,
     "Thou brave young Obbe Yern,
  "And well my brothers and myself
     "Thy kindness will return."

44   So battled Folker Spilleman,
     The clamour fill'd the sky;
  Would rather perish like a man,
     Than meanly skulk or fly.

NOTES.

St. 3.* l. 3. The original is very obscure, and probably imperfect. 'oc raske hellet, der jeg neffne kand'.

St. 4. Birds 'fogle' mistaken for 'fole' horses.

St. 7. Merwomen on land assumed the form of beautiful women.

St. 16. l. 4. **round him reek'd the blood.** So in the Niebelunger's Fall l. 6278.

Do sahen s'in dem schiffe riechen daz blut.

St. 19. This Vikingr mode of rowing is not in the Niebelunger's Lay. Gunter and Gernot in that poem are the brothers of Grimild (Chriemhilt), and the former the king of the Burgundians.

St. 30. **Obbe Yern.** The brother alluded to may perhaps be Ulf of Yern, the subject of another ballad, No. XI. In the Niebelung Lay Rudiger lends Hagan a shield, l. 8889

Wie gerne ich dir wære gut mit minem schilde,
Torst ich dir'n bieten vor Chriemhilde!
Doch nim du in hin, Hagene, unt tragen an der hant:

"Fain with the same I'd serve thee to th' height of thy desire,
"But that I fear such proffer might waken Kriemhild's ire;
"Still take it to thee, Hagan, and wield it well in hand."
Lettsom's transl.

St. 42. In the Niebelunger's Lay Folker is killed by the hand of Dieterich of Bern.

Grimild's Revenge. B.

Grundt. I. p. 47. Dan. Vis. I. p. 117. Raszm. II. p. 112.
Grimm p. 7.

1 It was the stately dame Grimild,
   Let brew the wine and mead,
   And sent for many a gallant man
   Renowned for mighty deed.

2 "Go, bid them come to feats of war,
   "And bid them come to strife;
   "There's many a hero young and brave
   "Is doom'd to lose his life."

3 The Hero Hogen's mother dream'd,
   She knew the purport well,
   That, as his rider rode him out,
   The foal slipp'd up and fell.

4 "Now what this dream betides, my son,
   "I'd have thee well aware;
   "Thy treacherous sister plots thy death;
   "Of her designs take care."

5 The Hero Hogen, he it was,
   Rode out along the strand,
   And there he found a Merwoman,
   Who bask'd upon the sand.

6 "Tell me, thou honest Merwoman,
   "Tell me thou cunning wife,
   "Shall I on When-isle slay my foes,
   "Or shall I lose my life?"

GRIMILD'S REVENGE.   47

7   "List, Hero Hogen, list to me,
       "Thou gallant knight so bold,
    "Here thou hast forts and castle towers,
       "And silver too and gold:

8   "But if to When-isle thou shalt cross,
       "And leave thy home so fair,
    "Thou fallest slain by traitor hand,
       "And buried stayest there."

9   Then wax'd the Hero Hogen wroth
       At such ill-boding spell,
    And smote the wretched Merwoman,
       That on the earth she fell.

10 "There lie thou still, thou wretched wife,
       "Stretch'd on the ocean sand;
    "I well know how to make my way
       "Back from the Whenish land."

11 Like lords they rode before the gate,
       And bright their weapons glanced,
    In silken raiment they were clothed,
       And high their horses pranced.

12 They beat the gate, till in the hall
       Was heard the dinning knock;
    "Up, Porter, up! why tarriest thou?
       "Thy gate to us unlock."

13 "That dare not I" the Porter said
       With mantle-muffled chin;
    "Without Grimild, my lady's, leave
       "I let no stranger in."

14 He went and ask'd the proud Grimild,
        Where at her board she sate;
    "Two knights before the castle stand,
        "And bid unbar the gate.

15 "There wait two lords before the door,
        "And bright their weapons glance;
    "In silken raiment they are clothed,
        "And high their horses prance.

16 "The one he bears a fiddle bow,
        "The other bears an ern;
    "That both are heroes stout and bold,
        "That I can well discern."

17 "Surely they are my brothers both,"
        The proud Grimild began;
    "The Hero Hogen it will be,
        "And Folker Spilleman."

18 And out went dames and maidens all
        To view those champions' gait;
    And slender were their belted waists,
        Their persons tall and straight.

19 And went the stately dame, Grimild,
        In scarlet robe array'd,
    And courteously the stranger guests
        To banquet table bade.

20 "But this is castle use and law,
        "No sword may here be worn,
    "Since traitor hand King Sigfrid slew,
        "Whose death I daily mourn."

GRIMILD'S REVENGE.

21   "Lady, 'twas I King Geffred slew,
      "With this my hand and glaive;
  "And I, who slew king Ottelin,
      "So strong a man and brave.

22   "Aye! camp'd before the walls of Troy
      "I made those champions bleed,
  "'Tho' lost my trusty coat of mail,
      "And gone my noble steed."

23   She led them into the banquet hall,
      Where sat her men at board;
  Against those two a hundred rose,
      And brandish'd each his sword.

24   "Will one among ye, warriors,
      "Who daily eat my bread,
  "My brother Hogen dare to slay,
      "And earn my gold so red?"

25   When that heard Folker Spilleman,
      He sprang across the board,
  He wrench'd the door from off its hinge,
      He bared a fearful sword.

26   He seiz'd the heavy bolt of steel,
      With glee he swung it round,
  And fifteen champions at a blow
      Laid lifeless on the ground.

27   "Bravo!" said Folker Spilleman,
      "Now doth my fiddle sing;"
  And then slew Hero Hogen too
      His twenty at a swing.

28 Up spake the stately dame Grimild,
      Her breast with anger glow'd;
    "'Twere better, had ye stay'd at home,
      "When from your land ye rode.

29 "A hundred widows ye will leave,
      "Before the fight is done."
    "That" Hero Hogen answer'd her,
      "Thyself thou hast begun."

30 The Hero Hogen rais'd his helm
      All burning off his brow;
    "My flesh beneath the coat of mail
      "With heat begins to glow.

31 "I feel with thirst and weariness
      "My heart within me sink;
    "Would God in heaven I had at hand
      "A horn of wine to drink!"

32 He loos'd his helm, the raging thirst
      With dead-man's blood to slake;
    "In nomine Domini!" were the words,
      The Hero Hogen spake.

33 Grimild's three hundred warriors all
      Dead on the ground had lain,
    By Hero Hogen's heavy hand
      And by his brother slain.

34 "God help thee, Folker Spilleman,
      "Who liest near me dead!
    "Well has thy bar of steel today
      "Serv'd thee in weapon's stead."

35 Full four and twenty fell for one,
  As there they stood in rank;
  He like a champion mow'd them down,
  Before, himself, he sank.

36 "If I live yet one other day,
  "Ere it begin to wane,
  "I'll make my sister rue thy death,
  "I'll have her burnt or slain."

37 To her, Grimild, a fearful fate,
  And day of reckoning came;
  For Hogen's son closed in a cave
  And starved that vengeful dame.

NOTES.

St. 13. **Saa listelig under sit skind.** Perhaps it means in a soft tone of voice. Grimm translates it 'unter dem Kleide so listig und fein.'

St. 16. The word here translated **ern,** that is an *eagle,* is in the original öffne, evidently miswritten for örn. In the copy letter A. he is said to bear a **hög** or *hawk,* in allusion to his name Hogen.

St. 18. 1. 2. **gait.** This seems to be the meaning that Grimm and Raszmann attach to the word 'Gang', which they render by the same word 'Gang' in German. It may perhaps admit the sense of *procession,* and the stanza would then be rendered

  To see those heroes marching up
    Went dames and maidens all,
  And slender were their banded waists,
    Their persons duly tall.

St. 21. **King Geffred,** the Markgraf Geffart whom Hogen and his brother Dankwart slew on their march to Hungary.

King Ottelin. It is unknown who is meant, and it is not at all clear why Hogen alludes to these two feats.

St. 22. It is a question what Troy is meant; but it seems most probable that it is the Tronege of the Niebelung Lay; and this was Xanten on the Rhine, called originally 'Troja santa'. Hagen in the Niebelung Lay is always called 'Hagen von Tronege', and in Simrock's version of it 'Tronje'.

St. 30. This stanza is unintelligible without reference to the Niebelung Lay, in which Hagen, when the house is on fire, recommends one of his followers to drink blood. He unlaces his helmet and quenches his thirst with a draught of it. In the 36th Adventure Simrock's version —

"Mir thut vor starker Hitze der Durst so schrecklich weh,
Ich fürchte, mein Leben in diesen Nöthen zergeh!"
Da sprach von Tronje Hagen: Ihr edeln Ritter gut,
Wen des Durstes Noth bezwingt, der trinke hier das Blut.
Hingieng der Recken einer, wo er einen Todten fand,
Er kniet ihm zu der Wunde, den Helm er niederband,
Da hub er an zu trinken.

"Ah me I'm so tormented by thirst from burning heat,
"That in this horrid anguish my life must quickly fleet."
Thereat outspake Sir Hagen, the noble knight and good,
"Let each by thirst tormented, take here a draught of blood."
With that straight went a warrior, where a warm corpse he
found,
On the dead down knelt he; his helmet he unbound;
Then greedily began he to drink the flowing blood.

Lettsom's transl.

St. 37. In the Niebelung Lay Grimild is killed by Dietrich of Bern. In the Wilkina Saga it is her second husband, Attila, who is enticed into the treasure cavern of Sigurd and starved there.

Grimild's Revenge. C.

Grundt. I. 48. Dan. Vis. I. 109. Grimm p. 3. Raszm. II. p. 114.

1 It was the stately dame Grimild,
 The mead she bade to brew,
 And gallant knights to share the feast
 From every country drew.

2 She bade them come, and tarry not,
 To battle-field and strife:
 And there it was, so young and brave,
 That Hogen lost his life.

3 The Hero Hogen, he it was,
 He walked along the strand,
 And there he found a Merwoman
 Asleep upon the sand.

4 "Good luck to thee, dear Merwoman,
 "Thou fair and cunning wife;
 "Shall I on Whenild's land be safe?
 "Or shall I lose my life?"

5 "Here thou hast forts and massive towers,
 "With gold thy coffers fill'd;
 "But if to When-isle thou shalt go,
 "As surely wilt be kill'd."

6 The Hero Hogen, he it was,
 His sword so hasty drew,
 And struck the wretched Merwoman,
 And cut her neck in two.

7   The dripping gory head he seiz'd,
      And slung into the Sound,
    And after it the body toss'd,
      To join upon the ground.

8   The Hero Hogen turn'd about
      And walk'd along the strand,
    And there he found a ferry man,
      Was waiting on the sand.

9   "Hark thee, good honest ferryman,
    "Row me across the strait,
    "I'll give thee then my golden ring,
    "Full fifteen pounds in weight."

10 "I will not row thee o'er the sound
    "For all thy gold so red,
    "For if thou treadest Whenild's land,
    "Thou fallest on it dead."

11 The Hero Hogen, he it was,
      His sword so hasty drew,
    And struck the wretched ferryman,
      And cut his neck in two.

12 The golden bracelet off his arm
      He gave the boatman's wife,
    "See, take thou this as friendship's gift
    "To pay thy husband's life."

13 Gunter and Gernot, gallant knights
      From land the vessel drave,
    But straight in fury rose the storm,
      And boil'd the briny wave.

14   In fury rose the stormy sea,
       And dash'd upon the shore;
     Asunder brake in Hogen's hand
       The massive iron oar.

15   That iron oar in sunder brake
       In Hero Hogen's hand,
     But those two lords with gilded shields
       Steer'd on their boat to land.

16   As on the shore their troop debark'd,
       They scour'd each man his blade,
     And watching, what the strangers did,
       There stood a gentle maid.

17. Her banded waist it was so small,
       Her person tall and straight,
     And yet her body duly short,
       And maidenly her gait.

18   To Norborg then they march'd away,
       And towards the gate drew near;
     "But where can now the Porter be,
       "Should aye be standing here?"

19   "Here 'tis the trusty Porter stands
       "Hourly to watch and wake;
     "If I but knew, whence ye are come,
       "Your message I would take."

20   "Hither from kingdoms three we come,
       "Both we and all our crew;
     "For sister lady Grimild claim;
       "The tale we tell is true."

21 In to the hall the Porter came,
    And stood before the board;
    A cunning man of speech was he
    To choose the fittest word.

22 "'There stand without before the gate
    "'Two men of noble mould;
    "'The one of them a fiddle bears
    "The one a helm of gold.

23 "'The one a bow and fiddle bears,
    "But not for master's fee;
    "Come whence they may, these noble youths,
    "Two duke's sons they must be."

24 It was the stately dame Grimild,
    Her head wrapp'd in her cloak,
    And went into the castleyard,
    And thus to her brothers spoke:

25 „Now will you to the chamber go,
    "And drink of mead and' wine,
    "Or rest your limbs on bed of silk
    "With two fair ladies mine?"

26 Thus spake the stately dame Grimild,
    In mantle wrapp'd her head,
    And into the marble banquet room
    To find her warriors sped.

27 "Here sit ye all, my men, at board,
    "Sit drinking day by day;
    "Now who will Hero Hogen face?
    "My brother who will slay?

28 "If any here to earn a prize
 "Can slaughter one so bold,
 "Lord of my castles he shall be,
 "And all my treasur'd gold."

29 Then up and spake a champion,
 A chieftain o'er a land;
 "It's I that will thy guerdon win
 "With this my proper hand.

30 "'Tis I that will the guerdon win,
 "And strike that hero dead;
 "The lord of all thy castles be,
 "And all thy gold so red."

31 Him answer'd Folker Spilleman
 With massive iron bar;
 "I'll surely leave my mark on thee,
 "Before thou goest far."

32 A first and heavy stroke, he struck,
 Laid fifteen champions low,
 "Ha, Ha, so Folker Spilleman
 "Can play his fiddlebow!"

33 So many were the men he slew,
 A bridge of them he built,
 And broad and long I ween it was,
 And much the blood he spilt.

34 Above were spread the wetted hides,
 O'er rolling peas so small,
 And forward Hero Hogen stepp'd,
 And first was he to fall.

35 The Hero Hogen turn'd about,
  Would up again with speed;
 "Stay, stay, my brother," cried Grimild,
 ""Twas otherwise agreed.

36 "Stay there, my brother, keep thy word,
 "As doth become a knight,
 "If on the ground thou shouldest fall,
 "No more to stand upright."

37 The Hero Hogen kept his word,
  As by his honour bound,
 He fought awhile upon his knees,
  And got his mortal wound.

38 Yet other champions three he slew,
  None of the least were they,
 And then to find his father's hoard
  To Hammer took his way.

39 Still on the hero fortune smiled,
  A lovely maid he won,
 And with fair Whenild, so she hight,
  Begat a worthy son.

40 Ranke that champion's name, and well
  He venged a sire so brave;
 For proud Grimild he starved to death
  In Niding's treasure-cave.

41 And then away through Lombardy
  He made his march to Bern,
 And with his kindred Danish men,
  Great glory did he earn.

42   His mother Whenild stay'd at home,
     From her took When it's name;
     To knights and gallant champions
     Is known that island's fame.

NOTE.

St. 25. A proposal of this character accords with the time of Attila, for Bleda's widow made the same offer to Priscus and his suite on their embassy to that monarch. See Herbert's Attila p. 384, and Gibbon ch. XXXIV.

These Ballads bear such a striking resemblance to portions of the Wilkina Saga and the Niebelung Lay, that there can be no doubt of their common origin, at the same time that there is such diversity between them and those ancient poems, as to render it doubtful whether the one were copied from the other. It is the historical circumstances that are different, and the small anecdotes that are alike. One of the Danish editors, Nyerup, remarks that, "as children draw the windows and tiles of a house with great care without regard to whether the house itself stands leaning or straight, or what proportion there is between this or the other accessory; so in the infancy of history anecdotes and small circumstances remain much more fixed in the memory than the relation of the actors to one another, or the locality of the events, and the order of time and connexion of them".

The island, When, which in these ballads is the scene of action, lies near Copenhagen in the passage up the Sound towards Elsinore. In Vedel's time the four fortresses Norborg, Sonderborg, Jarlshoy, and Hammer were still traceable. The island chronicle relates, rather differently from the ballad, that Folker had slain the warriors opposed to him, and was then told by Grimild that his brother Hogen had been killed at Norborg, upon which he drank of the blood of the slain and died: that she then went to Norborg, and seeing that Hogen was getting the better of her warriors there, made the agreement with him, that whoever fell in combat, should rise no more. She then had wet hides laid over peas at the doorway, and set three men upon him from whom he received his death-wound. The chronicle proceeds to say that after this by the wish of Grimild he slept with the maiden Whenild and begot a son, in order that the noble race might not be extinguished. This son, Ranke, took Grimild to Hammers-hoy to show her the treasure of Niding, to which his father had left him the key, and locked her up in it to die of hunger.

In the 'Niebelung Lay' the scene is in Germany and Hungary, and every thing on a grand scale. It is the great conqueror Attila, king of the Huns, at whose palace the feast is held in honour of his marriage with Chriemhilt, (Grimild) and it is Gunther, king of the Burgundians, her brother, who accepts the invitation, and takes Hagen (Hogen) as a warrior with him. Folker is another warrior, not related to them. It is in crossing the Rhine that Hagen meets with merwomen, who prophecy the destruction of Gunther and the whole of the large army, which marches with him. He does not resent the ill news as in the Danish ballad. He next has a scuffle with the ferryman, who refuses to take him over, and who strikes Hagen with his oar, upon which the hero decapitates him, and himself rows the boat and breaks the oar. Arrived at Attila's palace they have intelligence of Chriemhilt's bitter resentment against Hagen for the murder of her first husband Sigfrid, and robbing her of her treasures. Hagen associates with him the stout minstrel Folker, and by watchfulness and courage escapes two attempts to assassinate him by night. The chieftain, to whom Chriemhilt promises unbounded wealth in gold and castles, is Blœdel, the Bleda of the interesting narrative of the embassy of Priscus to the Hun king. Through the conduct of Hagen, who insults the Queen, and strikes the infant son of Attila dead at a banquet at which the Burgundians are entertained, the two armies become embroiled. After every effort has been made to capture Hagen, and has failed, the Queen orders the house in which he and his followers are defending themselves, to be set on fire. It is during the heat of the conflagration that Hagen recommends his men to quench their thirst with blood. He is eventually slain in single combat by Dieterich of Bern, his friend Folker having already fallen under the sword of Hildebrand.

The Danish ballad seems like an imperfect echo of this fine poem. The grandeur of two mighty nations at war is reduced to the quarrel of little Danish chieftains, and the circumstances misrepresented, as they might be by persons who had heard the poem in a foreign language, and had not understood it well. Of the stratagem with the hides and peas there is no mention in the Niebelung Lay. The Icelandic Saga is on the same subject, but differs so widely in all the circumstances, that the ballad could not have been derived from it.

All these poems, Sagas and Ballads alike, refer to the period of the great Attila, king of the Huns, but the persons and events are mixed up in a confusion perfectly inextricable. The reader will find more on the subject, than he is likely to read in the Appendix to W. Herbert's poem of Attila. This author considers Attila, Sigurd and Sigfrid to be the same person. But the best and fullest compilation of poems on the subject, and the most able disquisition on them will be found in Raszmann. Vol. II. ch. V.

VI.

SAMSON.

This ballad is founded upon a tale in the Wilkina Saga, which in Hagen's Helden-Sagen is told nearly as follows. Vol. I. p. 1.

'At Salerno there ruled a powerful chief named 'Rudiger or Rodgeir, who had a daughter named Hil-'deswid, a most beautiful girl and clever in every ac-'complishment. The Earl loved her extremely, and all 'the people of the castle praised her for her beauty, 'grace and condescending manners, and virtues of every 'kind. There was a knight at the court named Samson, 'a man distinguished above all others for strength and 'bravery, with hair and beard as black as pitch, and 'of gigantic stature, and in every respect a model of 'a warrior. He served Earl Rudiger faithfully, and was 'highly honoured, as he deserved to be. This knight, 'Samson, was much enamoured of Hildeswid, and de-'termined to obtain her. One day that he was serving 'the Earl at table, he was desired by him to take two 'silver-gilt dishes of meat to his daughter Hildeswid, 'which he did, carrying one in each hand, and so enter-'ed her castle with his squire. He bade this squire to 'get his horse ready, and his weapons, and all his 'valuables, and wait in the yard with them. He then 'went up to the lady, who was sitting with her com-'panions in the highest tower. She begged him to sit

'down and eat with her and her ladies. He did so,
'and made his proposal to her. As soon as dinner was
'over, she collected her valuables, and went with him,
'charging her maids to keep it a secret from her father.
'In the yard he armed himself, sprang on his horse,
'took her up on his lap, and rode into the forest with her
'and built her a house there. Several days afterwards
'the Earl, her father, heard of it and was exceedingly
'angry, and seized upon Samson's property and burnt
'it, and commanded his troopers to slay him, whereever
'they could find him. Samson retaliated by burning and
'destroying the Earl's property and cattle and people.
'The Earl pursued him with sixty men, but Samson
'defeated and killed him. He continued the war against
'Brunstein, the Earl's brother and successor, and de-
'feated and killed him also, and became master of the
'country. He was the father of Ermanrek of Rome,
'and of Dietman, the father of Dietrick of Berne.'

The above is abridged from the Wilkina Saga, ch. 1.

Samson.

Dan. Vis. IV. 81. Grundtv. 1. 59. Grimm p. 107. Arwids.
I. p. 137. Raszm. II. p. 351.

1 Young Samson at court in service stood,
And there he his king's fair daughter wooed.

2 "O Kirstin, now listen, fair maid, to me,
"And tell me, will you my trulove be?"

3 "Dear Samson, thy bride I gladly were,
"But thwart my father I do not dare."

4 The maid he wrapp'd in his mantle blue,
And up on his charger gently threw.

5   He held her fast on his gallant gray,
      And off to his home with her rode his way.

6   His hat he joyfully waved on high;
      "And now then, king of the Danes, Good bye!"

7   The news to the king was quickly sped;
      "Your daughter has e'en with Samson fled."

8   The king bade over his castle call,
      "Up, troopers, and d'on your harness all!

9   "Up! up! my men, up! to horse! to horse!
      "My daughter is carried away by force.

10 "Up, troopers! up, all! take spear and bow,
      "In Samson ye'll find a dauntless foe.

11 "Ride, follow up hard on the villain's track,
      "Till dead or living ye bring him back."

12 Nor were they tardy, his guardsmen leal,
      But arm'd, and buckled their spurs on heel.

13 They rode, and as soon as they reach'd the mead,
      Their horses urged to their utmost speed.

14 They rode and they came to Samson's gate,
      Where Metté, his stately mother, sate.

15 "Speak, Metté, lady so fine and fair,
      "Where 's Samson thy son? o tell us where."

16 "My Samson yesterday rode away,
      "And will not be back till Christmas day."

17 "We'll give thee heaps of the ruddy gold,
      "To tell us where Samson has his hold."

18 "Right pleasant the sight of gold in store,
   "But Samson is now at home no more.

19 "As gay as in chest are gold's bright hues
   ""'Tis painful an only son to lose."

20 They down on the grass a mantle spread,
   And pour'd upon it the gold so red.

21 "A house is on yonder northward side,
   "And Samson is there and his royal bride."

22 So false was his mother, she basely sold
   Her only son for a heap of gold.

23 The troopers they rode to Samson's yard,
   Were thinking to win a rich reward.

24 They batter'd the door with spear and shield,
   "Out, Samson, and meet us upon the field!"

25 Young Samson he back the casement threw;
   "Ye count so many and we so few;

26 "But wait, good troopers, sit down and rest,
   "Till I for the combat am duly drest."

27 To help him his lady did not fail,
   But buckled about him his coat of mail.

28 Well arm'd he sprang from his chamber door,
   And thinn'd their ranks so close before.

29 He first slew four of them, then slew five,
   Of thirty he left not one alive.

30 He hew'd them, till hew he could no more,
   He trampled in thirty troopers' gore.

SAMSON.

31 "And now from his stall my charger bring,
   "I'll mount him and ride to see the king."

32 He stopp'd as he pass'd the homestead gate,
   Where waiting his traitress mother sate.

33 He drew from his scabbard the reeking steel;
   "My mother art thou, or its edge shouldst feel."

34 He drew from the sheathe his glittering knife,
   "My mother art thou, or it cost thy life.

35 "The cruellest mother thou hast been,
   "Hast sold my life to my foes yest'reen.

36 "For yonder glittering heap of gold
   "A mother her own son's life has sold!"

37 As Samson rode to the palace gate,
   There stood the king in a robe of state.

38 "Hark, Samson, my man, and answer me,
   "Where tarry the troopers I sent for thee?"

39 "Your troopers are all on my courtyard spread,
   "Are wounded some of them, some are dead:

40 "Some sick, some likely enough to die,
   "And some on the bier as corpses lie.

41 "So tell me, my king, so brave and fine,
   "When send you to fetch your mastfed swine?

42 "Let five of your baggage waggons come,
   "And load them, and bring the slaughter'd home."

43 His sword from the scabbard Samson drew,
   "And were you not king, this should you rue."

44 "Nay, gallant Samson, put up thy blade,
"Thou provest thee worthy a royal maid.

45 "E'en take my daughter and sheath thy knife;
"I give her to thee to be thy wife."

46 He turn'd him about and homeward hied,
To visit in peace his royal bride.

47 He turn'd him, and gave his horse the rein,
And rode to his lovely bride again.

VII.

VIDRICK VERLAND'S SON AND THE GIANT LANGBANE.

This ballad is founded on an episode in the Wilkina Saga introduced into the description of King Diderick's Expedition to Birtingsland ch. 170—177. The name of the giant in the Saga is Etgeir. Hagen's Heldensagen V. II. p. 20. Raszm. V. II. p. 478.

'"Now," said king Diderick, as he looked to the 'one side and the other, "a great force of these pre‑ 'cious heroes is collected here in my hall: and what 'mortal were bold enough to wage war against them? 'Here sit upon one bench thirteen men, who when they 'are armed and mounted on horseback, methinks 'might ride unchallenged through the world, and no 'one match himself with them, or have the courage to 'point a spear at them. Aye! and if any there should 'be bold enough, or arrogant or senseless enough not 'to fear our great courage, and bravery, and our 'sharp swords, and hard helmets, and unbending 'shields, and careering horses, which slay men like· 'lions, they would soon pass on themselves sentence 'of death." Herbrandur, the wise bearer of the king's 'banner, felt irritated at these words, and said. "Cease, 'my lord, and speak no longer of that matter, till

'thou knowest whether what thou sayest is true.
'Thou art a child, and certainly speakest from pre-
'sumption and ignorance, if thou thinkest, that there is
'no one a match for thy men. I can tell thee of a
'land, that is called Bertangaland, over which rules a
'king, who is called Isungur: and he is the strongest
'and most intrepid man in battle that we have heard
'of. He has eleven sons, and they are like their
'father; he has a banner-bearer, named Sigurdur Sveinn,
'who is so bold a man in all emprizes, that no one
'can be found any more to fight with him. His whole
'body is as hard as horn, and it is but little that wea-
'pons wound him, and he is so strong that I think he
'might bind and carry off prisoner any one of us who
'might combat with him. The sword he wears is
'not less excellent than the one the king has: the
'sword's name is Gramur. He has a horse called Grani,
'which is a brother of Falka, Skemming and Rispa,
'and the best of all these. Gramur also is the best
'of swords, and can easily cleave helmets and shields,
'and cut men's limbs in two. Of the same quality are
'all the rest of his weapons; and it is my opinion,
'that if thou engagest with this man, of whom I have
'even spoken, thou wilt say, ere thou comest home,
'that thou hast never been in such imminent danger
'before. This wilt thou confirm, when thou comest,
'and so will every one of thy men." King Diderick
'spoke with great spirit: "If it is the truth that thou
'sayest about this brave king and his sons, and the
'intrepid banner-bearer whom thou hast praised so
'highly, then thou shalt at once go from this table,
'and arm thyself the best way thou canst, and mount

'thy horse and carry my banner; and I know no hind-
'rance to my following thee with all my eleven bre-
'thren in arms. March towards Bertangaland and lead
'the way. Before I sleep again in my realm of Bern
'(Verona) I will know whether they or we have the
'most bravery and courage. One of us shall conquer
'and subject the other, before we part." Herbrandur
'went and fetched his arms and dressed himself
'handsomly, mounted on his horse in knightly array,
'and with his best weapons, and took in his hands the
'banner of king Diderick, and rode into the middle of
'the king's yard and called with a loud voice, "If I
'am to show thee the way to Bertangaland, thou mighty
'king Diderick, I am now ready, so tarry not longer."
'Diderick was now quite ready, and all his men, and
'mounted on their horses in full armour.

'Herbrandur now rode off from Bern with king Di-
'derick's banner in advance of all of them, and next
'to him king Diderick, and the rest one after another.
'So they rode on upon their journey, as before related,
'with the good will of the king himself and his noblest
'knights and best fighters. They marched through long
'tracts and immense forests, inhabited and uninhabited,
'to which king Diderick had never before come, nor any
'of his men. And so they reached a great forest,
'through which lay their road. Herbrandur now stop-
'ped and turned to the king and said;

'"My Lord," said he, "here lies Bertanga forest be-
'fore us, and in this forest is a giant who is called
'Etgeir, a son of king Nordian, and brother of the
'giants, whom our comrade Wildifer slew at the resi-
'dence of king Osantrix, the giants Aventrod and

'Widolfur with the bar. The giant Etgeir is here to 'guard the land of king Isungur, who fancies that his 'land and his realm are safe, where he is. If you 'will come to Bertangaland, there is no other road than 'to ride straight on through this forest, and no chance 'of getting there any other way. This giant is so 'strong, that I know no other equal to him. Now ride 'foremost into the forest either one of you that will, 'but do not suppose that I shall proceed any farther 'than this, unless we all ride together. In that case 'I will stay with you. I have now told you the dan-'gers there are there, so that you will not be taken 'unawares. So arrange, as you know what is before 'us, and let us all ride in company."

'Widga spake: "As matters are so, as thou hast said, 'Herbrandur, then the king and all of you shall pull 'up your horses, and I will ride into the forest, and 'hold a parley with the giant, and it may be that on 'my entreaty he allows us all to ride forwards; I have 'been told that we are possibly related to each other, 'and it may be that he allows that plea to avail us. 'But if he will not permit us to ride on, then my horse 'will return with no less speed than he goes, and we 'will take counsel together, and do what king Diderick 'shall determine to be best." The king and all his 'comrades left him to manage it.

'Widga now rode on into the forest, and saw before 'him a man lying asleep. The man was immensely 'large, his legs were thick, his body strong stout and 'tall, and between his eyes there was at least an 'ell, and the rest of his person in the same propor-'tion. In his countenance was expressed fierceness

'and malignity, and he blew so in his sleep that all
'the twigs on the trees in the neighbourhood were
'torn and bent back. Widga then dismounted from
'his horse and bound him to an olive tree, and went
'to the giant, and drew his sword Mimmungur, and
'kicked the giant with his left foot, and called to him
'and said. "Stand up, giant, and defend thyself; a
'man is come here to take thy life. He should not
'be always sleeping so, who is set to guard the land
'of a rich sovereign."

'The giant now waked up and looked at him, and
'saw that there was a man come. Etgeir had no fear
'of one like this, and said to him: "I am not always
'sleeping, but am awake when there is need, and I
'think I may do what I please, wake or sleep, as far
'as thou art concerned. But why wakest thou me? and
'who and what art thou? I advise thee to take care
'of thyself, and go thy way, and give up such arrogant
'language. It seems to me rather too much to stretch
'my legs and stand up for just to slay thee." And
'the giant then fell asleep again no less soundly than
'before. Widga gave him another kick with his foot,
'and broke him two of his ribs, and now the giant
'sprang up in great wrath, and seized his iron bar
'and flew at Widga. But he, as he saw which way
'the bar was coming, sprang aside from under it, and
'the giant struck it into the earth so that he jammed
'it between two rocks. King Diderick heard the crash
'as the bar came down. "There" said Herbrandur;
'"That must be Widga's death-blow that we hear.
'Let us ride away as fast as we can, for if we do
'not, it will be our own death next."

'The giant now took his spear, and launched it at
'Widga, but Widga ran towards him, so that the spear
'flew over his head, and drove so deep into the earth,
'that nothing more could be seen of it. Widga now
'cut at the giant's loins, and carved off a piece of
'his hip, as much as a horse could carry. Then he
'cut from the other hip a large piece of flesh, and one
'piece after the other, till the giant fell, and deep
'and great were his wounds. As he had no more
'weapons, he knew that he could not win the victory,
'and fell to the ground with the hope of falling upon
'Widga and crushing him. But Widga ran between his
'legs, as he was in the act of falling, and so he saved
'his life this time too. This heavy fall was also heard
'by Widga's comrades, and some of them said; "Yet
'it may be too that Widga has won the victory, and
'that the giant has fallen this time." Widga now said
'to the giant. "What ransom wilt thou pay me, not
'to cut off thy head?" The giant said; "Good Sir,
'slay me not; I will ransom myself with more gold and
'silver than thou hast ever seen." Then said Widga.
'"So go thou thither with me." The giant stood up
'very faint from loss of blood, and they went into the
'forest, where lay a great stone, and an iron ring
'forged round it. Then said the giant; "Lift thou
'up that stone, and thou wilt find great riches." Wid-
'ga strained with all his power, but could not even
'move the stone. Then said Widga; "If thou wilt
'reprieve thy life, lift off the stone." The giant then,
'as he could not help himself, seized the stone and
'lifted it up with one hand, and under the same stone
'there was a door, and the giant took hold of the

'door, and opened it, and there was an earth-house 'or cavern beneath it. "Now" said the giant "take, 'my good fellow, the riches that I spoke of, for this 'stone is no hindrance any longer." "Aye, aye," 'thought Widga, "if I go down into the house, the giant 'may close the door, and put the stone upon it, and 'I shall never come out again." So he said to the 'giant "Go into the house, and show me the riches." 'The giant went down, but, as he was descending, 'Widga swung round his sword with both hands and 'struck him on the neck, so that the head flew off; 'and the giant fell. Widga now seized his tongue, 'and cut it out of his head, and smeared himself with 'the giant's blood, and his horse too; and the tongue 'of the giant he tied to his horse's tail, to serve him 'for proof that he told no falsehood. He then sprang 'on his horse, and rode, as fast as he could, back to 'his comrades. As he approached them, he raised his 'sword high in the air, and called out as loud as 'he could, and said; "Away, good friends; the giant 'has given me my death-wound, and it will be your 'case too, if you do not each of you run as fast as he 'can." When they heard these words of Widga's, 'they were all frightened, and ran each as he best 'could, except king Diderick, who guided his horse 'towards Widga, and rode courageously, and drew his 'sword, and said; "Good comrade, let us now ride back 'with all speed and think on what we said, that we 'would not fly, even if we saw certain death before 'us; and there is no need to fly if we two are to-'gether." When they met, Widga told the king Di-'derick all that had occurred, and king Diderick thought

'Widga had behaved gloriously, as he was wont to do.
'And now when king Gunnar, and those who accom-
'panied him, found that neither were king Diderick
'and Widga near them, nor any body following after
'them desirous of harming them, they discovered that
'Widga had played a contemptuous joke upon them;
'and returned back to king Diderick and Widga, and
'felt ashamed of their flight. Now said Widga to king
'Gunnar and all his comrades. "Good friends, I beg
'you not to complain of me for not telling you the
'truth, nor be angry with me about it. I know very
'well that there are men among you' no worse soldiers
'or weaker men than myself; and the offence I am
'willing to atone with gold and precious things." 'They
now all spake together. "We are quite as willing to
'forgive thee that, as thou canst wish: and God grant
'that we never again incur such disgrace: We are our-
'selves entirely to blame, and not thou." They now rode
'all together and saw how deep was driven into the
'earth the bar that the giant threw, and the place
where the spear had gone in and was entirely out
'of sight. After that they went to the earth-house or
'cavern, where the giant had fallen, and took away im-
'mense riches in gold and moulded silver, and precious
'things. There had been collected there all the treas-
'ures of king Isungur, and the treasures which Etgeir
'the giant had brought with him from Denmark.'

The Bertanga land, the scene of this exploit is supposed by Grimm to be Bretagne, but appears to be a
vague name for any foreign country. Vidrick Verlandson on all occasions acquits himself like a hero,
and in the course of the tale fights a duell with king

Isungur, and releases from captivity a great number of his companions in arms, who had been beaten and taken prisoners by king Isungur's sons. His sword Mimmung or Mimmering was given to him by his father the famous armourer, Wayland Smith, 'Velant'. This Velant like Vulcan was lame, having had the sinews of his feet cut by order of king Nidung, whose daughter he carried off in revenge. *

The Swedish ballad is nearly identical with the Danish.

Vidrick Verlandson and Giant Langbane.
Grundtv. I. 90. Dan. Vis. I. 25. Grimm p. 17. Arw. I. 13.
Oehl. p. 7. Raszm. II. p. 514.

1 King Diderick he sits at home at Bern,
    And boasts of his power and might,
  Of wondrous feats he has done in war,
    And many a humbled knight.

2 King Diderick is peering from castle tower
    As wide as his eye can see;
  "Would God, that a Hero so stout I knew,
    "As dared to contend with me!"

3 Him answer'd the Master Hildebrand,
    For travell'd had he so far;
  "There dwells a champion at Birtingsberg
    "Thou darest not meet in war."

---

* This story is perhaps the most ancient of all that are current in the North of Europe, and was equally popular among all the Germanic nations. See Beowulf line 908.

4 "Now hark thee, good Master Hildebrand,
   "So brave on the battle field!
  "Ride foremost thou in the wood to day,
   "And carry my royal shield."

5 "Nay" answer'd the Master Hildebrand,
   For prudent as brave was he;
  "I will not carry thy shield to day,
   "Such honour becomes not me."

6 Then up and spake Vidrick Verlandson,
   So hasty and warm of mood;
  "'Tis I that will lead the band today,
   "And march through Birting wood."

7 'Twas so spake Vidrick Verlandson,
   And rous'd himself to wrath;
  "My sword is a finely temper'd blade,
   "Cuts iron as well as cloth."

8 Three hundred champions brave they were,
   Came marching to Birting's ground,
  And hunted the giant Langbane out,
   And him in the forest found.

9 Then up and spake Vidrick Verlandson,
   "Strange game it is we shall try;
  "Let me to the wood first ride alone,
   "If ye can on me rely."

1 And answer'd him Diderick thus, the king,
   For jealous of fame was he;
  "If Langbane the giant thou dost find,
   "Conceal not the truth from me."

11 He waited not, Vidrick Verlandson,
    But off to the forest sped,
  And there he a narrow footpath found,
    That straight to the giant led.

12 As onward and onward Vidrick march'd,
    O'er Birting's heath away,
  He came to where, all so grim and black,
    The giant Langbane lay.

13 The slumbering giant he rous'd from sleep
    With thrust of his spear so rough;
  "Awake thee, Giant! Wake, Langbane, wake!
    "Methinks thou hast slept enough."

14 "On this wild heath for many a year
    "I've rested me day and night,
  "And never has one come here before
    "To wake me from sleep to fight."

15 "But now it is Vidrick Verlandson
    "With sword of the keenest steel,
  "I'm come from dreaming to wake thee up,
    "Its edge I'll make thee feel."

16 The Giant Langbane he turn'd him round,
    And wink'd with his sleepy eyes;
  "What paltry foolish young swain is this,
    "A Giant like me defies?

17 "But hark thee, I will not fight with thee,
    "Unless of a knightly race;
  "So tell to me who and whence thou art,
    "And all thy lineage trace."

18 "My father was Verland, the cunning smith,
　"And well he deserv'd his fame;
"My mother, the child of a king was she,
　"Fair Bodild she hight by name.

19 "My shield's call'd Skrepping, and on its face
　"Has many an arrow play'd;
"And this my helmet of steel, call'd Blank,
　"Has broken many a blade.

20 "And Skimming is named my noble horse,
　"Of wild mare foal'd in the wood;
"And Mimmering is call'd my trusty sword
　"Well temper'd in hero's blood.

21 "Myself I am Vidrick Verlandson,
　"And well I am clad in steel;
"And stirrest thou not thy lengthy legs,
　"My strength thou wilt quickly feel.

22 "And further, thou Giant Langbane, hark!
　"My message is quickly told,
"The king outside of the forest waits
　"To take thy tribute of gold."

23 "As much as I own of treasur'd gold,
　"I keep it in safety stored;
"And never will let it be told of me,
　"That stable-boy won my hoard."

24 "As young and as little as I may seem,
　"Thy strength I will surely break;
"From off its carcase I'll lop thy head,
　"And all thy treasures take."

25 The Giant Langbane would fain in peace
    A little while longer lie;
    "Young hero, return in safety home,
    "Unless thou art will'd to die."

26 Then rear'd him Skimming on both his legs,
    And right on the Giant ran,
    And seven of his ribs he broke at once,
    The battle with that began.

27 All foaming with wrath the Giant rose,
    And whirled his massy bar;
    At Vidrick he aim'd it, but sped the steel
    Away to the hill afar.

28 Full surely the Giant Langbane thought
    To slaughter his puny foe,
    But Skimming so nimbly had leap'd aside,
    That Vidrick had miss'd the blow.

29 The Giant he gnash'd his teeth with rage,
    And loudly began to wail;
    "As firm in the hill-side sticks the bar,
    "As hammer could drive a nail."

30 Nor longer did Vidrick then delay,
    For wrathful of mood he grew;
    "Turn, Skimming, about! and, Mimmering, ware!
    "See thou, what thou canst do."

31 Sword Mimmering he took in both his hands
    And straight at Langbane ran,
    And down to his entrails through his breast
    He clove that monstrous man.

32 The Giant Langbane had now from sleep
      Woke up with the deadly pain,
    And if he had only had the power,
      Had paid it him back again.

33 "A curse on thee, Vidrick Verlandson!
    "A curse on thy trenchant blade!
    "Such pain and anguish thy hand has dealt,
    "So deadly a wound has made."

34 "I'll mince thee up into bits as small
    "As leaves in an autumn wind,
    "Unless thou tellest, where in this wood
    "Thy treasure heaps I may find."

35 "Have mercy, good Vidrick Verlandson,
    "Forbear thee to strike me dead;
    "And I will show thee my treasure house,
    "Its roof of the gold so red."

36 The Giant he crept, and Vidrick rode
      So deep in the murky wood,
    And found, where, shining as bright as fire,
      The house with the gold roof stood.

37 "Now roll from the mouth that massy stone,
    "And raise from its hinge the door,
    "And more the gold than in all thy land
    "Thou findest therein in store."

38 Vidrick could scarcely stir the stone,
      Though he with his two hands strove;
    But Langbane with ease the weighty mass
      With only two fingers hove.

39 "Now turn thee homeward, my pretty page,
    "And make me no more ado,
  "For more than thou with both thy hands
    "I carry with fingers two."

40 "Nay, nay," said Vidrick Verlandson,
    "Thy cunning is too well known;
  "No man that is wise will waste his strength
    "In heaving a block of stone."

41 "A greater treasure of gold is here
    "Than fifteen kings can show;
  "Step down to it, Vidrick Verlandson,
    "The foremost thou shalt go."

42 "Nay," answer'd him Vidrick Verlandson,
    His crafty designs he knew,
  "'Tis thou the foremost shalt enter in,
    "As usual it is to do."

43 But while the giant was stooping low,
    As in at the door he crept,
  Vidrick with only a single blow
    His head from his shoulders swept.

44 The bleeding carcase he lifted up,
    And leant it against an oak,
  And then to his friends rode back again,
    And thus of his combat spoke.

45 But first he smear'd with the Giant's blood
    Himself and his gallant steed,
  And rode up slowly before the King,
    As tho' he were lamed indeed.

46 "And here ye are standing, good comrades, still,
    "All under the shady leaf!
    "The Giant today has worsted me,
    "And heavy will be your grief."

47 "If fell upon thee today so hard
    "The blows of the Giant's hand,
    "Then venture we not another life,
    "But ride to our native land."

48 "Nay! nay! King Diderick, turn thee round;
    "But turn thee and come with me;
    "And all the treasure the Giant own'd,
    "I'll show it in store for thee."

49 "If Langbane the Giant thou hast slain,
    "Thy fame spreads over the land;
    "Nor is there a champion born on earth,
    "Thou mayest not well withstand."

50 King Diderick's heroes, and all his men,
    The Giant they wish'd to see,
    But stood afar off like laughing stocks,
    Nor dared to approach the tree.

51 They fear'd he might stretch his giant legs,
    And after their army run;
    They stood aghast at his monster size,
    And wake him there dared not one.

52 And much and heartily Vidrick laugh'd,
    And ask'd in a merry vein;
    "But how had ye faced the living man,
    "And dare it not, now he is slain?"

53 He poked the corpse with his lance's shaft,
    And down he toppled the head,
    And truly it was, as all confess'd,
    A giant most stout and dread.

54 They dragg'd the glittering treasure out,
    And parted the gold anon,
    And Vidrick he claim'd the greater part
    By dint of his valour won.

55 But hardly so much was Vidrick glad
    Those treasures of gold to gain,
    As for that himself he had all alone
    So mighty a giant slain.

56 In triumph they homeward rode to Bern,
    King Diderick joy'd the most;
    He gave to Verlandson after him
    The first and the highest post.

NOTES.

St. 3. The title of *Master*, so constantly given to Hildebrand, was due to him as Master of the Wollings or Ylfinger. He seems to have been skilful in curing wounds, and the most accomplished swordsman in Diderick's army.

St. 13. So Arthur wakes the Giant to fight him. Layamon 1. 26033.

St. 20. **sword tempered in heroes' blood.** This is exactly the Anglo-Saxon
        ecg ahyrded heatho-swate.   Beowulf l. 2924.

St. 23. **Stable boy.** 'Stall dreng'. The word may not be meant to imply lowness of calling, but merely youth. Lads of the highest rank had to serve their time as varlets or pages.

St. 31. We need not be surprized that the Giant lived and spoke after such a wound, for the same sword or another made by the same smith, Verland, was so sharp, that it cut a man through his body without his feeling more of it, than as if cold water had run through him, though he fell apart upon shaking himself a little.

St. 53. Grimm tells us that the Cid played the same joke upon his comrades, and enumerates several other instances of it from the romances of the Middle Ages.

VIII.

THE TOURNAMENT.

The subject of this Ballad is taken from the Wilkina Saga, which it follows very closely. The story comes next after that of Vidrick and Langbane, and is as follows. Hagen's Helden-Sagen V. II p. 43. Raszm. II p. 487.

'One day that King Isungur and his sons were 'sitting at their castle, and all in good humour, Si-'gurdur Sveinn came to them and told Isungur the 'king — "My lord," said he, "I have seen something 'that seems to me to be of no trifling importance. I 'have seen a tent pitched on the plain before thy 'castle, and the tent is fashioned as I never before 'saw any. In the middle of it stands a pole, and 'at the top of this pole is a great knob of gold; and 'in front of this tent is another tent of a red colour, 'and in that also a pole with a knob of gold; and 'behind it is a third tent, a green one, and upon 'it a pole and a gold ball; and on the right hand 'stands a tent of golden cloth, and upon that too a 'gilded pole with a knob of gold; and on the left hand 'is a white tent, and upon it a similar pole that is 'entirely of gold up to the knob; and it is my belief 'that no man ever saw a more beautiful tent. In front 'of the tent were hung thirteen shields.'

Then follows a description of them all.

"'From this," said Sigurd, "It seems pretty certain, 'that there are come to our land some unknown 'champions, let them come whence they will, and 'whatever be 'their object. Now I propose, o king, 'with your approval to ride to them and learn who 'they are, who have so boldly pitched their tents and, 'make such a grand appearance, and have had the as-'surance, without your approval, to come into your land."

"Then said the king "I will send to these men one 'champion only, to take them my message: that, if 'they wish to preserve their lives, they must send me 'toll and tribute, as our laws ordain. The champion 'must at the same time find out who they are, whence 'they come, of what country native, and whither they 'are marching, and what other business they have than 'to pay us the toll." Then spoke Sigurd, "The cham-'pion thou sendest thither, shall be no other than my-'self." Sigurd then took his weapons and clothes and an 'inferior horse without any saddle, and so he rode out 'of the castle, and forth over the mountain; and did 'not stop till he came to the tent of king Diderick. 'He then dismounted, and went to the tent of king 'Diderick, and spake thus. "Hail, brave warriors! I 'would greet each of you, if I knew your names." 'They answered him in the same tone, and bade him 'welcome. Then said Sigurd, "King Isungur, my so-'vereign lord, sends me hither with the commission to 'fetch tribute from you, as the law of the land here 'entitles the king to demand; and this tribute you will 'be pleased to pay. But if the king does not obtain 'his tribute, I would not have you conceal from your-

'selves, that, before any long time has passed, you 'will have to forego life and property at the same 'time." Then spake Diderick the king; "We started 'on our march to this land with something else in 'view than the paying tribute to your king. It is much 'more our desire that thou shouldest announce to thy 'king, that I challenge him to fight, and request him 'to come with as many men as I have; and before 'we part, he will be able to say what kind of people 'have visited him." Then said Sigurd; "With your 'permission I will now ask you, what are the names 'of your attendants, and from what land ye come? 'for what you have done has never been done before, 'the challenging king Isungur and his men to combat. 'Have ye not heard say of him, what power he has? 'Methinks he will not refuse to fight with you, who-
'ever ye are." Then said Vidga "Whether or not 'thou art acquainted with any of these men who are 'come here, I will not conceal any thing from thee. 'Over these men rules king Diderick, king of Bern, '(Verona) and there is another king here who is called 'Gunnar (Gunther) of Niflungaland; and there are 'other brave knights here, although we only name 'these. But what thinkest thou? Will king Isungur 'and Sigurd certainly fight with us, or will they avoid 'it?" Then spake Sigurd; "It is my belief that king 'Isungur and Sigurd Sweinn will not without a trial 'flee before you here in their own land, although there 'be come here Diderick king of Bern and his men. 'Be that as it will, you certainly will not break the 'law, and cheat the king of his tribute. You might 'easily send him from a feeling of propriety, of your

'own free will and accord, such as would be a mark
'of respect for him and do you no harm." Then
'said king Diderick. "Since thou hast executed his
'business with much skill and courtesy, I will send him
'a present, such as is worthy his acceptance." Then
'said king Diderick to his men, "What shall we send
'him, that it would become him to receive? Let us
'send him a horse and a shield, and cast lots which of
'our men shall give him the horse and shield we send."
'And they did so. The dice were accordingly thrown
'and the lot fell on Aumlung son of Earl Hornboga. So
'his horse was taken, and his shield, and sent by king
'Diderick to king Isungur, and Sigurd rode away.
'Aumlung was extremely vexed that he should have
'lost his horse, and would have preferred to have
'given up much of his property at home; and was
'desirous to ride after Sigurd, and not submit to it.
'He went therefore to his father, and begged him to
'lend him his horse, as he desired to recover his own
'from him who had ridden off with it. But the Earl
'disapproved of his riding after him, and refused him
'the horse, and wished him to let matters be. So
'Aumlung went to Widga, and begged him to lend him
'his horse. "Methinks" said Widga "thou wilt not get
'back thy horse from that knight, if he is really who I
'suppose him to be: and if thou gettest not back thine
'own horse, and losest mine, what shall I have for it?"
'Then said Aumlung "If I lose thy horse, then thou
'shalt have all my realm, and those are five of the
'strongest fortresses in Vineland, which my father
'gave me, and thou shalt be his heir, as I am now,
'if I bring thee not back thy horse: but if I bring back

'thy horse, then I keep my property as before, and
'one of these two I will have, my horse or my death-
'blow." Then said Widga "On that condition then thou
'shalt take my horse, as thou art disposed to venture
'the utmost on this ride." Aumlung then mounted on
'Skemming's back, and rode as fast as he could, till
'he overtook him: and that was near the king's castle,
'and there stood there a linden tree.

And now Aumlung shouted to the man, and begged
'him to stop for him, which he did. "Now," said Aum-
'lung, "dismount from the horse thou ridest, for I will
'not give it up, as I have far to ride home." Then
'said Sigurd; "Who and what art thou, who so boldly
'claimest this horse on which I am sitting? I do not
'think thou wilt get it, whether thou hast had it be-
'fore or not." Then said Aumlung; "Dismount from
'the horse, or thou mayst lose thy life as well as the
'horse." Sigurd now guessed that this man must be the
'son of Earl Hornboga, who was a relation of his,
'and he said; "I see plainly that thou desirest to fight
'with me for this horse, and it may be thou hast met
'with a man, who will fight with thee in a short time,
'if thou dost not fight now: and the proposal that I
'make is, that we try some other means to determine
'whether thou shalt give up the horse thou claimest,
'or abandon that on which thou art sitting. Now fix
'thy lance and ride at me, and I will stand still against
'it; and if thou throwest me from my horse, then take
'thou thine and enjoy him: but if I withstand thy
'charge, then I will try and ride at thee with my lance;
'and we cease not this game, till one of us has lost
'his horse." This pleased Aumlung well, and he agreed

'to it. Aumlung then rode at Sigurd, and gave Skem-
'ming the spur, and struck with his lance in the midst
'of Sigurd's shield so hard, that Sigurd's horse fell on
'his haunches; but himself he sat unmoved in his saddle,
'and the lance broke in two in the middle. Then said
'Sigurd: "That was well delivered for a young man,
'and it may be that thou hast relatives in thy family
'who have well understood such chivalry. Now dis-
'mount from thy horse and girth him well, and prepare
'him and thyself for the encounter; and then mount
'and stand against me, as I stood against thee, and
'recollect that thou wilt have to do thy utmost not to
'lose thy horse." Aumlung did so, and soon made
'himself ready, and now Sigurd gave his horse the
'spur, and drove his thick lance at the middle of
'Aumlung's shield, so hard and strong, that with that
'charge he drove Aumlung far backwards from off
'his horse. Sigurd then took Skemming by the bridle
'and said: "My brave knight, now thou hast not gained
'thy horse for which thou hast ridden, and hast lost the
'other, which I believe must have cost thee a large
'sum, if it is, as I think, Widga's horse, Skemming.
'I imagine thou wilt have pledged him a large sum,
'before he lent it thee, and wilt yet be in ill favour
'with him for having lost it. It would have been better
'for thee to have remained quiet this time." Then
'spake Aumlung "So may think those who are not
'men of courage. But our enterprize may yet turn
'out well, if thou wilt, although at present appearan-
'ces are against it." Then said Sigurd; "What wilt
'thou now give more, to receive thy own horse, and
'the one besides which thou hast lost?" Then said

'Aumlung "I will give thee for it all I possess, so 'that it do not bring disgrace on me or my family." Then 'said Sigurd: "Before our combat I asked thee what was 'thy name and race, and thou wast too proud to tell 'me, but now thou must tell me both, before thou 'gettest thy two horses." Then said Aumlung; "Since 'I concealed from thee my race and name, when I 'had my horse, my comrades will say, that I tell it 'now out of fear; I shall therefore certainly not do 'so now for the sake of my horse, or any thing else, 'though all my property and my realm depends on it, 'and so bring on myself shame and scandal." Then 'said Sigurd, "I do not ask thee this in order to re-
'proach thee, but because I suspect, that thou art the 'son of Earl Hornboga, my kinsman, and I would rather 'do thee honour than dishonour. So I will now tell thee 'my own name first: I am Sigurd Sweinn." Then said 'Aumlung; "Although thou hast first told me thy name 'without compulsion, yet I will not tell thee mine, but 'upon condition that thou swearest by God that no dis-
'grace shall accrue to me from it." Then said Sigurd, "That 'I certainly promise thee." Then said Aumlung "My 'name is Aumlung, I am the son of Earl Hornboga, 'as thou hast guessed; and we are indeed related." 'Then said Sigurd "Thou hast now done well not to 'conceal any longer that thou art my relative; and I 'will manage it so, that it shall turn out to thy honour 'and not to thy dishonour." Sigurd then sprang from his 'horse and said: "Come, my dear kinsman, and take 'thy horse, take both of them, and ride back to thy 'tent, and say that thou hast won this one from me 'by force. But before thou goest, thou shalt bind me

'to this linden, and carry off my spear, my horse, and 'my shield." And so they did. Now rode Aumlung back 'with both his horses, and as he came before the tent, 'he galloped up proudly. King Diderick and Widga 'were standing outside the tent and saw Aumlung ride 'up. Then said Widga "Here rides Aumlung our com-'rade, and has got his horse. I dare guess that if 'that was Sigurd Sweinn, as I believe it was, Aum-'lung has begged him very courteously for the horse, 'and told him first of their relationship, and entreated 'him for it in all humility. He would never else have got 'his horse." Then said king Diderick. "Nor do I think, 'myself either, that he took horse or any thing else 'from Sigurd against his will: but it may be that that 'was some other man, from whom he could take what 'he liked." Aumlung now rode to the tent, and his 'father and his comrades came out to meet him, and 'welcomed him, and asked him, how he had won his 'horse. Then said Aumlung; "When I came to the 'plain at the foot of this hill, there was the man be-'fore me, who had taken away my horse, and I rode 'against him as hard as I could, and thrust my spear 'at his shield, and here you may see his shield; the 'shaft broke in two, but I nevertheless unhorsed him 'and beat him with the pieces of the shaft. As I parted 'from him, I bound him to a linden tree, for which 'purpose I used his girdle, and the straps from his 'shield, and split up my own sword-straps too, till he 'was bound as fast as I desired, and there he is stand-'ing now, and I think he will not have loosed himself." 'Then they all said that he had won his horse in a 'chivalrous manner, and thanked him. Then said Wid-

'ga to king Diderick; "I will now ride to the place
'where he says that he bound this man. If it is Sigurd
'Sweinn, as I think him to be, then it has been done
'by craft and deceit; and if he stops at the tree we
'shall so part that I shall know for certain, whether
'it is Sigurd or some other man." That pleased the
'king well; and Widga then took his horse and said;
'"It is a great disgrace if the man stands there bound,
'and cannot loose himself: I will certainly release him."
'And he rode forth in haste. When Sigurd saw that
'a man was riding towards him, he broke asunder all
'his bands and ran up the hill; and would not have
'any thing to do with this man. Widga rode forward,
'till he came to the tree, and saw the bands lying
'there torn and the spear-shafts shivered. He then
'rode home, and thought now that it was all true, as
'Aumlung said; and told his comrades so.'

This story in the Wilkina Saga is supposed to be
the prose version of a versified romance composed in
Lower Germany. The ballad seems to have been
known to the author of that Saga about A. D. 1300.
The original Low German poem is long since lost,
as well as so many more, which have furnished material to the songs of the Middle ages.

The places mentioned, such as Hald and Bratingsborg, have no real locality, but are used in these
ballads, sometimes as the residence of the one party,
and sometimes as that of the other. The following
piece and the Fight between Vidrick and Langbaue,
which was originally a part of it, are supposed to be
among the oldest ballads extant in the language. They
are both in the Swedish also.

Who the Diderick really was, whose name is so famous in romance, is a matter of dispute and for the sake of these translations it is not necessary to go far into the question. It was formerly assumed that he was the Theodoric of history, the king of Italy who ruled at Verona, and after all that has been said and written, I am inclined to think this the correct view of it. But he has a rival in a Frankish king of the same name, one of the Merovingian family, who lived in the 6th century, and both are probably confounded with older kings, and their deeds mixed up with those of other heroes.

The name, there can be no doubt, is the same as Theodoric, and under this there have been the deeds of two Gothic kings confounded, the one contemporary with Attila, the Etzel of the Nibelung Lay, the other of a later period. The first was king of the Visi-Goths from 419 to 451. It was he who marched with the Roman General Aetius, and defeated Attila and his Huns at Chalons, but himself perished on the field A. D. 451. The other Diderick, usually called in romances 'Diderick of Bern' from the place of his great victory, Verona, was king of the Ostro-Goths from 475 to 526. At seven years of age he had been sent as a hostage to Constantinople, and resided there at the court of the Greek emperor for ten years, but unlike our Alfred, whom a temporary visit to Rome awakened to the beauties of literature, and a desire to promote it among his barbarous countrymen, Theodorik never learnt even to write his own name, but used a gold plate in which were cut the letters ΘΕΟΔ, and inked the interstices with a pencil.* He seems however to have been a man of great natural talent and commanding presence, and accomplished in all the athletic exercises fashionable at that time, and to have possessed in an eminent degree the power of controlling those with whom he came into contact. In 488 he was engaged by the Greek Emperor Zeno as an ally or auxiliary, but was defrauded by him of the provisions promised, and decoyed into a barren mountainous region, where his army was in imminent danger of perishing. To revenge himself he desolated Thrace, and besieged Zeno in his capital, who bought him off by ceding to him his claim upon the kingdom of Italy. Thither Theodoric and the whole nation of Ostro-Goths, men, women, children and cattle moved in a body A. D. 489. They fought their way up the Danube, through what is now Hungary and Austria, and crossed the Julian Alps to Isonzo near Verona, where he defeated Odoacer, the virtual king of Italy, in three battles. He eventually took him prisoner in Ravenna after a three years' siege, and so became the undisputed master of Italy. A third part of the lands he gave up to his Goths, but after

---

* The name Theodoric is not derived, as the first letters might mislead one to suppose, from the Greek $\Theta EO\Sigma$ God but from the Gothic Θiuda *people* and riik *rich* or *powerful*, meaning 'lord of nations'. The first word is the same from which the German appellative 'Deutsch' or 'Teutsch' comes, about which it is still undecided, whether it should begin with D or T. If etymology could settle it, it should be neither one nor the other, but Θ. It means 'national' contrasted with what is 'welsch' or foreign.

this first spoliation seems to have treated his Italian subjects with great lenity. It is probable that he merely transferred the seignory to other hands, as the Normans did on their conquest of England, leaving the mass of the people little affected by the change. It is to his credit that he used every endeavour to save the remains of antiquity from destruction. Theodoric was an Arian, but treated those of a different faith with perfect tolerance, till the persecutions to which his own sect was subjected by the Greek emperor, induced him to show great severity towards the Trinitarians. He died at Ravenna A. D. 526 where his highly interesting tomb is still preserved. See Ferguson's Architecture. Vol. II. p. 518. As guardian to the young king of the Visi-Goths he ruled over Spain and Southern Gaul.

The Tournament.

Grundtv. I. 108. Dan. Vis. I. 1. Grimm p. 23. Oehl. p. 1.
Arw. I. 28.

1 A troop they were of seventy-seven,
    As out from Hald they went,
  And forth they march'd to Bratingsborg,
    And boldly pitch'd their tent.

2 The king he stood on Bratingsborg,
    And look'd around so far:
  "Are yonder champions tired of life,
    "That here they come to war?

3 "Now hark thee, Siward, Hasty swain,
    "Thou wanderer far and wide,
  "Go thou and view these warriors' arms,
    "Up off to their army ride."

4 Siward stepp'd in beneath the tent,
    And duly greeted all;
  "Is one among you, gallant knights,
    "Will try with me a fall?

5 "Whoever rides a tourney best,
    "Here 's one that him defies;
  "Our prowess let us fairly test,
    "Our horses be the prize."

6 On table-board the dice were thrown,
    And roll'd about so wide,
  And on Childe Hummer fell the lot
    A joust with him to ride.

7 To Verland's son Childe Hummer went
    To help him in his need;
  "Lend me to-day against a pledge
    "Skimming, thy noble steed.

8 "Eight castles, all so strongly built,
    "These will I give thee first;
  "And then the sister I love the best,
    "Of pledges not the worst."

9 "Yon Siward he is a hairbrain knight,
    "Sees not his weapon's end;
  "If Skimming 's hurt, not all thy kin
    "Could make me due amend.

10 "For were these castles all of gold,
    "And all their water wine,
"All would I not for Skimming take;
    "Thank God! the horse is mine."

11 Vidrick his hand struck on the board;
    "Four winters now are past,
"Since with a girth for battle fray
    "I girded Skimming last."

12 Childe Hummer mounted upon his back,
    Glad such a horse to ride;
It seem'd to Skimming wondrous strange,
    When spurs stuck in his side.

13 The gold shone bright on Hummer's shield
    As sun in summer's heat;
"And now God help me, poor young swain,
    "Firmly to keep my seat!"

14 Against him rode a gallant knight,
    A hero stout and bold,
And both their shield-straps burst in twain,
    And far their shields were roll'd.

15 "Young man, thy horse thou sittest well,
    "And like a gallant knight,
"Dismount, I'll wait thy thrust awhile,
    "Make thou thy saddle tight."

16 The second bout those heroes rode,
    They proved their prowess well,
Childe Hummer's shield was struck so hard,
    That on the ground he fell.

THE TOURNAMENT.
101

17 "The good horse Skimming now is mine,
   "From off his back thou'rt thrown;
   "So now, brave youth, say, what the race
   "Thou claimest for thine own."

18 "My mother is Lady Helwig call'd,
   "And dwells at Lesen-eye;
   "My father's name is Jensen Boe,
   "And Hummer hight am I."

19 "If thou art Holmboe Jensen's son,
   "My next of kin art thou;
   "So take thy horse and go in peace,
   "I knew thee not till now.

20 "But first with shield straps bind my arms,
   "Bind me to yonder tree,
   "And ride and tell King Diderick,
   "That thou hast beaten me."

21 Childe Hummer stepp'd beneath the tent,
   On table toss'd his blade;
   "I've bound to an oak the stalwart knight,
   "Who late such boasting made."

22 "Hark thee, Childe Hummer, Vidrick said,
   "'Tis spoken but in joke,
   "Or Siward with his own good will
   "Was bound to yonder oak."

23 Vidrick then took a little horse,
   And rode away to the wood;
   He fain himself would see the place,
   And learn how matters stood.

24 As Siward there was standing bound,
    And saw him on the way,
    Up by the roots he tore the tree,
    He dared no longer stay.

25 The king he stands on Bratingsborg,
    And looks o'er dale and down;
    "Hither comes Siward Hasty swain,
    "And summer brings to town."

26 The Queen is looking far and wide,
    From out her lofty bower;
    "Siward has in the forest been,
    "And brings us back a flower.

27 "But hark thee, Siward Hasty swain,
    "What now, my son, I say:
    "Where is the horse that thou hast won,
    "And brought me home today?"

28 "That horse to one my next of kin
    "I've given for friendship's sake,
    "Nor hast thou here a knight, would dare
    "That horse from him to take."

29 "Then tell me, Siward Hasty swain,
    "For thou wast in their tent;
    "What is their several shields' device?
    "And what therewith is meant?"

30 "Blazon'd upon the first shield stands
    "A lion stout and bold;
    "And Diderick's that, the king's device,
    "A lion crown'd with gold.

31 "Blazon'd upon the second stands
　"A lion and giant tall:
　"And that is Master* Hildebrand's,
　"The bravest knight of all.

32 "Blazon'd upon the third shield stand
　A hammer and pair of tongs;
　"And that to one, no quarter gives,
　"To Verlandson belongs.

33 "Blazon'd upon the fourth shield stand
　"Two spurs with gold so bright;
　"And those the Hero Hagen wears,
　"That forward eager knight.

34 "Blazon'd upon the fifth shield stand
　"A fiddle and fiddle-bow;
　"And that bears Folker Spilleman
　"To play them never slow.

35 "Blazon'd upon the sixth shield stand
　"Two arrows clean and white;
　"And that one claims Childe Wifferlin,
　"Who never shrunk from fight.

36 "Blazon'd upon the seventh shield stands
　"A linden all in leaf,
　"And that bears Holmboe Jensen's son,
　"Young Hummer, gallant chief.

---

* See Appendix A.

37 "Blazon'd upon the eighth shield stands
  "A table of gold so red,
  "And that bears gallant Wolf of Yern
  "A champion courtly bred.

38 "Blazon'd upon the ninth shield stands
  "A lindworm's monster length,
  "And that is bearing young Sir Orm,
  "Who fears no mortal strength.

39 "Blazon'd upon the tenth shield sits
  "A hawk so swift of flight;
  "And that childe Detloff bears, the Dane,
  "So prompt of hand in fight.

40 "Blazon'd upon the eleventh shield
  "A naked sword-blade lies;
  "And that the rich Sir Herman bears
  "In every bold emprize.

41 "Blazon'd upon the twelfth shield stand
  "A cowl and bar of steel;
  "And that the stout monk Alsing bears
  "And makes the foeman feel.

42 "And now as many as I have seen,
  "Their shields I've truly told,
  "And sooth to say, there carry them
  "As many heroes bold."

43 The gladness spread through all the court,
  Outside and in the hall;
  The knights they parted best of friends,
  And home went joyous all.

NOTES.

St. 3. The hero in the Icelandic original is called Sigurd, which is the same as Siward and Sigfrid.

St. 7. The importance of a good horse in the days of chivalry could not be better proved than by the valuable pledges offered for the loan of one. In the fine Spanish romance of Gayferos (Wolf & Hofmann II. 230) we find a similar entreaty addressed to Roldan.

> "Por Dios vos ruego, mi tio,
> "Por Dios vos quiero rogar,
> "Vuestras armas y caballo
> "Vos me las querias prestar."

> "In heaven's name, dear uncle mine,
>   In heaven's name I pray,
> Your arms, dear uncle, and your horse
>   Lend me this single day."

St. 10. **Were these castles all of gold** a common expression in the ballad poetry of the period.

> 'Dat alle berghen goude waren
>   En alle waters wijn.'
>
> Königstochter. (Fallersleben p. 51.)

St. 17. It was only after being worsted that a knight would tell his name. So in 'Hildebrand' See App. A. the father first discovers his son after having unhorsed him. The expression 'fauren Unger-svend,' here translated 'brave youth,' is often used in scornful pity as to a mere boy. See No 7 st. 39.

St. 23. **A little horse** that is one that was not a war horse.

St. 30. This description of shields was in the days of chivalry a most important matter, for when the features and the whole person of a knight were cased in armour, it was only by the device on the shield that he could be recognized.

St. 41. l. 2. In some copies he bears a cowl 'kappe' in some a club 'kölle,' or a bar of steel.

IX.

KING DIDERICK IN BIRTINGSLAND.

The beginning of this ballad is much like that of the Tournament, and is very probably taken from the same source. The story of giants eating human flesh occurs in many other ballads of this collection, as 'Olger and Burmann', and 'Sir Folding', and indeed in the legends of most countries. Vedel has made several alterations in it, which were quite unnecessary. The following translation is from the ancient manuscript published by Grundtvig.

It will be observed that, with a confusion of places not uncommon, Birtingsland is now the country of Diderick's enemies, and Bratingsborg his own residence, while in the preceding ballad this is reversed.

Upon the absurdity of the conclusion no remark need be made. It is probably a burlesque from beginning to end, as the 13th stanza can hardly have been meant seriously.

King Diderick in Birtingsland.

Grundt. I. 124. Dan. Vis. I. 15. Grimm p. 54. Raszm. II. p 521.

1 The king rules over the castle tower,
    And lords it over land,
  And many a gallant champion leads
    All arm'd and sword in hand.

2 Then let the peasant till his farm,
　　His horse the trooper guide,
　The king of Denmark, him alone,
　　O'er fort and tower preside.

3 King Diderick sits on Bratingsborg,
　　Looks over land and sea;
　"I know not one in all this world,
　　"Dares match himself with me."

4 "And yet," said Brand of Wifferlin,
　　For he had wander'd far,
　"There's one whom I could show thee, king,
　　"A match for thee in war.

5 "King Isak is that champion's name,
　　"He dwells in Birtingsland,
　"And leads such warriors in his train,
　　"As can a wolf withstand.

6 "He leads such warriors in his train,
　　"As oft have fought the bear;
　"The flesh and blood of Christian men
　　"His foul but only fare.

7 "Each morning, soon as dawns the day,
　　"Hell-food he loves to gnaw,
　"Toads, vipers, efts and poisonous herbs
　　"To spice his fiendish maw."

8 In stepp'd to the hall a little page,
　　And stood before the board;
　"The tribute fix'd a year ago
　　"'Tis time ye pay my lord."

9 "I'll nevermore the tribute give
   "I hitherto have paid;
  "Will rather march to Birtingsland,
   "And there unsheathe my blade."

10 With joy rose Hwitting Helfred's son,
    And laugh'd with all his heart;
   "If you to Birtingsland will go,
    "I'm here to take my part."

11 "Last year thou wast in Birtingsland,
    "And there thy horse hast lost;
   "'Twere best, I trow, to stay at home,
    "Or dear thy game may cost."

12 "Rather than stay at Bratingsborg,
    "I'd lose a foot and hand;
   "Nay, if no horse I have to ride,
    "On foot I'll join your band."

13 The troop that rode from Bratingsborg,
    So solid was and great,
   The stones were crushed, the trembling earth
    Gave way beneath their weight.

14 Foremost of all king Diderick rode,
    A lion upon his shield,
   And on it shone the golden crown
    Afar across the field.

15 With gleaming crown of ruddy gold,
    The royal Diderick rode,
   And next him Vidrick Verlandson
    His tongs and hammer show'd.

16 Next follow'd Siward, Hasty swain,
   With brightly polish'd spear,
   And then came Brand of Wifferlin
   Who knew no sense of fear.

17 Next him the Hero Hogen rode
   All blooming like a maid;
   And then rode Folker Spilleman,
   In hand his naked blade.

18 Next after them young Ulf of Yern,
   His horse a noble dun,
   And then the young knight Hommerlom,
   Sir Holmboe Jensen's son.

19 Bold Gynther next and Gernot rode
   With arrows laid on bow,
   And then rode Sonne Folkerson
   With courage on his brow.

20 Next them the little Grimmer came
   With burnish'd coat of mail,
   And Seier, in battle field so prompt,
   Was never seen to quail.

21 The next rode Master Hildebrand,
   Who sat so well his steed,
   And then the stout monk Alsing rode,
   Had earn'd a champion's meed.

22 They went away from Bratingsborg
   In full array and force;
   Behind walk'd Hwitting Helfred's son,
   For he had lost his horse.

23 So long ran Hwitting Helfred's son,
   His face with anger glow'd;
  He struck a warrior off his horse,
   And mounted it, and rode.

24 The good king Diderick turn'd him round,
   Was riding in the van;
  "On horseback now I see the swain
   "Who barefoot lately ran.

25 "But hark thee, Hwitting Helfred's son,
   "And hear what I would say;
  "'Tis thou shalt march to Birtingsland,
   "And make them tribute pay."

26 "Aye!" answer'd Hwitting Helfred's son,
   And laugh'd with hearty glee,
  "And if I go to Birtingsland,
   "We'll go but only three."

27 "Then take thee Vidrick Verlandson
   "And Diderick, him of Bern;
  "These are of all my gallant men
   The last their backs to turn."

28 They mounted horse, those stalwart three,
   And long the way they rode,
  And, but the simple truth to tell,
   Most fiery tempers show'd.

29 The watchman high on turret stands,
   And looks around so far;
  "Yonder I see three champions come,
   "Methinks they're bent on war.

30 "The one is Hwitting Helfred's son,
   "A tried and stubborn foe;
   "The same was here and lost his horse,
   "'Tis now a year ago.

31 "The next is Vidrick Verlandson,
   "His hammer and tongs withal;
   "The third is Diderick, he of Bern,
   "Three champions stout and tall."

32 Their horses in the yard they left,
   And into the castle strode,
   And, truth to tell, without delay
   Their ruthless spirit show'd.

33 The porter near the gate they seized
   And chopp'd in morsels small,
   And in they strode before the king,
   Into the lofty hall

34 Isak, the king of Birtingsland,
   He rose, and this his word;
   "Now whence are come these desperate men,
   "Who stand before my board?"

35 Up then the royal butler spake,
   Who pour'd the wine and mead;
   "Let us but take our spears in hand,
   "We'll drive them back with speed."

36 But Helfred's son the braggart seiz'd
   All by his shaggy beard,
   And beat his head, till floor and wall
   With reeking brains were smear'd.

37 Aye further, Hwitting Helfred's son
    A dismal jest to make,
    He toss'd the body upon the board;
    "Who broils for me the steak?"

38 Stepp'd forward Didcrick, he of Bern,
    And sword from scabbard drew,
    King Isak in his navel stabb'd,
    And ran his body through.

39 And on rush'd Vidrick Verlandson,
    And clear'd himself a ring;
    He left full forty champions dead
    Around their slaughter'd king.

40 In tears king Isak's mother came,
    And old was she and gray;
    With her those heroes, truth to tell,
    Strange games began to play.

41 In anger Hwitting Helfred's son
    His sword upon her drew,
    But she in sunder kiss'd the blade,
    And shiver'd off it flew.

42 His trusty blade she kiss'd in twain,
    In shivers made it fly;
    But her he seiz'd by both her legs,
    And whirl'd her up on high.

43 She changed her form to a screaming crane,
    And off to the welkin flew,
    But he drew on a feather dress,
    And flew to the welkin too.

44 They flew all day, they flew for three,
 Untired still on they went,
 Till by her legs the crane he seized,
 And into morsels rent.

45 And that day's pastime ending so,
 All arm'd and sword in hand,
 They left king Isak's warriors dead,
 And rode from Birtingsland.

X.

KING DIDERICK AND THE DRAGON.

This tale, which was a great favourite with all the western nations of Europe during the middle ages, appears to have been derived from a Welsh original, the "Owain and Gabain" of Lady Guest's Mabinogion. V. 1. p. 67. In this romance Owain finds a lion and a serpent fighting, and kills the serpent; whereupon the lion out of gratitude follows him, and plays about him, as though it had been a grey-hound that he had reared. The lion collects fuel for him, and catches a roebuck for his meal, and watches over him by night. At a strange castle he lies all night in the horse's manger to guard him, and at the banquet crouches between Owain's feet, and partakes of his food. He assists him to fight and destroy a giant and two powerful champions.

It is unnecessary to allude to all the different forms which this tale has assumed in the literature of France and Germany, through which latter country it reached Denmark in the poem of Wolfditerick, long extracts from which are given by W. Grimm in the notes to his Altd. Held. p. 441—467, and by Weber in North. Antiquities p. 121.

The story of king Hertnid's destruction by a dragon, and the discovery of his remains in the cave by Diderick, is given by V. d. Hagen in Vol. II p. 440 and by Raszmann Vol. II p. 658 as translated from the 383d chapter of the Wilkina Saga, a poem that is undoubtedly of German origin.

The original poem of 'Owain and Gabain' was known to the Scandinavian nations by a translation of it into Norse made by Monk Robert A. D. 1226.

King Diderick and the Dragon.
Grundt. I. 139. Dan. Vis. I. 41. Grimm p. 13. Oehl. p. 14. Raszm. II. p. 667.

1 The good king Diderick mounted horse
    And rode to Bern away,
And found a lion and lothely worm
    In fierce and bloody fray.

2 One day they had fought, and eke the next,
    And all the third as well;
At night the lion could no more,
    And down on the green-sward fell.

3 In great distress the lion cried,
    As near him rode the king;
"O good King Diderick, pity me,
    "And speedy succour bring.

4 "Come to my aid, thou gallant king,
    "Make good thy glorious name,
"Since blazon'd upon thy shield I stand
    "All glowing like a flame."

5 King Diderick stood in anxious thought
    Some little while aside;
"This noble lion help I must,
    "Whatever may betide."

6 Thereon king Diderick spurr'd his steed,
    And drew his trusty sword,
And with that lothely lindworm closed,
    And deep the monster gored.

7 Right stoutly laid the king about,
    He hew'd with might and main,
Till at the hilt by dint of blows
    His good sword brake in twain.

8 Him grasp'd the worm beneath her tail,
    His horse beneath her tongue,
And bare them into a mountain cave
    As meat to feed her young.

9 The king she into a corner toss'd,
    But gave her young the steed;
"There, children, eat that morsel up,
    "I'll sleep before I feed.

10 "Content ye, children, while I rest,
    "With this the coarser fare;
"The man, when I wake up again,
    "With all of you I'll share."

11 Pent in that lothely lindworm cave
    He search'd it round and round,
And found the sword call'd Adelring!
    That famous sword he found!

12 He knew the finely temper'd blade,
      He knew the gilded knife;
    "Ha, Sigfred! rest thy soul in peace!
    "Thou here hast lost thy life.

13 "In many a fight I've stood with thee,
      "In many a long campaign,
    "But never did I know before,
      "That here my friend was slain."

14 With joy the king his weapon grasp'd,
      Its temper sought to know,
    And struck the cavern's flinty side,
      Till all was in a glow.

15 As saw the lindworm's elder son
      Their cavern flash with flame,
    "Who now," said he, "in her own house
    "The hostess puts to shame?"

16 With wrath that little lindworm boil'd,
      And fierce and fiercer grew;
    "Who dares in her own dwelling house
    "The hostess harm to do?"

17 Then spake the other lindworm young,
      That in the corner lay;
    "Should but our mother wake from sleep,
    "How thou wilt rue the day!"

18 In wrath king Diderick thus replied,
      For fierce of mood was he;
    "From sleep I'll quickly rouse her up,
    "And cold her dream shall be.

19 "Thy dam a knight of noblest birth,
    "The brave King Sigfred slew;
   "His death I'll with a heavy hand
    "Avenge on each of you."

20 Up then the mother lindworm woke,
    And much she shook with fear;
   "Who then is this, disturbs my rest?
    "Who makes such clamour here?"

21 "'Tis I — king Diderick, king of Bern,
    "A word with thee I crave,
   "The same whom coil'd beneath thy tail,
    "Thou broughtest to thy cave."

22 "O good king Diderick, slay me not,
    "My heaps of treasure take;
   "We'll here instead of useless strife
    "A bond of friendship make."

23 "Full many a knight hast thou devour'd,
    "Allur'd by crafty wile;
   "But never more so shalt thou me
    "Or other one beguile."

24 "O good king Diderick, hear my prayer,
    "And deign my life to save,
   "And I will show thee where thy bride
    "Lies hidden in the cave.

25 "Above my head the keys are hung,
    "Which lock her prison door,
   "And at my feet thy trulove lies
    "Beneath the cavern floor."

26 "Above and with thy lying head
    "Shall be the work begun,
"And down below and at thy feet
    "Thy slaughter first be done."

27 He straight the mother lindworm slew,
    And then the eleven young,
But through the venom fear'd to step,
    That dripp'd from off her tongue.

28 Before his feet he dug a trench
    To drain away the blood;
For well he knew, with death was fraught
    That boiling poisonous flood.

29 King Diderick loudly curs'd the lion,
    And angry he became;
"Light every curse and foul reproach
    "Upon that lion's name!

30 "'Twas he brought me to this distress,
    "May God reward his deed!
"Had he not stood upon my shield,
    "I had ridden out my steed."

31 His voice the noble lion heard,
    For loud king Diderick cried;
"Now wait, good king; I'll with my claw
    "Dig through the cavern's side."

32 The lion dug, King Diderick hew'd,
    The cave was all ablaze;
The king but for the lion's help
    Had ended there his days.

33 He now had fell'd his monster foe,
    And all her young ones slain,
  And arm'd with shield and coat of mail
    Came out upon the plain.

34 But though from prison he was free,
    He much bewail'd his steed,
  For oft they had each the other help'd
    In time of urgent need.

35 "Now hear me, Diderick, hear me, king,
  "And cease thy grief and care;
  "Up! mount thee on my shaggy back,
    "And thee I'll gladly bear."

36 So over meadow, hill, and dale
    Right gaily rode the man,
  As homeward through the forest glades
    The grateful lion ran.

37 And comrades were the lion and king
    In every field of strife;
  For each had proved the other's friend,
    And saved each other's life.

38 Beside him, when he rode afield,
    Would run the faithful beast,
  And laid his head in Diderick's lap,
    When sat the king at feast.

39 From this his name of 'Lion knight'
    The brave king Diderick bare,
  And lifelong true in war and peace
    Remain'd that faithful pair.

XI.

WOLF OF YERN.

This ballad seems to have been popular, as it is found in Sweden, the Faroe-islands, and Iceland. Revenge for a father's death, as we see in so many other instances in this collection, was the most sacred duty of a son, and the more ruthlessly he executed it, the more honour he claimed for the deed. Ballads of this sanguinary character seem to have been the especial favourites of the Danish people. The name of the king varies in all the copies Biergen-wendiil and Brathis-wendill, Blide-vinder and Blinde-vinder, Bregge-windt, Boldevin, and Brattens-vendel. It seems to be some Netherland name. Whence the tale came, is unknown. There is nothing on the subject in any of the Sagas. It is most likely of Low-German origin.

Perhaps it was composed in the first place by foreigners to hold up their coarser neighbours in the North to ridicule, and their own southern gallantry to admiration. This we might suspect from the insolence of the envoy at a foreign court, St. 31 and 32, and the noble conduct of the Brattens Vendel king going to battle, although certain of death, St. 43.

Vidrick Verlandson and Wolf of Yern.

Grundt. I. 154. Dan. Vis. I. 73. Grimm p. 44. Oehl. p. 25.
Arw. I. 49.

1 Childe Wolf of Yern to sessions rode,
 And stood before the King;
 "O lend me men for a father's death
 "A full revenge to wring."

2 "I'll freely lend thee a troop of men,
 "Myself will with thee go,
 "But pray thou Vidrick Verlandson
 "To aid thy feebler blow.

3 "I lend thee troopers, mailclad all,
 "My bravest men and best:
 "Vidrick and Diderick the stout
 "Bring low the loftiest crest.

4 "Two heroes they both strong and brave,
 "Victors in many a fight;
 "Their very names in every land
 "The boldest fill with fright."

5 In strode to the hall the Danish King
 Bright as a burning flame;
 "Now who of you, ye Danish men,
 "Will aid my kinsman's claim?"

6 The king came forward, where they sat,
 A silver cup in hand;
 "Who of my gallant troopers here
 "Will join my kinsman's band?"

7 They answer'd naught, but to their lips
   Their hoods in silence press'd,
  Save only Vidrick Verlandson,
   Who turn'd their fears to jest.

8 "For me" said Vidrick Verlandson
   In tone of merry cheer,
  "'Twould be like drinking a cup of mead,
   "If once we cross'd a spear."

9 Diderick to hear what Vidrick said
   So fierce and angry grew,
  Their heads he lopp'd from troopers twain,
   And at the King's feet threw.

10 "'Twere best," said Vidrick Verlandson
    For glory all athirst,
   "We steal not on them unawares,
   "But send an envoy first."

11 That errand took young Helmer Gray,
    And sped so fleet from town,
   That dumb were all who saw him pass,
    And every eye cast down.

12 The bold young Helmer Gray it was,
    So bright with golden lace,
   Whom neither hawk nor hound could beat,
    Or hold him equal pace.

13 In came the bold young Helmer Gray,
    And stood before the board;
   A clever wight in parley he
    To choose the fittest word.

14 "Hail, king of Brattens Vendel, hail!
"And Knights, who form thy train!
"Tomorrow comes Childe Wolf of Yern
"To venge a father slain."

15 "Wiser did Wolf to stay at home,
"And drive afield his kine,
"Than challenge send, and seek to match
"His puny strength with mine.

16 "Wiser would he, like some vile worm,
"Go creep beneath a stone,
"Than combat where a stouter man,
"His sire, was overthrown.

17 "Wiser did he to stay at home,
"And under brambles hide;
"His father stood me blows but nine,
"Still less will he abide."

18 "Hark! king of Brattens Vendel, hark!
"Keep teeth before your tongue;
"The whelp grows up with rending fangs,
"Remains not always young."

19 "There's not a man in all the world,
"For whom I need to fear,
"Save only Vidrick Verlandson,
"And he's not very near."

20 "Ah no!" replied young Helmer Gray,
And struck the boaster dumb,
"'Tis even Vidrick Verlandson,
"Who with his men will come."

21 Then up and spake a trooper bold;
      "Who that is, I can tell;
    "His father was the famous smith,
      "I know that champion well.

22 "Once on a time at Birtingsborg
      "Our warriors all were met,
    "And Vidrick play'd a wondrous game,
      "I never shall forget.

23 "Fifteen our stoutest men he fell'd
      "With many a jest and jeer;
    "I stood close by, and saw it all,
      "And pale I was with fear."

24 "Now hark thee, good young Helmer Gray,
      "A prayer I make to thee;
    "What thou canst tell of Verlandson,
      "Conceal it not from me.

25 "If Vidrick lay in his chamber sick,
      "And could no longer ride,
    "There's left to meet your force afield
      "Enough brave men beside."

26 Then spake the Brattens Vendel king,
      Spake like a man, did he:
    "I'll meet him on the battle-field,
      "If horse can carry me."

27 But up a trooper rose, and thus
      His braggart speech begun;
    "Vidrick! we'll never shrink from him,
      "A low-bred collier's son."

28 Young Helmer Gray was standing near,
   And, fired at what he said,
   Struck him but once, and on the earth
   Down fell the trooper dead.

29 "What!" said the Brattens Vendel king,
   And spake in angry heat,
   "What! strike my bravest champion dead
   "Before my very feet!"

30 "My maxim", said young Helmer Gray,
   "I need not seek to hide;
   "I'll never bear that any man
   "Vidrick or me deride."

31 Then said that bold young Helmer Gray
   That raging thirst he found;
   "So prithee, Brattens Vendel king,
   "Let drink be handed round."

32 They brought him eighteen quarts of ale,
   He drank them one by one,
   And 'fore the king to fifty bits
   He kick'd the empty tun.

33 Then off he ran, young Helmer Gray,
   The news to his lord to bring;
   "Now sharpen spear, and polish sword,
   "Tomorrow comes the King."

34 Across the black and pathless heath
   They rode in murk of night,
   But from their armour, bright as day,
   There gleam'd a guiding light.

35 They rode by night o'er Birting's plain,
   They rode through Birting's moor,
  Seven hundred warriors they were strong,
   And costly armour wore.

36 Soon as they came to Birting's town,
   Their men in ring they drew,
  And valiant Vidrick Verlandson
   For captain chose anew.

37 A flag, whereon a lion gleam'd,
   They raised on Birting's heath,
  And doom'd was many a guiltless man
   That day to meet his death.

38 They hack'd with sword, they shot with bow,
   They did not stint nor tire;
  The crimson sweat ran off their limbs,
   Their bucklers sparkled fire.

39 Then spake the Brattens Vendel king,
   As through his helm he peer'd,
  "What captain leads their troops today
  "By all my men so fear'd?"

40 Thereto replied the little page
   Who rode next at his side;
  "There's none but Vidrick Verlandson,
  "That fiery horse could ride."

41 Said one who knew the champion well,
   One of the royal band;
  "'Tis truly Vidrick Verlandson
  "And Mimmering in his hand."

42 Then look'd again the Vendel king
    Through visor's narrow bar;
"Against that Tongs and Hammer shield
    "'Tis useless waging war.

43 "I march to certain death today,
    "Vidrick leaves none alive;
"Against that Tongs and Hammer shield
    "It's vain for me to strive.

44 "Heathen or Christian man alike
    "To battle I defy,
"Save only Vidrick Verlandson,
    "For him no match am I."

45 And off the Brattens Vendel king
    Spurr'd fiercely o'er the down,
And Vidrick Verlandson assail'd,
    And fain had overthrown.

46 His blows the Brattens Vendel king
    Let fall so fast and hard,
That Vidrick nothing else could do,
    Than stand awhile on guard.

47 "I've stood thee fairly eighteen blows,
    "As fast as blows could fall;
"I charge thee on thy kingly name
    "To stand me one for all."

48 "If thou hast stood me eighteen blows,
    "I'll do for thee the same;
"I'll stand unflinching eighteen blows,
    "Nor stain my kingly name."

49 About his helmet bright with gold
    A silken thread he bound;
  "My bride hear not that hand of smith
  "Dealt me the mortal wound!"

50 A word to Mimmering Vidrick spake,
    "Now, Mimmering, do thy best,
  "'Tis many years, since last the time
  "I hew'd with equal zest."

51 He firmly clench'd his Mimmering's hilt,
    With all his might he hove;
  And the proud King from gilded helm
    Down to his saddle clove.

52 Then shouted Vidrick Verlandson
    Under the mountain side;
  "Is none of all your troopers left
    "A joust with me to ride?"

53 Dead lies the Brattens Vendel king,
    His blood streams on the heath,
  And glad at heart is Wolf of Yern
    To 've venged his father's death.

54 Around him o'er the battle-field
    Young Helmer gazed his fill;
  "These boasters lie like sleeping mice,
    "So mute they 're all and still."

55 With Wolf rode home the King's men all,
    And joy on every tongue,
  That Vidrick for a father's death
    A full revenge had wrung.

NOTES.

St. 5. **Bright as a burning flame**
If we suppose a fire to have been blazing in his hall, the comparison is not so violent. The same expression occurs in the Niebelung Lay l. 7403.

och lohent im di ringe, sam daz viuwer tūt
and the mailrings glow on him like fire does.

And in Lettsom's translation stanza 1901
Look how his helmet glitters! 'tis not more bright than stout,
To dint of steel impassive, and temper'd well throughout;
His mail like fire is glowing; by him stands Hagan too;
The guests may sleep in safety with guards so stout and true.

St. 9. This conduct of Diderick seems so unreasonable that we might be tempted to think the stanza not genuine. Nevertheless we have instances recorded of similar outbursts. Saxo Grammaticus speaking of Harthen says "Ad postremum, omni sævitiæ genere debacchatus, in sex athletarum suorum præcordia furenti manu ferrum convertit." And Holberg in his Dannemarēk's Riges Historie I. 198 says that Eric king of Denmark was so excited by the minstrelsy of a harper that he broke open a closet and seized a sword with which he slew four of his ministers.

St. 18. This is a proverbial expression and recurs in several other ballads.

St. 24. He perhaps means some peculiar stratagem of Vidrick Verlandson's, but it is more likely to be one of Vedel's injudicious tamperings. In another copy, C. the envoy does not tell the king that Vidrick is coming, but, on the contrary, the king says that he is the only man whom he fears, and asks the envoy if he knows him, upon which the latter says that Vidrick is lying sick; with the view apparently of enticing the king to come to battle.

St. 28. A similar inciden*, that of an envoy killing a courtier before the sovereign's face occurs in Layamon. l. 26454.

St. 45. This binding of a silk thread round the helmet before receiving a blow occurs also in No 170 St. 42, but for what purpose it was done, is unknown. The allusion to the bride might suggest that it was a token from her, which he wished to show that he only surrendered with his life. Arwidsson says Vol. I. p. 66 that there was a superstitious belief that a silk thread bound round the helmet had a magical power to protect it against the blow. of a sword. We read in the Sagas of a silken dress which one of the heroes of old, Orvar Odd, brought from Ireland, and which rendered him invulnerable, but that a mere thread tied round the helmet had any such power, we can hardly suppose them to have believed.

St. 50. Vedel with his usual amusing extravagance makes Vidrick say that for a *hundred* years he had not struck a blow with greater zest. The other copies say fifteen. Enough surely.

XII.

CHILDE ORM AND THE BERM GIANT.

This is a ballad the subject of which the Danish editor has been unable to trace in ancient Sagas, and considers Grimm's conjecture untenable, that Regnar Lodbrok, who was killed in England, is the king who was killed in Ireland, his son Sigurd Snake-eye the king Sigfred of this ballad, and this Sigfred's son, Childe Orm. Yet it is possible that the fact of Regnar Lodbrok having perished in a snake-pen 'Ormegaard' may have been confused with Sigfred's death in the Dragon's cave.

The Giant of Berm is represented in 'Diderick and Olger', No 18, as one of the 18000 who marched against Denmark, and who could look over the tops of the beech trees. Berm or Biarmaland is supposed to be Perm in Russia, once a commercial and wealthy country.

Childe Orm and the Berm Giant.

Grundt. I. p. 160. Dan. Vis. I. 55. Grimm p. 39.

1 It was the mighty Bermeriis,
   A monster large and tall,
So mad was he, no strength of man
   His fury held in thrall.

2 It was the mighty Bermeriis
   Girt on his sword so bright,
   And rode away to the royal court
   A worthy foe to fight.

3 "Hail, Danish king! here then you sit,
   "And at your board preside;
   "Your daughter you shall give to me,
   "And realm with me divide.

4 "Either your daughter you shall give,
   "And kingdom with me share,
   "Or find a champion bold enough
   "A joust with me to dare."

5 "Neither my daughter shalt thou have,
   "Nor yet the half my land,
   "But e'en a bold and gallant knight
   "To fight thee hand to hand."

6 It was the stately Danish king
   Strode up his castle hall;
   "Now who will win a lovely maid
   "Among my warriors all?"

7 There sat those champions all so still,
   None answer'd him a word,
   Except childe Orm, the youngest swain,
   And lowest at the board.

8 "Your daughter will you give to me,
   "And share with me your land?
   "Then here there stands the champion,
   "Will meet him hand to hand."

9   It was the stately Danish king
      Met him with scornful taunt;
    "And who is then the puny mouse,
      "Dares make this haughty vaunt?"

10 "It is no puny mouse I am,
      "Tho' such the name you gave;
    "For father I king Sigfred claim,
      "Who perish'd in the cave."

11 "And is King Sigfred then thy sire?
      "His features I can trace,
    "But scarcely fifteen years, I ween,
      "Have bronzed that beardless face."

12 At evening tide, the hour when swains
      Their steeds to water bring,
    It listed Orm, the youthful swain,
      To wake the sleeping king.

13 So hard childe Orm, the youthful swain,
      The tomb began to pound,
    That all its massive marble walls
      Were shaken to the ground.

14 "Who wakes me up before my time?
      "Who dares disturb my bones?
    "Can I not e'en repose in peace
      "Beneath these heavy stones?"

15 "'Tis I wake thee before thy time,
      "'Tis I this deed have done,
    "But not to cause thee grief or pain,
      "Childe Orm, thy youngest son."

16 "And is it thou art come, childe Orm,
   "My youngest son so dear?
   "And is it gold, or silver plate,
   "Or coin, thou seekest here?"

17 "I want nor gold, nor silver plate,
   "Nor coin from out thy grave,
   "But all to win a lovely maid
   "Sword Birting come to crave."

18 "Birting, my sword, thou shalt not get
   "To win for thee the bride,
   "Till thou hast venged thy father's blood
   "In Iceland, where he died."

19 "And if I Birting cannot get,
   "And win the boon I crave,
   "With massive rock I'll pound thy tomb,
   "And crush thee in the grave."

20 He gave him Birting from out his tomb,
   The hilt into his hand;
   "Grasp it with firm and dauntless mood,
   "And thee shall none withstand."

21 Childe Orm it was, the youthful swain,
   Girt on the sword so bright,
   And strode into the castle hall,
   And long'd his foe to fight.

22 Up went childe Orm, the youthful swain,
   Before the board to stand;
   "Where skulk those vaunting troopers now,
   "Last evening were so grand?"

23 All mute those Danish courtiers sat,
       Nor answer'd him a word;
    But one, the mighty Bermeriis,
       He sprang across the board.

24 Thus spake the mighty Bermeriis,
       And this reply made he,
    "Swear that sword Birting thou hast not,
       "Before I fight with thee."

25 "Birting I swear I do not hold,
    "Nor know that famous brand,
    "Under his tomb my father lies,
    "And grasps it in his hand."

26 They drew with two bright gilded shields
       A circle on the mould,
    And sooth were standing there to fight
       Two champions stout and bold.

27 And on the pear-bush drizzled rain,
       And rain on the pear-tree,*
    And he, that mighty Bermeriis,
       Was cut across the knee.

28 "With many a knight and champion
    "I've fought with stab and blow,
    "But never yet was warrior law
    "To strike a man so low."

---

* Probably two lines from another song put in for the rime's sake by some one who forgot the right ones.

29 "So short was I, and thou so tall,
      "And thence the seeming breach,
    "I struck no higher than thy knee,
      "Nor higher could I reach."

30 Childe Orm it was, the youthful swain,
      To Iceland steer'd his snake,*
    Would for his father foully slain
      A deadly vengeance take.

31 Childe Orm it was, the youthful swain,
      Stepp'd out upon the strand,
    And there he Gerd and Arland met
      Walking upon the sand.

32 "Welcome ashore, thou brave young man,
      "From off the stormy main!
    "And tell us, is to manhood grown
      "Childe Orm the youthful swain?"

33 "That Orm, the youthful swain, ye see,
      "Sail'd hither o'er the brine;
    "I come to venge a father's death,
      "Or claim of you the fine."

34 Arland and Gerd with point of sword
      Began to spirt the earth;
    "Fine for thy father thou shalt get
      "Never a penny's worth."

---

* Snekke, the long row-boat.

35 They drew with three bright gilded shields
    A circle upon the mould,
And, sooth, were standing there to fight
    Three champions stout and bold.

36 They fought a day, they fought for twain,
    The third day even so,
And hold or vantage neither one
    Could get upon his foe.

37 Then thus a friendly mermaid spake
    Down in her ocean cell;
"Now hark thee, Orm, thou youthful swain,
    "Thy sword is under spell.

38 "And hark thee, Orm, thou youthful swain,
    "Thy sword in spell is bound,
"But swing it three times round thy head,
    "And stick it in the ground."

39 He swung it three times round his head,
    And stabb'd it in the mould,
Heav'd then one blow, and at his feet
    Both Gerd and Arland roll'd.

40 When so he had venged his father's blood
    In Iceland, where he died,
He back to the royal court return'd
    To claim his lovely bride.

41 And happy now the youthful swain,
    That all his toil is done;
He nightly sleeps in peace and bliss
    With her his valour won.

42 Quit is Childe Orm, the youthful swain,
    Of care and all alarm;
    And sleeps, as pleased and glad as he,
    His trulove on his arm.

NOTES.

St. 10. See No X. Diderick and the Dragon. st. 11.

St. 14. This reply from the tomb, and indeed the whole passage, is taken from the Vegtamskwida. See Simrock p. 45. The prophetess there answers Odin

"Who is this unknown that dares disturb my repose, and drag me from my grave, where I have lien dead so long, all covered with snow, and moistened with the rains?"
Mallet. Vol. II. p. 221

>What call unknown, what charms presume
>To break the quiet of the tomb?
>Who thus afflicts my troubled sprite,
>And drags me from the realms of night?
>Long on these mouldering bones have beat
>The winter's snow, the summer's heat,
>The drenching dews, and driving rain!
>Let me, let me sleep again.
>Who is he with voice unblest,
>That calls me from the bed of rest?
>   Gray's Descent of Odin
Mitford's Ed. p. 102.

So Samuel asks Saul "Why hast thou disquieted me to bring me up?" 1. Sam. XXVIII. 15.

The same demand of a sword from the tomb of a deceased parent is made by Hervor in the Hervorar Saga. Lewis has translated the discourse at the tomb under the name of the "Sword of Angantyr," in his Tales of Wonder p. 34.

St. 2.   "Reach me, warrior, from thy grave
         "Schwafurlama's magic blade;
         "Fatal weapon, dreaded glaive,
            "By the dwarfs at midnight made."
St. 10. "Hervor, Hervor, cease thy cries,
         "Nor oblige, by impious spell,
         "Ghosts of slaughter'd chiefs to rise;
         "Sport not with the laws of hell."

Childe Swennendal also calls up his mother from the grave to assist him. See No 84. st. 7—16 and obtains a magic sword among other presents. A remarkably fine sword was perhaps occasionally plundered from an ancestor's grave; and the theft and sacrilege gilded with these poetical fancies.

The remarkable value attached to a good sword in ancient times is proved by the numerous allusions to them by their proper names, as 'Birting,' 'Adelring,' 'Mimmering' &c. and their real excellence is seen in the fine specimens taken from the tombs of deceased warriors, that are now preserved in the Museum of Copenhagen. When armour was worn, it was of the utmost consequence to have a blade of exquisite temper to cut through it. To judge from the Sagas, the event of a conflict wholly depended upon the weapon, and this ballad is not the only tale, in which a combatant makes the express stipulation that a particular sword shall not be used; nor is it the only one, where a falsehood is told on the subject. See Diderick's fight with Sivard in Hagen's Heldensagen Vol. II. p. 83 and Ravengard and Memering below No XIV.

The custom of burying a favorite sword with a deceased knight prevailed in England too: for instance

Atte North gate of London heo buryode this gode knyght,
And buryede with hym in hys chest that swerd that was so
                                                      bryght.
                    Robert of Gloucester, 50.

XIII.

RODENGARD AND THE EAGLE.

This ballad has no great intrinsic beauty or merit of any kind, but is on that very account the more remarkable as an instance of the fidelity of tradition. A copy of it lately taken down from recitation in the Faroe islands is almost word for word identical with one 300 years old, which is preserved in Denmark. How many centuries it may have been sung from generation to generation in those remote islands, it is impossible to say. If it related to any great historical fact, or if it contained an interesting tale, its preservation would be the less surprizing. Rodengard is mentioned among King Diderick's warriors

> There glitters upon the eleventh shield
> An eagle all so brown;
> And that bears young Sir Rodengard,
> So skill'd to write a rune.

His castle stood at Karup in Jutland, and was 6 stories high, but in Vedel's time, 250 years ago, was already a ruin. The name is the same as that of Hrobgar in the Anglo-Saxon poem, Beowulf, but belonged probably to a different person.

This tale seems to be an allegory, and to relate the destruction of one of his adversaries, whose device was an eagle, and who was living in the woods as a

Werwolf. In the same manner the Prince of Rheged's army of ravens is explained by the armorial bearings of that house, in Lady Guest's Mabinogion Vol I. p. 129; and the Breton tale 'L'Hermine' describes under the allegory of a Bull coming from the water to attack a Wolf, an invasion of Charles de Blois (the wolf) by the English (John Bull), while the Ermine (Brittany) looks on and, wishes them both destroyed. Barzaz Breiz I. 543.

Rodengard and the Eagle.
Grundtv. I. 174. R. Warr. p. 62.

1 It was the rich Sir Rodengard
   In green-wood went to ride,
And met the eagle of Beedelund
   At early morning tide.

2 "Now list, thou rich Sir Rodengard,
   "Why ridest thou alone?
"Where is thy hawk, and where thy hound,
   "And where thy followers gone?"

3 "Some are on land, and some at sea
   "Are ploughing through the foam,
"And I myself to shoot the deer
   "In green-wood forest roam."

4 "If these wild deer, that are my meat,
   "Thou darest thus to slay,
"Right dearly, rich Sir Rodengard,
   "Thy shooting thou shalt pay."

5 "I 've beasts at home, both ox and cow,
    "And foal, and fatted steed;
  "'Tis little, eagle of Beedelund,.
    "That I thy visit heed."

6 "'Tis not for ox, 'tis not for cow,
    "Or foal or steed I come;
  "But trust me, rich Sir Rodengard,
    "I'll visit thee at home.

7 "I'll on thy castle yard descend,
    "I'll choose me out the best,
  "And both thy handsome sisters too
    "Shall have me there for guest."

8 "Those maids I've loved and cherish'd both,
    "E'er since their father died;
  "Forbid it heaven, that aught of ill
    "Those blossoms should betide!"

9 "If with thy right good hearty will
    "I cannot feed on these,
  "Then on that mirror of womanhood,
    "Thy trulove, I will seize."

10 So stoop'd the rich Sir Rodengard,
    And on a linden rind
  He wrote with skill the potent runes,
    He long had borne in mind.

11 He bound the eagle of Beedelund
    High on the linden bough;
  "And so, fierce eagle, think no more
    "To get my trulove now."

12 There sits the eagle of Beedelund,
    And starving droops his wing,
    And on rides rich Sir Rodengard,
    And makes his charger spring.

13 There starves the eagle of Beedelund,
    All sitting on the spray,
    And glad is rich Sir Rodengard,
    And holds his wedding day.

NOTE.

St. 5. This passage is singularly like one in the Edda lay of Helgi the son of Hiörward.

Atli
Wilt thou with Atli,
Idmund's son,
Most crafty bird,
Further speak?

Bird
Yes, if the noble
Would offer to me;
Yet choose I what I will
Out of the king's house.

Atli
If thou choosest not Hiörward,
Nor his children,
Nor the prince's
Beautiful wives.
Choose not any
Of the king's brides:
Let us bargain fairly,
That is a friend's fashion.

Bird
A court will I have
And holy reliques,
Gold-horned cows
Out of the king's stall.

See Simrock's Edda Stuttg. 1855. p. 148.

XIV.

RAVNGARD AND MEMERING.

This ballad, as Grundtvig remarks, is a remarkable instance of the tenacity of life in popular tales. He traces it back to a very remote antiquity, and finds it still in vogue in Denmark, the Faroe islands, and Scotland at the present day, differing in particulars, but agreeing in essentials after the lapse of many centuries.. And it is not only sung in ballad form in these countries, but is the subject of many poems, legends, romances and dramas in Germany, France, Italy, Spain, England and Scotland.

It is unnecessary to follow the accomplished editor through the literature of all these countries, and to unravel with him the original legend from numerous others with which it has been mixed up. At a period when the virtue of ladies, as well as every other question, was subjected to the ordeal of a duel, similar events must have occurred over and over again, and seem to have been thrown by the minstrels into the ready made mould of the ancient ballad of Gunild.

In our English literature we find it in 'Sir Hugh le Blond', Scott's Bord. Min. II 274, where the traitor's name is Rodingham, and in 'Sir Aldingar' in Percy's Anc. Rel. II 53. where 'Aldingar' is his name, both of them distantly connected in sound with Ravengard. In both these, which are probably only different forms of the same original, (and how much Percy has garbled his copy is uncertain,) the traitor lays a leper upon the queen's bed, as a proof of her infidelity, and it is to save her from being burnt, that the champion fights her accuser. In Percy's copy this champion is a little boy who proves to be an angel. Of this our English tale the earliest notice that we find, is in the writings of William of Malmsbury, and therefore 700 years old. He says 'Hardiknute gave his sister Gunhilde, a daughter of 'Canute, and a girl of remarkable beauty, for whose 'hand during her fathers life many had sued in vain, 'to the German Emperor, Henry. The wedding was 'much celebrated, and indeed is sung in the streets 'in our century. The maiden was conducted to the 'ship by all the great men of England, and large sums 'of money both from the public purse and the king's 'private treasury were lavished upon the occasion. Ar-'riving at her husband's residence she lived with him 'for some time as his wife, but being charged with 'adultery, she appointed a little boy, whom she had 'brought with her from England, to meet her accu-'ser in the field. This was a man of gigantic stature, 'and all her other retainers had shrunk from a com-'bat with him. They met, and by God's grace the 'calumniator was wounded in the knee and defeated. 'Gunhild rejoicing in the unexpected victory, separated 'from her husband, and could never afterwards be 'induced by threats or prayers to return to him, but 'took the veil, and passed the rest of her life in tran-'quillity and the service of God.'

Will Malm. Gesta Reg. Angl. l. II. § 188.

This wedding took place in the year 1036.

The next notice of it is in an author 200 years later, John Bromton, who repeats William's account of it, and adds that the little champion's name was 'Mimicon, and his antagonist's 'Roddyngar'.

The third English author who relates it, is Matthew of Westminster in the 14th century, partly from William's account, but also from the ballads which were in vogue in his day, and to which he expressly refers. His story is nearly the same, but he says that the little champion was a dwarf, who from his smallness was called 'Mimecan'.

From this, says Grundtvig, we see that a song respecting Gunild's marriage was common in England in the 12th and in the 14th century, and although it is nowhere expressly stated, there can be little doubt that it was the same as still exists in English, Danish, Faroese and Icelandic, and refers to the daughter of Canute.

Yet notwithstanding this agreement and antiquity of popular tradition, the fact is false, for Gunild lived on the best terms with her husband, and died of the plague in Italy only two years after her marriage and scarcely 20 years old, in the year 1038.

It appears that her story became confused with that of Saint Kunigunde her contemporary, and perhaps also with that of another English princess Gunild, a daughter of Harald Godwin's son, who in the same century retired to a convent at Bruges after the Norman conquest. Kunigunde upon her virtue being called in question had proved her innocence by walking barefoot over hot plough-shares. This took place at Bamberg, and there is a picture of it in the Cathedral of that town, but she died and was buried at Spire A. D. 1040.

The tale however is not confined to nations of the Germanic or Gothic stock.

In an ancient Catalonian chronicle written by Bernardo Desclot about A. D. 1300 it is said that 'a Ger-'man emperor married the daughter of the king of Bo-'hemia, who was falsely accused afterwards of infidel-'ity to her husband, and thrown into jail, till she could 'find a champion, and, failing to do so, was to be burnt 'at the end of the year on a faggot pile. No Ger-'man knight would defend her cause, but a minstrel 'or juggler 'juglar' went out in search of one, and in-'duced Count Raimund Berengar of Barcelona to come 'with a single attendant the long journey to Cologne. 'On his arrival there he visited the empress in prison, 'disguised as a monk, convinced himself of her inno-'cence, and fought and killed one of her accusers, and 'so frightened the other, that he confessed his false-'hood. The gallant knight returned to Barcelona 'without telling his name, but the emperor sent his 'empress to follow and bring him back to receive the 'highest proof of his gratitude.' This tale much altered in the circumstances came round again to England as the 'Erle of Tolouse'. See Warton's Eng. Poetry. Vol. II. sect. XXIV. We have it complete in the Spanish romance 'En el tiempo que reinaba'. Wolf & Hofm. II. 102.

Further, we find the same tale in Lombardy. According to Paulus Diaconus, who wrote in the year

800, the wife of king Rodoald being falsely accused, her servant Carel requested permission to meet the man who had calumniated her, defeated him, and reinstated his queen in her proper rank. The lady's name was Gundiberta, which is in fact the same as Gunild — the 'berta' being an ordinary termination.

A nearly similar tale is told of a queen with the same name by another rather later writer Aimoin.

While however we find this tale the same in all essential points in the different branches of the Germanic family, and in Spain, France and Italy, there are still such variations in it, that one is tempted to believe it must have had its origin in remote antiquity, and have followed the migrations of the Germanic and Gothic races, adapting itself to different names and events. It is mixed up with the Diderick Songs, but does not seem to have originated with them. The English story agrees best with the oldest of the Danish ballads (A). In this (A) there occurs a circumstance in common with the story of Diderick's fight with Sigurd Swain, the shuffling trick with the sword. Diderick had stuck the point of his borrowed sword, Mimung, into the earth, and leant his back on its hilt, but held in his hand his own sword, 'Ekkisax', and swore 'So help me God, I know not the point of Mimung above the earth, or its hilt in any man's hand'. This throws light on Orm the youthful swain's perjury about his sword Birting in No. 12.

Grundtvig concludes

'Our ballad's more accurate description of the com-
'bat, with the above mentioned ancient trait, the two
'swords that bear names, Memering's more respectable

'appearance, as an ancient, faithful servant of small 'stature from the lady's father's house, in contradiction 'to the old English notion of her combatant being a 'dwarf, the more equal battle that follows without 'any accompaniment of miracle, as well as the whole 'stamp of antiquity that it bears, leads me to con- 'sider it (that is our ballad A) not inferior to the 'rest in authenticity, and superior to all others in 'fullness of detail. Now according to all analogy it 'may be assumed that a tale, which has spread so 'widely, and maintained itself so long, with so little 'alteration, could have only done so by being framed 'in a metrical form, and we therefore have every right 'to conclude that the Danish ballad, which is here 'given (letter A), is the very same, not taking the 'words quite literally, as was sung a thousand years 'ago by our long-bearded kinsmen the other side of 'the Alps.' Here we must make due allowancef or national partiality.

It is unnecessary to follow the Danish editor through all the phases which it assumes in the Charlemagne ballads, the later French, and the German tales. In the ancient Icelandic there is a poem, 'The Gudrune Lay', on the same subject, but apparently of German origin. In classical literature, Greek and Latin, he finds no trace of it; nor does he in the Celtic, or Oriental, except in a modern Persian tale which is probably taken from a European work, although the Bible story of Joseph and Potiphar's wife is in some degree a counterpart to it, especially if we take those forms of the ballad where Ravengard's malice is ascribed to the lady's refusal of his love. A com-but for a lady's honour was a common affair in those days, at least in their romances, and it was only to add such an incident as the above, that of her defendant being a little man, to complete the story as we have it in Sir Hugh le Blond and others of that stamp alluded to. Duelling for the ladies is a thing unknown in Oriental countries, partly because they rank too low in society for men to risk their lives for them, and partly because they are too closely secluded within their harems to receive the overtures of lovers. This was perhaps the case in some measure with the Greeks and Romans of antiquity.

The heroes in the Middle ages entered the lists with the firm conviction that

>   el que de verdad se ayuda,
>   de Dios siempre es ayudado.   W. & H. I. 151.
>   He whose cause on truth is stay'd,
>   Him in battle God will aid.

Ravngard and Memering.
Grundt. I. 204. A.

1 The Dame Gunild, she dwells in Spire,
 And her the great and rich admire,
  The Dame Gunild.

2 To woo her suitors come from South
 In rich array and prime of youth,
  To Dame Gunild.

3 To woo her suitors come from West,
 The wealthiest, bravest and the best,
  To Dame Gunild.

4 To woo her suitors come from North,
   Men of well-earn'd renown and worth,
      To Dame Gunild.

5 To woo her suitors come from East,
   For wealth and bravery not the least,
      To Dame Gunild.

6 To woo her too Duke Henry came,
   And fate decreed them woe and shame.
      The Dame Gunild!

7 He woo'd and brought her home for wife;
   Behind them followed storm and strife,
      The Dame Gunild.

8 The Duke to war must march away,
   And her to guard bade * Ravngard stay,
      The Dame Gunild.

9 "Of Brunswick, Sleswick, Spire take care,
   "But chiefly watch my consort dear,
      "The Dame Gunild."

10 As steer'd the Duke his ship from land,
   Rode Ravngard off along the strand,
      To Dame Gunild.

11 He round him wrapp'd his scarlet cloak,
   And up to the lady went and spoke,
      To Dame Gunild.

---

* Pronounced 'Rowngore.'

12 "Hear now, I pray, my lord's last word,
   "And fetch me Adelring, his sword,
      "My Dame Gunild."

13 "No such behest gave me the Duke,
   "When lately leave from me he took."
      Said Dame Gunild.

14 "Unless you give me Adelring,
   "A charge against you I shall bring,
      "My Dame Gunild."

15 "Lie as thou wilt, on thee the shame,
   "For God will prove me free from blame."
      Said Dame Gunild.

16 The Duke from war march'd home again,
   And Ravngard met the glittering train;
      From Dame Gunild.

17 "How has it fared with Spire this year?
   "And how is she, my wife so dear,
      "The Dame Gunild?"

18 "Your land is in its wonted state,
   "But ill has lived your wife of late,
      "The Dame Gunild."

19 "Ravngard, thy charge I deem untrue,
   "For faithlessness I never knew
      "In Dame Gunild."

20 "'Tis what myself have seen with pain,
   "Gunild has with th'Archbishop lain,
      "The Dame Gunild."

21 "I'll smite her down with heavy hand,
"And none shall dare my wroth withstand,
"Her, Dame Gunild."

22 The Duke his scarlet mantle hent,
And up to his consort's chamber went,
To Dame Gunild.

23 Gunild, as near her door he drew,
Rose up to show him honour due;
The Dame Gunild.

24 "Welcome my noble Lord again!
"How fared you in your late campaign?"
Said Dame Gunild.

25 "Most lucky had I deem'd this year,
"Such deeds of thee did I not hear,
"My Dame Gunild."

26 "My gracious lord, oh, say not so;
"Of wrong or crime I nothing know."
Said Dame Gunild.

27 "It little boots to plead or feign,
"For with th'Archbishop thou hast lain,
"My Dame Gunild."

28 With ruthless hand he dealt the blows,
Nor one to help his lady rose,
The Dame Gunild.

29 None but two courtly dames would dare
To pray the Duke her life to spare,
The Dame Gunild's.

30 "My lord, be not this charge believ'd;
"With lying tale you've been deceiv'd
"Of Dame Gunild."

31 "Let her then seek her out a knight,
"Who does a joust with Ravngard fight,
"The Dame Gunild."

32 Bare, head and foot, her garments rent,
From out her door in sorrow went
The Dame Gunild.

33 With tears she sought the banquet hall,
Where sat and drank the champions all,
The Dame Gunild.

34 Those knights, as towards the door she drew,
Stood up to show her honour due,
To Dame Gunild.

35 "Is here within a gallant knight,
"Will for an injured lady fight,
"For Dame Gunild?"

36 Her cause would no one undertake,
Mute all, till Memering rose and spake,
"O Dame Gunild!

37 "For fifteen years I serv'd your sire,
"Fed at his board, and took his hire,
"My Dame Gunild;

38 "But saw you never in such a plight,
"With thin and tatter'd raiment dight,
"My Dame Gunild;

39 "Never my master's child have seen
"Walk barefoot o'er the castle green,
"My Dame Gunild.

40 "To some the merchant coin he told,
"To some with cups he measur'd gold,
"My Dame Gunild;

41 "On Ravngard he the most bestow'd,
"The one who first has treason show'd
"My Dame Gunild:

42 "I've ever sat at table-end,
"Whither good gifts are wont to wend,
"My Dame Gunild;

43 "And now for you I'll take the field,
"If Adelring to me you'll yield,
"My Dame Gunild."

44 "If thou wilt take the field for me,
"The sword I'll gladly fetch for thee."
Said Dame Gunild.

45 On the bare mould they drew a ring,
Where each his sword and shield should bring
For Dame Gunild.

46 "A solemn oath thou now shalt swear,
"That Adelring thou dost not wear,
"For Dame Gunild."

47 "So help me God! to me is known
"Above the ground its hilt alone."
The Dame Gunild!

48 "And now an oath thou too shalt swear,
   "That thou sword Southwind dost not bear."
     The Dáme Gunild!

49 "So help me God from pain and woe!
   "That Southwind sword I do not know."
     The Dame Gunild!

50 The first blow Ravngard on him laid,
   In twain he sunder'd Memering's blade.
     The Dame Gunild.

51 "Now," said the Duke, "may all men see,
   "How true is what is charg'd to thee:
     "My Dame Gunild."

52 "The charge, my lord, is still untrue,
   "Tho' broke my champion's sword in two."
     Said Dame Gunild.

53 The first blow Memering on him laid,
   In twain he sunder'd Ravngard's blade,
     For Dame Gunild.

54 "Hold up now, Memering, stand aside,
   "And wait till I my shoe have tied."
     The Dame Gunild!

55 Down to the greensward Ravngard bent
   And so his good sword Southwind hent.
     The Dame Gunild!

56 "This villain perjury thou shalt mourn;
   "Thy guilty soul hast thou forsworn."
     The Dame Gunild!

57 The first blow Ravngard on him laid,
   In twain he sunder'd Memering's blade.
        The Dame Gunild!

58 "Stay, Ravngard, now stand thou aside,
   "And wait till I my shoe have tied."
        The Dame Gunild!

59 Down to the greensward Memering bent,
   And Adelring his sword he hent.
        For Dame Gunild!

60 "This perjury thou too hast to mourn,
   "Thy guilty soul hast thou forsworn,
        "For Dame Gunild."

61 "Nay, for I sware to me was known
   Above the earth its hilt alone."
        The Dame Gunild!

62 The first blow Memering on him laid,
   In twain he sunder'd Ravngard's blade;
        For Dame Gunild.

63 Memering heav'd yet one other blow,
   And headless fell his guilty foe
        'Fore Dame Gunild.

64 "See there, my lord, thy champion's fate,
   "And now thy groundless wrath abate."
        Said Dame Gunild.

65 "For now, my lord, yourself may see,
   "That Ravngard basely lied on me."
        Said Dame Gunild.

66 Duke Henry tapp'd her cheek so fair,
"Forgive me, and be again as dear,
"My Dame Gunild."

67 The gallant Memering homward sped,
With broken shins and bleeding head,
To Dame Gunild.

68 "Now, Lady, for thy father's soul
"My life long give me bread and bowl,
"My Dame Gunild."

69 "Memering, my champion, stout and leal,
"Fear not, thy wounds myself will heal."
Said Dame Gunild.

70 "And all thy days I'll give thee bread,
"And clothe thee too in scarlet red."
Said Dame Gunild.

NOTES

c. 20. This seems to have been the heaviest charge that could possibly be brought against a lady. It occurs in Ingerlille No. 58 and others.

c. 31. Characteristic enough of those rude and ignorant times, where no pains were ever taken to discover the truth by enquiry, but the question settled by hard fighting. See the romance of Amys and Amylion in Ellis's Metrical Romances. p. 584, and indeed almost any of the romances of that period. The more we study the age of chivalry, the more we shall see under all their pretentious gallantry the feelings of our own vulgar.

c. 32. and 38. These couplets will be explained by a statement in K. Weinhold's Altnordisches Leben p. 173. "The adulteress according to West-Gothic law had her mantle torn off her, and the back part of her gown 'skyrta' cut off, so that only her apron remained to cover her". See also the ballad of the 'Boy and the Mantle' in Percy's Anc. Rel. and the original of it in the French Fabliau analysed by Le Grand, and versified by Way under the name of 'The Mantle made amiss.' Vol. I. p. 87 which will be seen to turn upon this usage.

c. 47. This infamous perjury is in keeping with the coarse manners of the time. Our romance writers may portray the Norman knights as the beau ideal of chivalry, but they really had very little the character of gentlemen till they settled in the South of Europe.

c. 53. The battle is very confusedly described. We have just read that Memering's sword was cut in two, yet here he uses it again, and in couplet 57 gets it cut in two a second time.

c. 60. The ladies were the surgeons in those days. Arthur's wounds were dressed in Avallon by the Elfin queen.

XV.

MEMERING.

The subject of this ballad is not found in any of the Sagas. Mimering means a dwarf, and is also the name of Vidrick Verlandson's sword. I am inclined to think it must have been originally an allegory, an impersonation of this sword, but misunderstood, and mixed up with inconsistent details, as it passed from mouth to mouth.

Memering.

Grundt. I. 214. Dan. Vis. I. 100. Grimm p. 62.

1 The smallest man was Mimering
In all the realm of Karl the king.
My loveliest maidens.

2 Before him yet his mother bare,
Were made the clothes he was to wear.

3 Before he well could walk upright,
His limbs with coat of mail were dight.

4 Before he e'en began to ride,
He girt a broadsword on his side;

5 And soon as he the sword could wield,
   He sallied out and took the field.

6 On battle bent he paced the strand,
   Where lay the merchantmen at land.

7 He saw beneath the mountain side
   A mailclad warrior towards him ride.

8 The stranger gallop'd up with speed,
   And fierce as lion look'd his steed.

9 "List, knight, and say, dost thou desire
   "To take in pay a faithful squire?"

10 "Methinks thou 'rt yet too young and frail
   "To bear my heavy coat of mail."

11 Enraged, and prompt to avenge a slight,
   From off his horse he knock'd the knight;

12 Nor wrought him that disgrace alone,
   But beat his head against a stone:

13 Then mounted horse, and long'd to fight
   With some more brave and doughty knight.

14 He reach'd a wood, and riding on
   Encounter'd Vidrick Verlandson.

15 "Well met, brave knight, art thou in heart
   "To fight and take thy lady's part?"

16 'Twas Vidrick Verlandson replied,
   "Ready, and be thy valour tried."

17 They fought one day, aye did they twain,
   But neither could the victory gain;

18 So swore they friendship, firm and pure,
That should till judgement day endure.

19 But how should they be friends for life?
And that same night renew'd their strife!
My loveliest maidens.

XVI.

THE BALD-HEAD MONK.

This tale seems to be taken from the Garden of Roses, the third book of the Heldenbuch. See North. Ant. p. 137, and the German edition of it published by F. H. v. d. Hagen.

Queen Chriemhilt had challenged Diderick of Bern to come with eleven of his knights to fight twelve of her own knights, and promised the victors as their reward a chaplet of roses and a kiss from her own lips. Diderick accepted the challenge, and, collecting his forces, came before the Abbey of Eisenburg, where dwelt the stout monk Ilsan, brother of Hildebrand, his own most trusty counsellor, and one of his best warriors. When Ilsan saw Diderick's army encamped before the walls, his face waxed green and yellow with anger. St. 174. of the German edition. None of his brethren dared to enquire the cause of his wrath. He bade them bring his armour, and declared his resolution to attack singly and drive away the supposed enemies, and took an iron pole twelve fathoms long, and issued from the abbey. His brother Hildebrand was the first to descry him, and perceiving his menacing attitude, bade the host beware, armed himself, and came out to meet him. Hildebrand in the fight was struck on the head with the pole, and his helmet fell, and discovered him to be the monk's own brother, to whom he then told the reason of their coming, and invited him to join them, which he did, promising chaplets to all his brother monks. When they came to the Rhine opposite Worms the ferryman and his twelve sons demanded a foot and hand from all whom he ferried over, and quarrelling with the monk struck him with his oar. The monk returned the blow so effectively, that they demurred no longer, but took over the whole party. Arrived at Worms they were handsomely entertained eight days, and then the tournament began. St. 236. After several duels the Monk was called upon to fight the Giant Staudenfuss. St. 306.

Among the blooming roses leap'd the grisly monk
With laughter ladies view'd his beard, his visage brown and shrunk
As he trod with angry step o'er the flowery green,
Many a maiden laugh'd aloud, and many a knight I ween.

Up spake Lady Chriemhilt, "Father, leave thine ire,
"Go, and chaunt thy matins with thy brothers in the choir."
"Gentle lady cried the monk, roses must I have,
To deck my dusky cowl in guise right gay and brave."

Loudly laugh'd the giant, when he saw his beard so rough,
Should I laughing die tomorrow, I had not laugh'd enough.
"Has the kemp of Bern sent his fool to fight?"
"Giant, straight thy hide shall feel, that I've my wits aright."
Weber's translation.

The lady is obliged to part them to save the giant's life, and bestows a chaplet and her kiss on the Monk.

"Hear, thou lady fair, more roses I must have,
"To my two and fifty brothers I promised chaplets brave."

Up spake the Queen, "Monk Ilsan, see your chaplets ready
dight;
"Champions two and fifty stand waiting for the fight."
Weber's transl.

The Monk of course beats them all, and claims fifty-two kisses, which the Queen is compelled to give him, though his rough beard makes her lips stream with blood. On his return to the Abbey he presents the monks with their fifty-two chaplets, and presses the thorns into their scalps.

He pressed a thorny chaplet on each naked crown,
That o'er their rugged visages the gory flood ran down.
The abbot and the prior and all the convent wept,
But no one for his life forth against him stept.

"Ye must help to bear my sins, holy brethren all;
"For if ye do not pray for me, dead on the ground ye fall."
A few there were who would not pray for Monk Ilsan's soul:
He tied their beards together, and hung them o'er a pole.

Ever since where'er he went, they knelt and fear'd his wrath;
And helped to bear his heavy sins, until his welcome death.
Weber's transl.

There is another legend of the same character, founded very likely upon real cases of aged warriors retiring from active life to pass their days in a convent, and being roused to martial deeds by the insult of an enemy. In the romances of the middle ages such characters present themselves not unfrequently.

The legend referred to is in the Danish Chronicle of Charlemagne.

'The Emperor said in joke to William Cornitz "Thou 'art an old man, I see gray hairs on thy head." William was displeased and answered him: "I have served 'my Emperor so long that my hair changes colour. I

'will now serve God." So he kissed his wife and
'children, rode to Lombardy, entered a convent and
'lived there a long time. One day the Abbot said to
'him "Drive into town and buy us some bread and
'wine." William asked "May I defend myself, if
'robbers or others attack me?" The Abbot answered
'"So long as thou art not robbed of thy breeches-band,
'thou mayest not defend thyself, but if that be taken
'from thee, thou mayest." William took his gold ring,
'strung it on his band, and rode forth on an ass. As
'he was returning home, he met twelve robbers, who
'took from him the bread and wine, and beat him, and
'went their way. William called to them: "You are
'a set of stupid fellows. There is a gold-ring on my
'breeches-band that is worth more than 20 nobles."
'They turned back, and attempted to take the band
'and ring from him. He had no weapon of any kind,
'but at once tore a hindleg of his ass out of the hip-
'joint, and beat the robbers with it, till they ran for
'shelter to the wood. William then set the leg of the
'ass in its proper place, fell on his knee and prayed
'to God with tears, and the leg grew fast in its socket,
'just as it was before. He then collected his baggage,
'and put it on the ass, and rode home to the cloister.
'The monks all hid themselves. As many as he found,
'he whipped with rods, the Abbot among the rest.
'William said "I see that you have no love for God,
'and I will not stay any longer with you," and away
'he went.'

But when a legend has once become popular, it
gets mixed up with other tales, and attached to different persons, as we see in the case of Diderick and

his heroes in the preceding ballads, and that is probably the case here. Grundtvig is more disposed to trace the tale to the story of Heimir in the Wilkina Saga. Hagen's Heldensagen V. II. p. 467. Raszmann V. II. p. 669.

In this Saga Heimir is represented as an aged warrior, a former comrade and friend of Diderick of Berne, who after a life of violence retires to a cloister under an assumed name, and conforms to all the rules, till a giant named Aspilian seizes on some property belonging to the brotherhood. No champion can be found to meet him, and Heimir arms himself, feeds his ancient horse well, sallies out, and destroys the invader. Being subsequently recognized by his old friend, King Diderick, and induced to leave the cloister, he resumes his former occupation of arms, and is sent by the king to levy a contribution on the monks. They resist his demand, and he kills them all, and burns their cloister down.

The Bald-head Monk.

Grundt. I. 219. Dan. Vis. I. 167. Grimm p. 313.

1 There lies a cloister behind a wood,
    Its vanes with gold ablaze;
  And standing before it are champions twelve,
    That cloister sworn to raze.

2 To plunder and raze those cloister walls
    Twelve stalwart champions stood,
  And seized and slaughter'd both ox and cow,
    That serv'd the monks for food.

3 The bald-head Monk from his window look'd,
   And rattled the beams and wall;
   "What! are then our foes no more than these?
   "I'll meet them and fight them all."

4 The Monk he call'd to his serving boy,
   "Knave, fetch me my massive club;
   "I'll up and off to the forest go,
   "And yonder champions drub."

5 Fifteen were the men who brought it in,
   As many they were, or more,
   The Monk his club with his fingers two
   As deft and as gaily bore.

6 The Monk he shoulder'd his massive club,
   And off to the greenwood hied;
   And waiting to seize him and bind his limbs
   Twelve champions there espied.

7 They drew a ring on the heathy ground,
   Sang each to the other a lay,
   And doleful enough, to say the truth,
   The measure they sung that day.

8 He first slew four, and he then slew five,
   And all at a blow the rest,
   And started away, the bald-head Monk,
   Of worthier foes in quest.

9 It listed him then, the bald-head Monk,
   To go on a wider tour,
   And off to the wood he paced his way
   So leisurely o'er the moor.

10 Away to the wood he boldly strode
    O'er meadow and mountain fell,
And met there the lothly and vicious Trold,
    The one call'd Sivard Giell.

11 "Now tell me, art thou the selfsame Monk,
    "Who wrought on our champions woe?
"And wilt thou rather like craven fly?
    "Or stand to me blow for blow?"

12 "In truth I am still that selfsame Monk,
    "Who wrought on the champions woe,
"Nor will I rather like craven fly,
    "But stand to thee blow for blow."

13 The Trold began, and he struck the Monk
    So flat on his shaven crown,
That blood from his brawny shoulders burst,
    And dripp'd from his garments down.

14 But now the Monk in his turn laid on,
    And stretch'd the Trold at his length;
"O curses on thee, thou bald-head Monk!
    "Too well do I feel thy strength.

15 "But stay thy hand, thou bald-head Monk,
    "And strike me, I pray, no more;
"I'll heap thee with gold and silver too
    "And coin that I have in store."

16 As tall as on foot the stalwart Monk,
    Was down on his knees the Trold,
And, creeping, he show'd him a secret cell
    With fifteen doors of gold.

17 He led him the road to a secret cell
  With fifteen golden doors,
 And all that the Monk could carry away,
  He took of the treasured stores.

18 The gold to his cloister and silver too
  Seven loads he carried away,
 And bade them to send another one out,
  Who better his club could play.

19 When daylight waned, and the cheerfull sun
  To slumber had sunk below,
 The Monk had still to his cloister home
  Fifteen long miles to go.

20 The sun from out of the glowing west
  Beneath the earth had sunk,
 And yet the dish that the first was serv'd,
  The Abbot's, — that took the Monk.

21 Because for the soup he had to wait,
  Fifteen monks' heads he broke,
 Because the fish was still in the pot,
  Fifteen of them hung to smoke.

22 "Alas!" said aloud the serving boy,
  While fetching the grits for soup,
 "Whenever the Monk to cloister comes,
  To this we shall have to stoop."

23 He struck the Abbot across the eye,
  And knock'd it out of his head,
 Because he was sitting beyond the time,
  That folk should be gone to bed.

24 Up started the Abbot, and left the board,
    No longer he dared to stay;
  And great indeed was the grief and pain,
    He had to endure that day.

25 The morrow had dawn'd, and cloister bells
    So merry began to ring,
  But matins or lesson the bald-head Monk
    Would neither read nor sing.

26 Among the monks and the nuns he went
    All sitting in cloister quire,
  Nor dared they one of them read or sing
    For fear of that bald-head's ire.

27 At last the Abbot, good holy man,
    Was forced to resign his stall,
  And then was seated the bald-head Monk
    As Abbot above them all.

28 That cloister for thirty years or more
    He govern'd with pomp and pride;
  Nor e'er has the like of the bald-head Monk
    Been Abbot there, since he died.

XVII.

SIR GENSELIN.

This in its present state is no doubt a parody upon a serious ballad of ancient times. The first part of it seems to be little altered, and is found almost the same, word for word, in three manuscript copies of the 16th century. The latter part varies a little. The form in which it appears in two Faroese copies, is a proof of its having been originally a serious production, like all the others. In the one of these we find nothing about the wedding and the burlesque festivities, but Gansalin receives a horse from his mother and rides out into the world, first has a combat with Sir Ivar Blue, and afterwards with Duke Valuvant, both of whom he kills, then marries Lady Sólinita and rides home to his father; it ends with the words 'Handsome are Isin's sons, but Gansalin bears the palm before them all.' In the other Faroese copy he kills Ivar Blue, but spares king Valuvant's life on condition of receiving his betrothed bride Sólita; he afterwards gives Valuvant his own sister Gunhild in return, marches home, and tells his father his achievements. King Isin and his eleven sons come to the wedding. There is not the least trace of burlesque in either of these copies.

The marriage feast of the Danish ballad appears to have been imitated from 'Thor of Asgard' No. 1.

The names Valuvant, and Solita seem to indicate some southern source from which the tale has been derived.

Sir Genselin.

Grundtv. I. p. 223.   Grimm p. 63.   Arw. I. 67.

1 It was the count Sir Genselin,
    He thus to his mother cried;
  "My manhood I would fain essay;
  "I'll up the country ride."

2 "And wilt thou ride then up the land?
    "Thy manhood there essay?
  "I'll give thee a good and gallant steed,
    "Men call him 'Carl the grey.'

3 "Gird thee no sword upon thy side,
    "Nor spur upon thy feet,
  "Unless the champion Iver Blue
    "Thou shouldest chance to meet."

4 It was the Count Sir Genselin,
    Rode under a mountain side,
  And there he met young Theedman Thinn,
    And call'd and bade him 'Bide.'

5 "Well met! well met! young Theedman Thinn,
    "What place have you rested at?"
  "On Bratinsborg, where men at arms
    "Were striking fire from hat."

6 Wrath was the Count Sir Genselin,*
    And crimson grew his cheek;
"I swear by heaven, young Theedman Thinn,
    "Thy death-doom thou didst speak."

7 With that he drew his glittering sword,
    And smote young Theedman dead;
That did the Count Sir Genselin,
    And ill the youngster sped.

8 So rode he forth to Bratingsborg,
    The gate with his spear-shaft beat;
"Is here a champion bold enough
    "Me in a joust to meet?"

9 Then up and spake Sir Iver Blue,
    A man so void of fear;
"Now help me God, but at the gate
    "A champion's voice I hear."

10 So fierce did Count Sir Genselin
    His hauberk on him fling,
That loud across three hides of land
    His mother heard it ring.

11 The lady woke at midnight hour,
    And loud to the Lord she pray'd;
"O heaven in mercy shield my son,
    "In danger lend him aid!"

---

* Thinn meant by 'hat' iron helmets, but Sir Genselin could not take a joke.

12 They rode and met, those champions two,
   Rode both so firm and bold;
   But off his horse Sir Iver Blue
   Afar on the field was roll'd.

13 "Now listen, Count Sir Genselin,
   "My life I prythee spare,
   "I've e'en a handsome bride betroth'd,
   "To thee I yield the fair."

14 "Keep thou thy bride, her need I not,
   "I take not her to wife;
   "Give me thy sister, Swollen-toe,
   "I'll thank thee all my life."

15 So to the marriage feast they rode,
   As best they found the way,
   And ask'd the bravest champions,
   That hands on they could lay.

16 They sent for Vidrick Verlandson,
   Stout Diderick, him of Berne,
   And Danish Olger, one whose heart
   For fight did ever burn.

17 They sent for Master Hildebrand,
   And Siward Hasty swain,
   And twelve more mighty champions
   To form the bridal train.

18 Thither the giant Langbane came
   T'escort the gentle bride;
   And thither young king Sigfred came,
   And ill his grief could hide.

19 And there the lady Kreem-molt stood,
    And dress'd the bride with care;
    She clad her legs in iron greaves,
    Her hands in jewels rare.

20 Thither the lady Brynild came,
    From off the northern wold,
    And with her came to share the feast
    A hundred champions bold.

21 To bridal house they led the bride,
    She thought the hint was good;
    She ate two whole ox-carcases,
    And found them pleasant food.

22 Five tuns of ale the lady drank,
    To swill the roast and broil'd,
    And then a mess of porridge craved
    In seven-tun kettle boil'd.

23 Into the hall they led the bride
    Array'd in scarlet pall,
    But, ere she through the door could pass,
    Came down seven ells of wall.

24 The bride they led to her bridal bench,
    And down thereon she sate;
    Of marble stone the bench was built,
    But crush'd beneath her weight.

28 Then up the bridegroom rose, and spake;
    His brain began to reel;
    "I never yet a bride have known,
    "Could eat so large a meal."

26 They next a little dance began
   Out on the grassy lea;
   The smallest dancer there had ells
   Fifteen below the knee.

27 Eighteen the tallest champions
   Follow'd the dancing bride;
   The rocks gave way, she trod upon,
   As round she thought to glide.

28 Out on the field they mark'd a ring,
   Where stood those champions bold;
   They fain would for the bride do fight,
   And tourney for her hold.

29 Up sprang the bride with heavy hand,
   And partner meet she caught;
   'Twas giant Langbane tripp'd with her,
   And wondrous feats they wrought.

30 For then it was the youthful bride
   Began her pace to mend;
   And fifteen champions dead she slew
   With but her stay-lace end.

XVIII.

STOUT DIDERICK AND OLGER THE DANE.

The stout Diderick of the following ballad is not the king Diderick of Berne, the hero of so many romances, but a heathen king of Berme land or Biarma land, a part of Sweden or Russia, probably Perm. Vedel with the most brilliant indifference to place and time has altered Berme to Berne and calls Stark Diderick 'Kong Tiderich', observing naively enough that "it is difficult to see how it agrees with history, since Diderick of Berne died in the year 520 after God's birth, and Olger in the time of Charlemagne about the year 800, but that his forefathers no doubt wished to show that Denmark was a free kingdom, and never paid tribute to foreign princes."

It appears to be a rifacciamento of some ancient Saga descriptive of a heathen invasion repelled by a Danish hero, but the names to have been changed to Diderick and Olger, names which were more familiar to the hearers, and were representatives, the former of German, and the latter of Danish nationality.

The description of the battle is highly picturesque, and spirited.

Stout Diderick and Olger the Dane.
Grundt. I. 232. Dan. Vis. I. 35. Grimm p. 51.

1 Stout Diderick up in Bermer land
 With eighteen brothers dwelt;
And each of these twelve sons could boast,
 Whose hand their foes had felt.

2 And twelve as stout and dauntless sons
 His fifteen sisters bare;
Thirteen sons had the younger one,
 Whom danger could not scare.

3 These champions stood before the cave,
 And were so lofty each,
Their heads rose — 'tis the truth I tell —
 Above the highest beech.

4 "For many a year, and far and wide,
 "We've fought, and not in vain;
"In Denmark lives a worthier foe,
 "King Olger, call'd the Dane.

5 "This Olger up in Jutland dwells,
 "If true what we've been told,
"And dares to set our power at naught,
 "And crown his head with gold."

6 Swerting, he seized a bar of steel,
 "King Olger I despise;
"Myself I 'd meet a hundred Danes,
 "And drive them back like flies."

7 "Nay, Swerting, hark thee, swarthy wight,
   "Deem not their prowess small,
   "For well I know king Olger's men
   "Are valiant heroes all."

8 Uprose the mighty Bermeriis,
   And spake in all his pride;
   "We'll thither march, and see if he
   "Our onset dares abide."

9 With eighteen thousand mailclad men
   They march'd from Bermer land;
   They vow'd to be king Olger's guests,
   And reach'd the Danish strand.

10 Stout Diderick straight an envoy sent,
   And bade King Olger say,
   If he would fight him on the field,
   Or yearly tribute pay.

11 With scorn King Olger made reply,
   Ill he could bear a taunt;
   "Meet us thy braggart king afield,
   "We'll make him rue his vaunt."

12 Olger to council call'd his men,
   The case before them laid;
   "Stout Diderick treads our Danish soil,
   "And tribute will be paid."

13 Then thus replied his champions all,
   And bold they spake and plain,
   "If Diderick's men to Denmark come,
   "They go not back again."

14 And these the names of Olger's men,
   Felding, and Wolf of Yern,
Hogen and Vidrick Verlandson,
   And Blue, and Koll the stern.

15 Olger the Dane and Diderick met,
   Kings both so fierce of mood;
And round them, all athirst for fight,
   Their countless champions stood.

16 They strove that day, for three they strove,
   Would none to the other yield;
And sooth it was a stubborn strife,
   And grim that battle field.

17 They met and fought with all their might
   Out on the dingy heath;
And wrathful were those warriors all,
   And fought for life and death.

18 The blood on hill and flowery vale
   Ran bubbling like a stream;
The very sun look'd red with gore
   Through clouds of dust and steam.

19 Then spake the lofty Bermeriis
   In grief and sore dismay,
"We've scarcely a hundred left alive,
   "How can we win the day?"

20 Stout Diderick took to his heels, and fled
   O'er wooded hill and dale;
Swerting, at risk of neck and limbs,
   Fled on his master's trail.

21 Stout Diderick call'd his scatter'd troops,
    And look'd to the angry sky;
    "My men, we find no shelter here,
    "To Berm land let us fly."

22 "Off then!" so spake young Wolf of Yern
    Beneath the hill so green;
    "'Tis little cause ye'll have to boast,
    "That ye 've in Denmark been."

23 Full eighteen thousand mailclad men
    Had march'd from Berm away,
    But five and fifty were the most,
    Came from that deadly fray.

NOTES.

St. 3. **before the cave** 'fram for bierig'. Trolds and supernatural beings and giants seem to have been assigned to mountain caverns. This would alone indicate that the present names are not those which originally belonged to to the ballad.

St. 18. This stanza is placed last in the original, but clearly belongs to this place, and has been inserted here by Vedel in his edition. Jamieson translating from Vedel's text gives us two fine stanzas.

> The yowther drifted sae high i' the sky,
>   The sun worth a' sae red;
> Great pity was it there to see
>   Sae mony stalwart dead!
>
> There lay the steed; here lay the man,
>   Gode friends that day did twin,
> They leuch na a' to the feast that cam,
>   Whar the het bluid-bath was done.
>
> North. Antiq. p. 291.

He observes on it 'This sublime picture of the sun looking dark and red over the field of the battle, through the clouds formed by the vapours which arose from the blood and sweat of the combatants, will call to the mind the admirable stanza in Campbell's Ode on the battle of Hohenlinden.

"''Tis morn, but scarce yon level sun
 Can pierce the war-clouds rolling dun,
Where furious Frank, and fiery Hun,
 Shout in their sulphurous canopy."

XIX.

CHILDE NORMAN'S RIDDLE RIMES.

The proper meaning and drift of this ballad is as great a riddle as any that Childe Norman asked. The Danish and Swedish copies, of which there are several, differ much from each other, but are equally obscure. N. M. Petersen in his Essay published in the Annalen for Nordisk Oldkyndighed 1842 — 3 has devoted several pages to elucidate it. He observes that the several names of the hero in different copies, Vonved, Urmand, Svanehvit, &c. seem all of them to imply insanity. 'Childe Vonved,' he says, 'is a young 'sanguine prince, who has hitherto devoted himself to 'poetry and minstrelsy and the day dreams of youth, 'and has never thought in earnest of avenging his 'father. His mother reminds him of his duty. He 'tears himself from his dreamy life; he yields to her 'remonstrance, but parts from her on ill terms, resent-'ing her offer to secure victory to his arms by witch-'craft.' (Here he is alluding to a different copy of the ballad from ours.) 'Nothing can show the hero's 'noble nature more than his passing from victory to 'victory without regard to his mother's wishes for his 'ruin. Upon his return he finds her still using her 'vile arts, and destroys her.' 'The song,' Petersen says, 'displays in the strongest traits a life torn asunder, 'strength of soul, which by nature had been destined 'to the most charming harmony, but which had been 'torn from its destiny by circumstances, and burst with 'a frightful crash.'

The resemblance between this Danish hero and Shakspeare's Hamlet cannot fail to strike the reader. There is no doubt that Shakspeare grounded his tragedy upon a Danish romance, and that romance may not improbably have been influenced, or even suggested, by the following piece. The ballad edited by Vedel under the name of 'Svend Vonved,' was a composition that he made up from several different ones with, apparently, large additions of his own, and this copy more or less altered has been translated into German by W. Grimm, and been reprinted in the Danske Viser. The following version is from an older manuscript published by Grundtvig, and free from Vedel's tampering. The name of the hero in this copy is Normand. It is undoubtedly a fragment or dim recollection of some very ancient romance. Similar riddling questions occur in the Icelandic Sagas, and in Norwegian and Faroese and Servian ballads. In English and German pieces the questions are usually ask'd and answered between a lover and his mistress, and lead to the agreeable conclusion of a marriage. Thus in German we have 'Räthsel über Räthsel' in Knaben's Wund. II. 429 and 'Es ritt einmal ein Ritter' Kn. W. IV. 139. Very closely corresponding to these two is the lively Scotch ballad 'Capt. Wedderburn's courtship' Jam. Pop. Ball. II. 155 and 'The Laird of Roslin's daughter.' Sheldon's Minstrelsy of the Border p. 230.

It is on riddles of the same character that turns the admirable old English ballad of the Abbot of Canterbury, Perc. II. 343 which has been cleverly paraphrased by Bürger, and is already naturalized in Germany. They occur also in the 'Bonny Hind squire.' Bell's Ballads p. 183. Grundtvig refers to the Legend of St. Andrew, in which the saint rescues his Bishop by answering the Devil's riddles, and to a similar legend of St. Bartholomew, both from the Swedish.

But that riddles of this kind were a common amusement at the tables of the great we learn from the account given by Alcuin of the court of Charlemagne at the beginning of the 9th century. See Guizot's History of Civilization Vol. II. p. 239 (Bohn's Ed[n]) where among other questions is ask'd 'What is the sea?' A. 'The highway of the daring, the hostelry of rivers.' 'What is the year?' A. 'The chariot of the world.' 'I saw a man standing, a dead man walking, a man walking who had never breathed. 'How may that have been?' A. 'An image in the water.' The conversations of Salomon and Saturn, and of Adrian and Ritheus, contain many questions that are little else than riddles. 'What is the heaviest thing on earth to bear?' A. 'A man's sins and his Lord's anger.' 'What is that which pleaseth one man and displeaseth another?' A. 'Judgement.' See Ælfric Soc[ys] Publications.

Such riddle poems are found in all languages in the world.

Childe Norman's riddle rimes.
Grundt. I. 240. Dan. Vis. I. 83. Grimm p. 227. Oehl. p. 29.
R. Warr. p. 208.

1 Childe Norman sat in ladies' bower,
With golden harp beguil'd the hour.
Look round about, Childe Norman.

2 He harp'd beneath his mantle skin,
Till came his mother stalking in.

3 "'Twere nobler game, methinks, to ride,
"And brunt of mounted champion bide;

4 "To venge a father foully slain,
"Than trill on lady's harp a strain."

5 Childe Norman belted sword to side,
And would in search of battle ride.

6 "When may I mix the wine for thee,
"And when expect thee back to me?"

7 "Soon as the stone shall take to flight,
"And grows the raven's feathers white."

8 "Never did stone take wing and fly,
"Or raven change his sooty die."

9 "True! stones were never wont to soar,
"And, mother, you see me no more."

10 "Here then with me I'll thee detain,
"Go thou shalt not, or go in vain.

11 "Ill luck thy every step betide!
   "Ill luck thy sword in combat guide!"

12 He tapp'd his mother's lily cheek;
   "In kinder tone, dear mother, speak."

13 "I'll blessings on thy journey call,
   "And thee shall naught of ill befall;

14 "But victory to thy sword be bound,
   "Thy horse with victory tread the ground."

15 He rode along the mountain side,
   And there he saw a champion ride;

16 A lynx upon his shoulder hung,
   A bear beside him stalk'd along.

17 "Hear, champion, what I say to thee,
   "These creatures thou shalt change with me."

18 "No knight has dared my blow abide;
   "Since at my hands King Carel died."

19 A bitter joy Childe Norman fill'd;
   "Thou then it was, my father kill'd."

20 They fought that day, they fought for twain,
   And all the third they fought again;

21 As near its close the fourth day drew,
   That doughty chief he fell'd and slew.

22 His sword to his side Childe Norman bound,
   And journey'd forth to foreign ground.

23 Where first he reach'd a farmer's stead,
   His flocks afield a shepherd led.

24 "Now hark thee, shepherd, what I say,
"The flocks thou drivest, — whose are they?*

25 "Say what is rounder than a wheel,
"And where is spread the daintiest meal?"

26 "The sun's more round than any wheel,
"In Heaven** is spread the daintiest meal."

27 "What is it fills these vallies all?
"And what sits robed in richest pall?"

28 "'Tis snow fills all the vales so white,
"And robed most richly sits the knight."

29 "What than a sloe can blacker stain?
"What louder sounds than voice of crane?"

30 "Blacker than any sloe is sin,
"Louder than crane the thunder's din."

31 "What bridge is't hath the broadest span?
"Whom thinkest thou the ugliest man?"

32 "Ice is the bridge with broadest span,
"The Dwarfking, he is the ugliest man."

33 "Where doth the loftiest highway go?
"Where doth the foullest liquor flow?"

34 "To Heaven** the loftiest highway goes,
"In Hell the foullest liquor flows."

* After this 24th couplet something seems to be omitted, but the tales were perhaps told in prose partly.
** That is the heathen Heaven, Valhalla.

35 "Where is the fort with moated wall,
   "Where champions drink in festive hall?"

36 "Here lies a fort with moated wall,
   "Where champions drink in festive hall."

37 Childe Norman took a golden band,
   And laid it on the shepherd's hand.

38 "Thine is the prize, and other none
   "Aught from Childe Norman ever won."

39 Childe Norman belted sword to side,
   Back to his mother's house to ride:

40 But when he reached it, near the gate
   Fifteen the foullest witchwives sate.

41 His trusty sword Childe Norman drew,
   And all those lothely witchwives slew.

42 But worst his mother fared of all,
   Chopp'd to a thousand pieces small.

NOTES.

c. 4. The sacred duty of revenge was equally acknowledged by our own Anglo-Saxon ancestors. See the conversation of Adrian and Ritheus. (Ælfric Soc. p. 200)

Q. What is the glory of the living man?
A. I tell thee the blood of the dead one.
Q. What son first avenged his father in his mother's womb?
A. The son of the serpent; for first the mother slew the father, and afterwards the young slay the mother.

c. 7. A proverbial expression. See Sven in Rosengard. Arw. II. 85.

Sv. Folkv. III. p. 4.

"När kommer du tilbaka,
  Du Sven i Rosengård?"
"När korpen han hvitnar,
  Kära Moder vår."

"Och när hvitnar korpen,
  Du Sven in Rosengård?"
"När gråsten han flyter,
  Kära Moder min."

"When comest thou back,
  Thou Swain of Rosengore?',
"When the crow whitens,
  Dear mother mine."

"And when whitens the crow,
  Thou Swain of Rosengore?
"When the grey rock flies,
  Dear mother mine."

c. 42. It does not appear from the ballad why he murdered his mother. It is probable that in the original tale he had reason to believe her to have been an accomplice in his father's death, as in our tragedy of Hamlet.

A Faroese Riddle rime is given in Appendix B.

XX.

ANGELFYR AND HELMER KAMP.

This ballad seems to have been composed from a dim recollection of the Hervarar Saga. The heroes belong to the society of Berserkers. These were warriors who worked themselves up to a state of insane fury and went to battle without armour, whence their name of Bare-sark. In their fits of frenzy, which were probably excited by the use of some drug — possibly the hemp or *bhang* still used in the East Indies, the *dacca* of South Africa — they were wont to perform the most astonishing feats of strength, and to perpetrate the most horrible excesses.

'Odinus efficere valuit, ut hostes ipsius inter bel-
'landum coeci vel surdi vel attoniti fierent, armaque
'illorum instar baculorum obtusa essent. Sui vero mi-
'lites sive loricis incedebant, ac instar canum vel lupo-
'rum furebant, scuta sua arrodentes: et robusti ut tauri
'vel ursi, adversarios trucidabant: ipsis vero neque
'ignis neque ferrum nocuit. Ea qualitas vocatur furor
'Berserkicus.'
Snorro Sturleson in Bartholin p. 344.

Polybius relates of the Gæsatæ, a tribe of Gauls, that they stripped themselves naked before battle, and fought in the first rank; but whether they were under artificial excitement, he does not say. He attributes their doing so to vanity and bravado φιλοδοξίαν καὶ θάρσος. Book II. ch. 28.

The following account of the Berserker family, who are the subject of our ballad, is taken from the Hervarar Saga. ch. III —V.

'Arngrim, the father of Angantyr, made an expe-
'dition against Swafurlami, killed him and took from
'him his sword, Tyrfing, and his daughter, Eyvora,
'whom he married. This woman was the mother of
'12 sons, all Berserkers like their father. Angantyr
'the eldest was taller by a head than all the rest,
'and equal in strength to two men. Even in early
'youth they undertook piratical expeditions, and found
'none their equals any where. They never had any
'but themselves on board their own ship, although they
'frequently had several other ships in their company.
'Their father in his expeditions had obtained for them
'weapons of great excellence, and Angantyr received
'from him Tyrfing, Hiorvardur (or Hervard) Hrotta, &
'Seming Mistiltein, which Thrainn afterwards robbed
'from his grave. It was their custom, when they were
'alone among themselves, and felt themselves seized
'with the Berserker fury, to disembark on land, and
'attack great rocks and trees; for it had sometimes
'happened to them, that upon being seized with this
'frenzy they had killed their own people, and deso-
'lated their ships. They never fought a battle any
'where without coming off victors, and there was not a
'king, who would not rather give them any thing that
'they asked, than suffer their attacks. It happened
one Christmas evening—that, as they were sitting at
'Bolm and making vows of great achievements of va-

'lour, Arngrim's sons made such vows too. Hiorvardur
'bound himself by oath to get possession of Ingeborg,
'a daughter of the Swedish king, Aun, who reigned
'at Upsal: which princess was renowned for good sense,
'beauty, and wit. He declared that he never would
'marry at all, if he did not get her. In the following
'spring they all marched off to Upsal, and went up
'to the king's table, where he was sitting with his
'daughter on his throne. Hiorvardur declared his er-
'rand, and the king remained thoughtful about it, as
'the brothers were powerful and of a great family.
'There were many illustrious warriors sitting at the
'king's table, of whom Hialmar the highminded, or
''hug-prude', and Oddur the far-travelled, generally
'called Orvar-Odd, were the most distinguished. They
'were both of them captains under the king Aun,
'and set by him to guard his land. Hialmar now
'stepped forward and said. "My liege, remember the
'assistance that I have rendered you, since I came
'hither, and how many years I have worked to re-
'cover your kingdom for you, and how ready I have
'always been to serve you. Now I pray you to show
'me the honour of giving me your daughter, whom
'I have loved so long. It is fairer that you should
'do a favour to me than to these Berserkers, who have
'done nothing but evil, as well in this realm as in
'other king's lands." The king was in great perplex-
'ity, for both the champions, who sued for his daugh-
'ter, were men of high family. He told them so,
'and that he left it to his daughter's own decision.
'Ingeborg then chose Hialmar, whom she knew best.
'Hiorvardur thereupon called him out to a duel on the

'island Samsey, adding that he, Hialmar, would be
'looked on as a pitiful fellow, a Nidding, if he de-
'clined it. Hialmar accepted the challenge. The Ber-
'serkers on their voyage home put in at a harbour
'in Garderige, where the Jarl, Biartmar, had a fair
'daughter named Swafa, and Angantyr courted and
'married her there, and they then sailed home to their
'father. Before he left Biartmar's court he had dreamed
'that he and his brothers were standing in Samsey
'and saw a multitude of birds, and killed them all,
'but that there then met them, in another part of the
'island two eagles, of which the one attacked him, and
'fought with him furiously, till the strength of both
'was exhausted, and they were obliged to sit down.
'The other in the meantime had fought with his
'eleven brothers and killed them all. The Jarl ex-
'plained the dream to mean the death of certain men,
'and to concern his brother chiefly. They then returned
'home to prepare for the duel. Their father furnished
'them with good weapons, and bade them farewell.
'They reached Samsey, and, being seized with the
'Berserker frenzy, attacked the trees as usual.

'In the mean time Hialmar had arrived at another
'part of the island with two ships called Askar, each
'manned with 100 men heavily armed.

'The Berserker brothers recognised these as the
'ships of Hialmar and Oddur the wide-wandered. The
'sons of Arngrim brandished their swords, and gnaw-
'ed their shields, and howled violently, and six of
'them attacked each Ask. The battle was waged vi-
'gorously, for they were all gallant soldiers and
'none quitted his post or expressed a word of fear.

'The Berserkers, going along one side of the ship,
'and returning along the other, killed them every one,
'and then with howling disembarked. Hiorvard thought
'his father had been mistaken as to the prowess of
'Hialmar and Oddur, but these two were not in the
'battle, for they had gone to another part of the island
'to learn if their foes were come, and met them as
'they landed, exhausted, as though from disease.

'Oddur then sang

'"Then for once Fear seized me, when they de-
'barked from the Asks bellowing and howling, and
'landed on the island: not clad in mail, twelve to-
'gether."

'"You see", said Hialmar, "that our people have
'all been killed, and it is probable that we shall all
'be guests of Odin in Valhalla this evening." This
'was the only word that Hialmar uttered expressive
'of fear. Oddur thought it were advizable to retire
'to the forest, but, encouraged by Hialmar, determined
'to meet them.

'The Berserkers were now coming towards them,
'brandishing their swords, and covered with blood.
'One was a head taller than the rest. They observed
'that the sword, which Angantyr held in his hand, was
'Tyrfing, for it emitted flashes like the rays of the sun.
'Hialmar claimed him as his antagonist on the ground
'that he was the Duke of the kingdom, born of royal
'blood, and promised the daughter of the Swedish king.

'As Hialmar met Angantyr, they each bade the
'other go to Valhalla. They agreed that the victor
'should not spoil the slain, but that Tyrfing should
'be buried with Angantyr, his silk dress with Oddur,

'and Hialmar's weapons with him, and that the sur-
'vivors should bury the dead under a tumulus. So hot
'was the fight between Hialmar and Angantyr that the
'flashes of their swords were like a blazing flame, and
'the earth shook, as if suspended on a thread. Oddur
'proposes to the eleven brothers to fight them one by
'one, to which they agree. Oddur's sword was so
'finely tempered that it would cut steel as easily as
'clothes. Hiorvardur soon fell and died. His bro-
'thers, when they saw this, distorted their faces, and
'gnawed their shields, till the froth fell from their
'mouths. Another then rose and attacked Oddur, but
'he also soon fell and died. The Berserkers roared,
'and protruded their tongues, gnashed their teeth, and
'bellowed like bulls, that the rocks reechoed it. Then
'Seming rose to the fight, and cut Oddur's armour all
'to pieces, but could not penetrate the silk dress.
'Seming was so cut and wounded, that all the flesh
'fell from his bones, but he did not give up till all
'the blood had flowed from his body. One after the
'other all the eleven fell before Oddur's sword. He
'then went to witness Hialmar's duel with Angantyr,
'and sang — .

'"What ails thee, Hialmar? Thou hast changed
'colour, I say that thou art exhausted with many wounds,
'thy helmet and mail cut to pieces: I say too that thy
'life has perished."

Hialmar sang —

'"I have sixteen wounds, my mail rent to pieces;
'darkness moves before my eyes; vision fails me to
'march. The sword of Angantyr has pierced my heart,
'the point hardened in poison. I possessed on the soil

'five estates together; but I never was satisfied with 'my territory. I am now compelled to lie dead, gashed 'with the sword, on the island Samsey. My attendants 'drink mead in the hall, ornamented with collars, at 'my father's house. But the scars of battles pain me 'on this island. I departed from the fair nymph in 'northern Agnasitia. That prophecy is verified, by 'which it was foretold that I should never return. 'Draw thou off my hand the glittering bracelet, and 'carry it to the youthful Ingeborg. Great sorrow will 'dwell in her mind that I do not return to Upsal. I 'departed from the beautiful song of virgins, anxious 'for these joys in the east at the rock of Soto, I hast-'ened my journey, I embarked on board ship, leaving 'at the commencement of my voyage my faithful friends. 'The raven flies from the east from lofty woods, he 'pursues on his track the eagle flying before him. To 'that bird I furnish food at last. He shall taste my 'blood."

'After both the combatants had fallen exhausted 'and died, Oddur passed the night there. In the morn-'ing he collected the bodies of the Berserkers and 'commenced a tumulus. He ordered the people of 'Eyarskegg to build up trees together upon which they 'threw sand and stones. This was a laborious work 'and strongly made, and cost a month's labour. The 'Berserkers were then carried into it with their arms, 'and the entrance stopped up. Oddur afterwards car-'ried Hialmar to his ship, and conveyed him to Sweden 'to the king's daughter, Ingeborg, but she would not 'survive her beloved, and killed herself.'

These two freebooters seem to have been comparatively civilized for they gave their retainers the following laws —

"That no one should eat raw meat — that no one 'should plunder peasants or merchants, but yet might 'take as much as they needed for food — that no one 'should rob women or carry them aboard ship against 'their will — and that any one who transgressed 'these laws, should lose his head without regard to his 'rank or character.'

Swafa bare a daughter after Angantyr's death, the celebrated Hervor, whose visit to her father's tomb is described in a subsequent part of the Saga, and has been paraphrased by Gray.

Upon comparing the ballad with this ancient Saga Grimm remarks that 'One may observe the agreement 'of the ballad with the Saga in general and in some 'particulars. Angelfyr represents Hiorvardur, who sues 'for the princess and also Angantyr, who fights a duel 'with the other suitor, in which duel both are killed. Helmerkamp is obviously Hialmar. Wolf of Otters-'cliff the father, who speaks with him before he dies, 'is Oddur. The ballad makes the former unsuited to 'be the brother of the other suitor, by describing An-'gelfyr and all his race as Trolds, that is Berserkers, 'which of course would equally apply to his brother too.'

Grimm's comparison certainly seems a little far fetched, but is undoubtedly the correct view of it. We must remember that ballads were not generally composed by literary men, but by the peasantry, who may have only half understood the language of the Icelandic Saga, and to whom any nice accuracy was a matter of indifference.

Angelfyr and Helmer Kamp.

Grundt. I. 254. Dan. Vis. I. 139. Grimm p. 171.

1 Alf, he dwelt at Otterscliff,
   A man of wealth and fame;
And sons he had two gallant youths,
   Had earn'd a champion's name.

2 Alf, he dwelt at Otterscliff,
   And sons he had so bold,
The king's fair daughter they would woo
   On Upsal's dreary wold.

3 Young Helmer Kamp his servants bade
   His saddled steed to bring,
"We'll up the country, and claim for bride
"The daughter of Upsal's king."

4 Then rose and bade young Angelfyr
   With speed his horse to girth,
"And we to Upsal too will ride,
   "Beneath us crack the earth."

5 There, as within the court they come,
   Their cloaks they round them fling,
And stride both into the lofty hall
   Before the Upsal king.

6 In walk'd young Helmer Kamp the first,
   And stood before the board;
   "Sir, will ye me your daughter give?
   "Deign me a gracious word."

7 Then up went haughty Angelfyr
   Before the board to stand;
   "King, thou shalt me thy daughter give,
   "And quit, thyself, the land."

8 "Nay," so the king of Upsal spake
   With stately mien and voice,
   "To none will I my daughter give,
   "But leave to her the choice."

9 "O hearty thanks, my father dear,
   "That choose myself I can;
   "Young Helmer Kamp will I betroth,
   "He is at least a man.

10 "But Angelfyr will I not have,
   "I loathe his fiendish face,
   "I loath his father and mother too,
   "And all his heathen race."

11 Short answer made young Angelfyr,
   Wroth at the maiden's slight;
   "We 'll down below to the castle yard,
   "And settle that in fight."

12 Content the king of Upsal was,
   And this for answer made;
   "Their swords are sharp, the lads are hale,
   "E'en let the game be play'd."

13 Alf listening stood at Otterscliff,
    What sounds came o'er the hill,
  And wafted heard in every breeze
    The clank of swords so shrill.

14 Alf heard it over at Otterscliff,
    As on the heath he stood;
  "How have my sons then fallen out?
    "And why so fierce of mood?"

15 He waited not a moment more,
    But sprang on his horse so red,
  And rode across, and Upsal reach'd,
    Before his sons were dead.

16 "Speak thou, and say, young Helmer Kamp,
    "What is't, my dearest son,
  "That pouring from thy wounded head
    "These streams of blood should run?"

17 Young Helmer Kamp his father heard,
    And thus he spake in pain;
  "That did my brother Angelfyr,
    "The bride he could not gain.

18 "Fifteen my wounds, and death-wounds all,
    "Stabb'd with a poison'd knife;
  "With only one, for a single hour
    "No art could save my life."

19 He turn'd him, Alf of Otterscliff,
    And rooted up an oak,
  And fell'd his son, young Angelfyr,
    Dead with a single stroke.

20 Now buried lie those champions two
   In the same grave at rest;
   And the Upsal king to his daughter gives
   The youth she loves the best.

NOTE

St. 20. This second choice of a youth she loved is, we see from the passage quoted in the Introduction, contrary to the Saga.

XXI.

HABOR AND SIGNILD.

This is without doubt one of the most beautiful tales to be found in the ballad literature of any nation. The earliest notice of it is in Saxo, who gives the incidents in prose, but, singularly enough, although this tale has been a favorite with the Scandinavians for more than a thousand years, there is no poem on the subject in their ancient language, nor any echo of it in Icelandic prose literature. The site of the event has been as much contested as the birthplace of Homer, and in each of the three kingdoms Denmark, Norway, and Sweden several different places compete for it. Sigarsted in Seeland seems to have the best claim to that honour, and as any but Danish or Norse readers can be very little interested in the question, it is useless to name the other places and their several claims. Perhaps few English readers will be able to accede to P. A. Munch's view of the matter. After speaking of the wide diffusion of the tale, he says

'Most traditions which, like this one, have become 'nationalised and localised in various Germanic nations, 'or races, belong properly speaking to no single race, 'but only to the original 'Stammfolk' or stock; they 'are, as we have already hinted in respect to the 'Wayland and Niflung tales, mostly old traditions

'brought from the original home of the nation, but locali-
'sed among the separate races in the lands where they
'came at a later period to settle.' It is with the
greatest diffidence that I venture to dispute any opinion of such a profound thinker and scholar as Professor
Munch of Christiania, but allowing the possibility of
what he says of the Wayland and Niflung tales, I
cannot concede that there is even the least shadow
of reason for assuming that this simple ballad is of
any such ancient date. There is no external evidence
of it, for the tale is confined to the Scandinavian
countries, and there is internal evidence of a higher
state of culture than was known to that rude period.
Still fewer perhaps will agree with Grundtvig's remark.

'On one point there can be no doubt, that it is *this*
'*very ballad*, which is the source of all that has been
'said and written upon the subject, Saxo's prose tale
'and Latin verses inclusive, and that it is this, which
'from time immemorial has echoed over all Scandina-
'via, and carried the tale from land to land; and we
'have in this a striking proof of the vital power that
'resides in such a little song, sprung from the very
'heart of a people and borne on its tongue as far as
'the Danish language is understood. For though its
'tones may be lower, and its voice more feeble, it is
'still the very same that sounded in the ears of Saxo,
'and still earlier in those of Thiodolf.' Now there
really does not appear to be any more reason for
supposing the complete tale to have consisted of ballads, than for this ballad having been formed from
the tale, and all evidence is in favour of the latter
supposition, that only a part of the original Saga was

popularized, that, namely, which we have here. It is to be remarked that the names of the parties are always the same, which they would not have been, had the ballad passed through many centuries of tradition. I have no doubt that somebody in the 14th or 15th century made it from Saxo's tale. The stratagem employed by Habor is common to several others — to that of Achilles and Deidamia among the rest, as well as to several Danish ballads, and the Flemish one, 'Das Weltweib,' Fallersl. p. 58. There is however a very much closer parallel in the ancient German romance of Hughdietrick. See North. Antiq. p. 62.

The hero is king of Greece and at his father's death assembles his nobles, and asks their advice respecting his marriage. The Duke of Meran tells him that the most beautiful damsel, he had ever beheld, was Hiltburg, daughter of king Waligunt, who kept her confined in a fortress, and had sworn never to give her to any man. Hughdietrick had recourse to the same stratagem as Habor.

Firmly my mind is fix'd Hiltburg the fair to win,
Then, if ye think it fitting, I will learn to work and spin,
To sew like cunning virgin, quaintly with silken thread,
All the mastery will I learn, which well-taught maidens need.
Richly will I clothe me in gentle lady's guise:
Then find me, noble Bechtung, a mistress quaint and wise,
Bid her to come and teach me works fit for ladies mild,
On the silk to broider beasts, both tame and wild.
Weber's Transl. in North. Antiq.

Having fully accomplished himself he set out for the castle with a large retinue of ladies and fifty knights, and pretended to be the sister of Hughdietrick flying from a compulsory marriage. He was kindly received by king Waligund, but immediately suspected by the queen, whose doubts however were overruled, and our hero admitted to the intimate society of their daughter Hiltburg. He astonished the whole court by working a table-cloth, on which he depicted many wild animals. Hiltburg prays that the stranger may be allowed to teach her, and they are shut up together in her tower. After some months Hiltburg discovers that she is in the family way, and Bechtung comes to fetch away Hughdietrick to Constantinople, whither he returns, leaving directions to his bride how to escape and follow him. The story ends with his returning to the castle and marrying her with her parents' consent, contrary to the Scandinavian tale, which is uniformly tragical.

In the copies of this ballad there are many variations in particulars, as for instance the hero in most of them is represented as cutting the animals and trees with a knife upon the table. From the great number of manuscript copies of it of the 16th century it seems to have been extremely popular at that period, and the variety in the expressions and small traits and incidents very great, yet the main facts are so bold and distinct, as to be preserved in all of them unaltered.

From comparison of these copies with the account that Saxo gives of the romance, Grundtvig maintains that our present ballad is merely a fragment of a longer tale, a brand saved from the fire, as he expresses it. Saxo's tale is as follows. See Grimm p. 510.

'Alf and Alger, sons of king Sigar, meet on their 'voyage the sons of Prince Hamund, named Helvin,

'Hagbarth, and Hamund with a hundred ships. A
'violent battle begins, and only ends at night-fall.
'Next morning, both sides being equally unable to re-
'new the fight, they make peace. At that time there
'was a German knight, named Hildigsleus, of noble
'race, but a great coward, who was courting Sigar's
'daughter Sygne. Hagbarth sails with Sigar's sons
'to Denmark, and obtains, unknown to them, an in-
'terview with Sygne, who promises him her favour.
'She afterwards sings a song in praise of Hake, an-
'other brother of Hagbarth, but all who hear it, un-
'derstand that Hagbarth is meant. Hildigsleus irri-
'tated at this preference of a rival, bribes Bolwis with
'handsome presents to turn the friendship between the
'sons of Sigar and Hamund into enmity. For Sigar,
'now an old man, allowed himself to be guided by
'two counsellors, of whom Bolwis was one. This man
'constantly seeks to stir up a quarrel among them, but
'the other to reconcile them. Bolwis at last wins over
'Alf and Alger, by representing to them that Hamund's
'sons will never remain true, and they fall upon Helvin
'and Hamund, when apart from Hagbarth, and kill
'them in a battle. Hagbarth brings up his troops, and
'avenges his brothers by killing both their murderers.
'Hildigsleus is wounded in a disgraceful part, and flies.

'Hagbarth now disguised himself in female clothes,
'and as though he had not offended Sigar's daughter
'by killing her brothers, went alone to demand the ful-
'filment of her promise, and greater was his confidence
'in her fidelity, than his fear on account of the deed
'he had done. As excuse for the journey, he pretend-
'ed to be a shield-maiden of Hake, and sent by him

'to Sigar's court. At night a bed was assigned him
'among the girls, and as the maids were washing his
'feet, they asked him, why his legs were so rough,
'and his hands so far from white and delicate. He
'answered "Now by sea and now by land and forest
'goes my march, and my breast in iron rings inclosed,
'and wont to receive the brunt of spears, cannot be
'tender like your's, which only a thin cloth covers.
'Not the distaff or the goblet has my hand borne, but
'gory arrows." Sygne helped him, and said that a
'hand hardened by the work of war and rowing could
'not be tender and soft. To show him the greater
'honour a place was assigned him in her own bed. As
'they lay there, Hagbarth asked Sygne "If I should
'be taken prisoner by your father and sentenced to a
'dismal death, wilt thou forget our engagement, and
'yield thy love to another? for if that should be my
'fate, I do not expect that he will forego the oppor-
'tunity, eager as he is to revenge himself for the death
'of his sons: as I have killed your brothers, and am
'with thee now, unknown to him, and against his wish.
'Tell me, my dear, what thou wilt do, when I can
'embrace thee no more?" Sygne answered. "Think
'not, my dear lord, that I could wish to live, if thou
'wert come to destruction, or to prolong my life, after
'a mournful death had brought thee to the tomb.
'Whatever death carries thee off, whether disease,
'sword, or accident by sea or land, I vow to die too,
'so that in death as in the bridal bed we may be
'united. The pain of thy death I shall feel, and never
'will I forsake him, whom I have deemed worthy of my
'love, who has first tasted the kisses of my lips, and

'enjoyed my blooming person. Promise could not be
'more binding, or more to be relied on, if ever word
'of woman was true."

'These words so inflamed Hagbarth, that her pro-
'mise gave him more pleasure, than his daring enter-
'prize caused him fear. Betrayed by the maidservants,
'he was attacked by Siward's men, but defended him-
'self well, and killed many of them, but was captured
'at last, and carried before the court of justice.
'Bilwis, the brother of Bolwis, advised that they
'should rather avail themselves of his bravery, than
'use him cruelly. But Bolwis said, that it was ill ad-
'vice to induce the king to forego revenging himself
'on Hagbarth, who had robbed him of the comfort of
'his two sons, and disgraced his daughter. The major-
'ity were of his opinion, and Hagbarth was sentenced
'to be hung. The Queen then came forward and offer-
'ed him a horn, and begged him to quench his thirst,
'with these harsh words "Now, thoughtless Hagbarth,
'whom the whole court condemns to death, put the
'horn to thy mouth, and drink, to banish thy fear, in
'the last moment with unquivering lips from the cup
'of death. Soon wilt thou arrive at the dwellings
'underground, and go into the opened realm of the
'severe God." The youth seized the horn, and an-
'swered; "With the same hand take I the last draught,
'with which I killed both thy sons. Not unavenged
'go I into the world below, to the wild souls, whom
'my victories have sent before me into the dark cavern.
'This right hand has dripped with thy blood. This
'hand took off in tender youth the children, whom thou
'broughtest into the world; dishonoured, frenzied wo-

'man! unhappy mother! robbed of thy children! No 'time will give thee back what thou hast lost. May 'every day renew thy mortal pain!" With that he 'threw the horn in her face, so that she was wetted 'all over with the mead.

'In the meantime Sygne asked her weeping maids, 'whether they had the courage to carry out with her 'what they had begun. They all promised to follow 'their mistress, and Sygne believed them. She then 'burst into tears, and said she would follow in death 'him who alone had shared her bed. So soon as the 'sign should be given, they should set her chamber 'on fire, twist ropes out of their veils, put them round 'their necks, and kick away the footstool. They were 'all willing to obey, and, to lessen their fear of death, 'she gave them mead. Hagbarth was presently led out 'for execution to the hill that has since borne his name. 'He there would fain put his bride's fidelity to the 'proof, and begged the hangman to hang up his mantle. '"He had a fancy" he said, "to see how he would 'look in death." They did it, and the watchman, 'thinking it to be Hagbarth, told the young women 'what had happened. They immediately set fire to 'their chamber, kicked away their stool, and the noose 'was drawn tight round their necks. Hagbarth saw 'the royal castle on fire, and the sleeping room that 'he knew so well, in flames, and felt more joy in the 'fidelity of his lady, than sorrow for his approaching 'death. He gave orders to those about him to pro-'ceed with the execution, and sang his deathsong, and 'the hangman drew the noose.'

Saxo further says that there is local evidence of the

truth of the story, for that near Sigarsted in Sceland there is a village that still bears Hagbarth's name, and the hill is pointed out, where he was hung. Stephanius in his notes to Saxo refers the event to the end of the second century, Messenius to the year A.D. 222 about 20 or 30 years later. The ballad, in the form in which we now have it, cannot have been written earlier than about the 15th century.

It is the opinion of Danish literati that this is the middle one of three ballads. The first one would have contained an account of Habor's visit to Sigar's court, and his quarrel with the sons, then would have followed the present one, and after that a third tale of Hake's revenge, with the stratagem of the wandering wood, one that occurs in several Danish and German tales as well as in Shakspeare's Macbeth.

An idea which I cannot but consider a false, or at least an unwarranted one, pervades the writings of all the Danish critics who have treated of these ballads, but Grundtvig's more especially, that, because they have formed the amusement of the peasantry, they must have been composed by them and handed down by them. This is most certainly not the case with our English and Scottish ballads, and still less so with the Spanish and Portuguese, many of which latter were composed by the best poets of their day. The Danish editors seem to regard it as a thing quite out of the question that the authors of their's should have studied Saxo Grammaticus and the Eddas and made ballads of their tales. But seeing what a very large proportion of them have been obtained from the recitation of country clergymen and their wives, why need we doubt that educated people of that order also composed many of them?

The differences between Saxo's tale and the following ballad are considerable. Saxo's tale makes no mention of the dream, although so agreeable to the old style of romance, and repeatedly occurring in the Edda and other poems. Again Signild, according to Saxo, immediately recognises him as her betrothed, and so there could have been nothing of the discourse in the bed chamber. He says nothing of Habor's cutting out the animals, nor of the maid stealing his armour, and as might be expected, nothing about the binding him with a hair of Signild's head, a trait well suited to the romances of the South of Europe, but very little in accordance with the feelings of Scandinavians towards the ladies; nothing again of the king's remorse, nor of the punishment of the maid.

The editors of the Danske Viser observe of this ballad that it presents an example of 'faithful love, inextinguishable hatred towards enemies, revenge, and contempt for death, that is a pure transcript of the spirit and mode of thought that formerly prevailed in the North.'

Of the two translations here given the first has been made from that published by Vedel, and apparently revised by him, and improved by the adoption of several incidents, that all occur in the different older copies, but not all together in any one of them. The second is from Grundtvig's letter B. It is evidently imperfect, especially the latter part of it. From the 3d and the 8th stanzas it appears to have been written in some other country than Denmark. In the main story it is much the same as Vedel's, but the dream is different, and the hero is represented as carving in wood but not working with the needle.

As a trait of the simplicity of ancient manners, it is perhaps worth remarking that the prince is described as starting up from his dream, and telling it to his mother and her ladies, as they lay awake, indicating that, as in farmhouses in Norway at the present day, all the members of a family, male and female, slept in the same room. It is rather remarkable that in the East too, where the seclusion of women is in many respects so strict, it seems to have formerly been the fashion, and perhaps it is so now, for a sister to sleep in the bridal chamber. In the Introduction to the Arabian nights we read. "The sultan passed the night with Scheherazadé on an elevated couch, and Dinarzadé her sister slept at the foot of it, on a mattress." In some of the many versions of Fair Anna she is represented as sleeping, like Dinarzadé, at the foot of the bride's bed. In a low state of civilization very great indelicacy is consistent with the purest virtue, and on the other hand when manners are refined and artificial, very great immorality is consistent with the strictest delicacy.

This beautiful ballad is introduced by Tegner in his Frithioff as sung by a minstrel at the banquet given by King Ring: ch. XVII.

Och skalden tog sin harpa, han satt vid kungens bord,
och sjung et hjertligt qväde om kärleken i Nord,
om Hagbart och skön Signe, och vid hans djupa röst
de hårda hjertan smälte i stålbeklädda bröst.

A minstrel sat beside the throne, he sang his best that day,
And told a tale of tenderness, an old Norwegian lay;
Of Hagbart's fate and Signe's love — his voice was sweet and low
That iron hearts began to melt, and tears were seen to flow.

Latham's transl.

Habor and Signild. A.

Dan. Vis. III. 3. Grundt. I. 300. Oehl. p. 51. Grimm p. 93. Svens. Folkv. I. 138. R. Warr. p. 243.

1 Habor and Siward, princely chiefs,
   A deadly feud had they,
All for the gentle Signild's sake,
   So fair that lovely may!

2 It was young Habor, royal Prince,
   At midnight hour awoke,
And all in haste of his vivid dreams
   He thus to his mother spoke.

3 "It seem'd I stood in heaven above,
   "Was in the beauteous town,
"And held my trulove in my arms,
   "And through the clouds fell down."

4 Her ladies heard the Prince's dream,
   Nor gave it heed or thought,
But well his royal mother knew,
   With fate that it was fraught.

5 "Now ride, my son, to yonder cave,
   "No moment check the rein,
  "And the Elfking's eldest daughter pray
   "Thy dream to thee explain."

6 In left hand Habor, royal prince,
   Held firm his trusty blade,
  As off to the Elfin cave he rode
   To see that graceful maid.

7 With fingers small in mantle roll'd
   He gently tapp'd her cell,
  She lay awake, the summons heard,
   And knew his purpose well.

8 "Hail! Elf-king's daughter, peerless maid,
   "Robed in thy pall of state!
  "For God's sake tell what means my dream,
   "And what shall be my fate.

9 "It seem'd I stood in heaven above,
   "Was in the glorious town,
  "And held my trulove in my arms,
   "And through the clouds fell down."

10 "The maid, for that you 've dream'd of heaven,
    "Shall in your bosom lie;
   "But falling through the cloud portends,
    "That for her you must die."

11 "And if I once should have the bliss
    "That lovely maid to gain,
   "To suffer death for one so fair
    "Will never give me pain."

12 Prince Habor let his hair grow long,
    Got ladies' dresses made,
And so disguised to Siward's rode,
    As though to learn to braid.

13 The Prince was dress'd in ladies' clothes,
    Had all in ladies' style,
And up the land to Siward's rode
    His daughter would beguile.

14 There, as he cross'd the castle yard,
    He d'oun'd his scarlet cloak,
And mounting up to the ladies' bower
    To dames and maidens spoke.

15 "My greeting, Matrons all, and Maids!
    "And dames of each degree!
"And you, the Princess, most of all,
    "If you indeed be she.

16 "Your skill, fair Signild, royal maid,
    "The silk to spin and throw,
"Prince Habor greets you and entreats
    "To me you'll deign to show."

17 "And if Prince Habor sent you here,
    "You 're come a welcome guest;
"With all the skill that I can boast
    "Shall you be soon possess'd.

18 "I'll teach you work in silk and gold,
    "No secret from you keep,
"And at my table you shall dine,
    "And with my maid shall sleep."

19 "With Princesses I am used to dine,
   "And at their side to lie;
   "If now with servants I must sleep,
   "For sorrow I shall die."

20 "Fear not, sweet lady, lack of care
   "For one so gently bred,
   "With me at table you shall eat,
   "And share with me my bed."

21 Around her sat her maidens all,
   And each her needle plied;
   But his laid Habor on his lip,
   And sat awhile aside.

22 They broider'd stag, they broider'd doe,
   That ran in woodland green;
   The Prince, oft as the wine went round,
   Drank out the goblet clean.

23 In sullen mood and ill-starr'd hour
   Came in the spiteful maid;
   "So fair a lady I never saw,
   "Who could not weave or braid.

24 "So fair a lady I never saw,
   "Who neither sew'd nor span;
   "So fair a lady I never saw,
   "So well could empt a can."

25 And aye she vented gibes and jeers
   In still more bitter strain;
   "So fair a lady I never knew
   "Such draughts of liquor drain.

26 "With needle sews she not a seam,
   "She keeps it 'tween her teeth,
   "But empts at once, be it e'er so full,
   "The cup that holds the meath.

27 "Was ever maiden known to gaze
   "With eyes so bold and keen?
   "Or with such hard and horny hand
   "A noble lady seen?"

28 "Now list thee, maid, whoe'er thou art,
   "Why scoffest thou at me?
   "Was thy work wrongly done or right,
   "I never chid at thee.

29 "Thy bitter gibes and foul affront
   "No longer will I brook;
   "Turn I mine eyes or in or out,
   "'Tis not at thee I look."

30 Then sate him down the royal prince,
   And broider'd work began;
   He pictur'd both the stag and doe,
   And hounds that yelping ran.

31 He work'd the lily, work'd the rose,
   And bird on leafy spray;
   His skill those maidens much admired,
   And begg'd him long to stay.

32 They stitch'd and broider'd all day long
   Till twilight dusk of eve,
   Then, rising, fain would all retire,
   And ask'd their lady's leave.

33 So late the hour, that o'er the court
    The dew was seen to sweep,
  As Signild, rising too from work,
    Herself would go to sleep.

34 Habor, the royal prince, would know,
    Where he should rest him too;
  "Up in the chamber you shall sleep
    "Reclined on cushions blue."

35 Up stairs and round the balcony
    The way fair Signild led;
  Within himself Prince Habor laugh'd,
    And follow'd her to bed.

36 The cheerful tapers there they lit,
    And were so well inclined;
  But came with ill designs at heart
    The spiteful maid behind.

37 The lights burnt out; they seem'd alone;
    The maid they thought was gone;
  And then the Prince his kirtle doff'd,
    And first his sword-blade shone.

38 So gently as he laid him down,
    And on the cushions sank,
  Was heard, and no mistaken sound,
    His shirt of mail to clank.

39 Fair Signild wonder'd much and spake,
    Her heart so ill at ease,
  "I never knew so fair a maid,
    "To wear so coarse chemise."

40 On Habor's breast so bright with gold
   Her lily hand she laid;
  "And why is not your bosom grown
   "Like any other maid?"

41 "Because my country's mode requires,
   "That when to court we go,
  "We damsels ride in coat of mail, *
   "And so it cannot grow."

42 They lay the weary hours of dark,
   The maid beside the knight,
  And talk'd so long, and still to talk
   They found so much delight.

43 "But now, dear Lady Signild, say,
   "While here we 're left alone,
  "Whom would you rather choose to wed,
   "Of all whom you have known?"

44 "To me no knight is half so dear
   "Of all in court are bred,
  "As brave young Habor, royal prince,
   "And him I may not wed.

45 "Though true, as yet his graceful form
   "Has never met mine eyes,
  "I 've heard him sound his golden horn
   "In riding to th' Assize."

* See note.

46 "And is the king's son, Habor, he
    "That is to you so dear?
    "Then Signild, turn, my sweetest maid,
    "'Tis he beside you here."

47 "Can you the King's son, Habor, be,
    "And put me thus to shame?
    "Why ride not in with hawk und hound
    "In court my hand to claim?"

48 "Within these walls with hawk and hound
    "I've made for you request;
    "And, sooth, your father spurn'd my suit
    "With scorn and bitter jest."

49 But while they thought they lay alone,
    And chatted hour by hour,
    That base and treacherous waiting maid
    Was listening near the door.

50 Foul shame befall the wicked maid
    For woe, she caused that night!
    She came, and stole away his sword,
    And shirt of mail so bright.

51 She carried off his trusty sword,
    His mail she stole away,
    And went in haste to the upper room,
    To where king Siward lay.

52 "Wake up! wake up! my Lord and King,
    "Quick from your couch arise,
    "For clasp'd in young Prince Habor's arms
    "Signild your daughter lies."

53 "Tell me no falsehood: he 'tis not:
    "Habor it cannot be;
"For off in th' East-land waging war
    "And far away is he.

54 "Forbear, thou lyeing wicked jade,
    "On her such charge to make,
"Or, ere the morning's light shall dawn,
    "I'll burn thee at a stake."

55 "But if, my noble lord and King,
    "You will not trust my word,
"Yet look at this, his coat of mail,
    "And this, his glittering sword."

56 In haste upstarted then the King,
    And shouted fierce with rage;
"To arms! to arms! my household all,
    "Hard fight is here to wage.

57 "With sword and shield strive each your best,
    "And stand not one aloof;
"Habor, the Prince, a dauntless foe,
    "Is now beneath my roof."

58 His voice the gentle Signild heard,
    And wrung her hands for fear;
"Up! Habor, up! what means this noise?
    "Give heed! There 's danger near."

59 "Be calm, my dearest, let them come,
    "I've means their force to meet,
"Here at my head my trusty sword,
    "My armour near my feet."

HABOR AND SIGNILD.

60 Up from his couch Prince Habor sprang,
　　To every corner flew,
　But gone was both his trusty sword,
　　And gone his armour too.

61 In grief and anger Habor spoke,
　　As there he stood so bare;
　"That traitress maid foul shame befall!
　"'Tis she has laid the snare."

62 Against his door in tumult wild
　　They beat with sword and spear;
　"Out! Habor, out to the tilting yard!
　"Wake up, and d'on thy gear."

63 Now proved he him a gallant prince,
　　For manfully he fought,
　Nor, while a bedpost yet was left,
　　To yield could he be brought.

64 With foot and hand he dealt his blows,
　　With table, bench, and stool;
　Full thirty of Siward's bravest men
　　Lay in a gory pool.

65 In vain with new-forged iron bolts
　　They chain'd him feet and hands,
　With ease, as though they 'd been of lead,
　　He burst their strongest bands.

66 Then up and spoke the crafty maid,
　　Whose rede was aye for ill;
　"Bind him with hair from Signild's head,
　"And hand and foot are still."

I.   15

67 From Signild's head to tie his limbs
    But two hairs did they take,
  And, such the love he felt for her,
    That band he could not break.

68 She spoke, and while she spoke, the tears
    Ran down her cheeks so fair;
  "Habor, you have my full consent,
    "In sunder snap the hair."

69 They dragg'd him then, the royal prince,
    Within the prison wall,
  And men and maidens crowded round,
    His trulove most of all.

70 His hands and feet, while there he lay,
    In heaviest bonds were kept,
  But to and fro Fair Signild went,
    And bitterly she wept.

71 "Habor," she said in saddest tone,
    "My mother's sisters three
  "Will of my father beg your life,
    "If you to that agree.

72 "For firm is else his stern resolve
    "To hear of no delay,
  "But hang you straight on the highest oak,
    "Ere breaks the dawn of day."

73 "What?" answer'd Habor, gallant prince,
    "And full of wrath was he,
  "Think you it were so small disgrace,
    "That women begg'd for me?

74 "Farewell, my Signild! one request —
"One proof of love I claim;
"When high you see me swing aloft,
"Your chamber set on flame."

75 And thus that gentle maid replied,
Tho' sorely did she weep;
"Habor, I pledge my word to this,
"And will my promise keep."

76 They led him forth, the royal prince,
Down from the castle gate,
And all the women sobb'd and wept,
And deeply mourn'd his fate.

77 But when to the open plain they came,
Where he was doom'd to die,
A little while he bade them stop,
Her love he wish'd to try.

78 "Hang up, I pray, my scarlet cloak,
"For first I wish to see,
"If yet perhaps the king regrets
"To hang me on the tree."

79 Fair Signild, when the cloak she saw,
More sad and desperate grew;
"What boots me now a longer life?
"The worst is all too true."

80 With sullen grief and anger fill'd
She call'd her maidens near;
"We'll in our chamber a pastime find
"These weary hours to cheer.

81 ."If there be any here with us
    "For Habor's death to blame,
"I'll fearful vengeance take on all,
    "And perish in the flame."

82 With that the brands she toss'd about,
    Till all the chamber glow'd;
How stern that haughty woman's will,
    To every eye she show'd.

83 Prince Habor turn'd him round to look,
    Where stood his Signild's bower,
And saw the fierce and greedy flame
    Its crumbling walls devour.

84 "Throw on the ground my scarlet cloak,
    "Nor let it longer wave,
"For had I ten more lives to lose,
    "Not one of them I'd save."

85 King Siward out of his window look'd,
    Sad scene there met his gaze;
Prince Habor hanging on the oak,
    And Signild's bower a-blaze.

86 "Oh! Had I known or heard before,
    "That loveties were so strong,
"For Denmark and for Norway both
    "Had I not done them wrong.

87 "Haste, ye, to save my daughter's life,
    "If still alive she be,
"And ye to save Prince Habor too;
    "No felon thief is he."

88 But when to Signild's bower they came,
    She lay in the cinder red,
And when those others reach'd the tree,
    Habor the Prince was dead.

89 Prince Habor's corpse they carried home
    In fair white linen roll'd,
And at his trulove Signild's side
    Laid him in Christian mould:

90 But seiz'd the maid by neck and hair,
    And right the death she found,
They buried her, fit bridal bed,
    Alive beneath the ground.

NOTES.

St. 3. **in the beauteous town**, 'udi den faure By', the heavenly Jerusalem, the brilliancy and beauty of which was a favorite subject with poets in the middle ages. See in Willems' Vlaem. Lied. p. 451. 'Het hemelsch Jerusalem' an address to the New Jerusalem —

>   Want boven aller schoonheit schoon
>   Sijt ghy van buiten en van binnen,
>   Soo dat tot uwen lof idoon
>   Noch mensch en kan noch Seraphinen.

>   For so beyond all brightness bright
>   Art thou without and eke within,
>   That sing thy beauty's praise aright
>   Can neither man nor Seraphin.

And so in the 'Deadman's song,' quoted in the Introductory remarks to No. 45 below, from Ritson's Ancient English songs p. 287.

Of diamonds perles and precious stones
It seem'd the walls were made;
The houses all with beaten gold
Were tiled and overlaid.

This allusion to the New Jerusalem, as well as several other expressions, betrays a much more modern date than the enthusiastic admirers of the ballad in Denmark would willingly allow. As a *ballad* it is not old, although the story may be so.

St. 7. **With fingers in mantle roll'd** a very common expression to imply that the person wished to tap as gently as possible.

St. 8. **Robed in thy pall of state,** literally 'You are well drest in pelisse' a common form of compliment to ladies of high rank.

St. 14. In crossing the yard he don'nd his cloak. We never find a stranger arrive at court, but we are told that he drew on his cloak before entering the presence chamber. The robes of state worn on ceremonious occasions at our modern courts and universities, derive their origin from this ancient fashion.

St. 18. This custom of sleeping with their servants, men with their pages, and ladies with their waiting maids, as inconsistent, as it seems, with the great deference exacted from them on other occasions, seems to have been general in Europe during the middle ages.

St. 40. Whether the gold shone on his breast or her hand, is dubious. The Danish text allows either interpretation. W. Grimm takes the latter, but the former seems more agreeable both to ballad usage and the structure of the sentence.

St. 41. He means to say that he was a Skiold-mö or shield-maiden, a character of not unfrequent occurrence in the Sagas. Ferrier in his 'Caravan journies' p. 104. speaks of a Tartar tribe near Herat in Afghanistan, the women of which bear arms as well as the men at the present day.

St. 45. The same winning effect of a horn is that upon which the ballad of 'Fair Mettelille' turns No. 105.

St. 47. The hawk and hound were the insignia of a gentleman from Norway to Spain.

Baldovinos ha llegado	Count Baldwin he is come
Con sus perros de trailla	to town
Y su halcon en la mano.	With hounds in leash and
Wolff & Hoffm. II. p. 276.	hawk on hand.

The Crusader knights are so represented by Anna Comnena; as entering Constantinople each with his hawk on his wrist. Ladies too in those ages bare a hawk as a mark of rank.

> On her fair hand a sparrow hawk was placed,
> Her steed's sure steps a following greyhound traced.
>
> Way's Fabliaux.

To such a height did they carry this privilege, that the treasurer of the church of Auxerre had the right to assist at divine service with a hawk on his fist, and the Lord of Sassai that of perching his falcon on the edge of the altar. The portraits of illustrious persons and their tombs are frequently embellished with these hawks and hounds. See Le-Grand Vol. I. p. 193.

St. 66. This exaggeration of the chivalrous respect shown to ladies is an addition to the original ballad in comparatively modern times.

St. 90. This mode of punishment by burying alive was a usual one till a late period, and several corpses have been disinterred from peat mosses in Denmark and Finland, which are evidently those of persons condemned to that mode of death. These were chiefly and almost exclusively females. M. Akerman has collected some very interesting facts on this subject in his Essay 'De furca et fossa.' See also No. 171.

The following ballad is from a much more ancient manuscript, and, although the story is in the main the same, it details the incidents differently.

Habor and Sinnelille. B.
Grundtv. I. p. 279 B.

1 Habor and Siward, princely chiefs,
  A deadly feud had they,
All for the gentle Signild's sake,
  So fair that lovely may!

2 Habor at silent midnight hour
  With vivid dream awoke,
And sleepless lay his mother dear,
  And listen'd, while he spoke.

3 "I dream'd that, as in Danish land
  "On Ossey bridge I came,
"There blazed a taper in my hand,
  "And then — went out the flame."

4 "The dream, my son, that thou hast dreamt,
  "Implies some lady fair:
"I'll send a message after one,
  "Its meaning will declare."

5 Beside his mother Habor sat,
  And hasty message sent
To fetch a wife well skill'd in dreams
  To tell him what it meant.

6 And it was she, the cunning wife,
  Into the chamber came,
And up stood Habor, royal prince,
  And told her all his dream.

7 "Doubtless 'tis in your fate, young Prince,
   "To win that lovely maid,
   "But heed you well, lest with your life
   "The gaining her be paid."

8 Prince Habor got a lady's dress,
   And left his hair to grow,
   To Denmark then a journey rode
   To many charged with woe.

9 Prince Habor o'er his shoulders threw
   A lady's scarlet cloak,
   And straight to the upper chamber went
   To Sinnelille, and spoke.

10 "My greeting, gentle Sinnelille,
   "And every dame and maid!
   "Prince Habor bade me come to you
   "To learn the art to braid."

11 "That art, so much as I have learnt,
   "To you I shall disclose,
   "And at my table you shall dine,
   "And with my maid repose."

12 "With Princesses I am used to eat,
   "And at their side to lie;
   "If with a servant I must sleep,
   "For shame and pain I die."

13 "Nay, lovely maiden, hear me now,
   "And fear no lack of care;
   "At table you shall sit with me,
   "May bed too you shall share."

14 There sat those graceful maidens all,
        And each her needle plied;
    His laid Prince Habor on his lip,
        And silent sat aside.

15 There work'd those maids, and pass'd the hours
        With many a merry word,
    But still and silent Habor sat,
        And sketch'd upon the board.

16 He sketch'd the nimble hart and roe
        Bounding on wooded hill;
    And then, with all the art he could,
        The lady Sinnelille.

17 But up and spake the waiting maid,
        Spake like a spiteful shrew;
    "So fair a maid I never saw,
    "Who less of broidery knew.

18 "No seam she sews, but idly keeps
    "Her needle 'tween her teeth;
    "Yet be it ne'er so large and full,
    "She drains the cup of meath."

19 "Cease thou thy gibes, base serving maid,
    "And jeer no more at me,
    "For whether I go in or out,
    "I little think of thee."

20 The day had now begun to wane,
        And yield its place to night,
    And Sinnelille her orders gave,
        That tapers they should light.

21 Her maidens two wax-tapers lit
        So neatly shaped and dress'd,
    And Habor towards his chamber led
        With Sinnelille to rest.

22 "Now tell me, gentle Sinnelille,
        "While no one else is here,
    "If there is any, who to you
        "Is more than other dear?"

23 "Knight, that I love, in all the world
        "None other do I know,
    "Except Prince Habor, him alone,
        "And him I must forego."

24 "And is Prince Habor then the knight
        "Who is to you so dear?
    "Oh! turn, my gentle Sinnelille,
        "He's resting with you here."

25 "But why then, Habor, royal prince,
        "Why put me thus to shame?
    "And not ride up in knightly guise
        "At court my hand to claim?"

26 "That could I not," with courteous tone
        Prince Habor answer'd so,
    "Your father is so hasty a man,
        "With him 'tis word and blow."

27 "Believe me, Habor, royal Prince,
        "These hours with woe are rife,
    "For when my father hears of it,
        "This visit costs your life."

28 "Oh! calm your fears; behind my head
 "There lies my trusty blade;
 "And tho' there came here thirty men,
 "Should I not be afraid.

29 "And at my feet there lies below
 "A new-made coat of mail;
 "Though come here thirty armed men,
 "I neither fly nor quail."

30 Ah! little did Prince Habor think
 But that they lay alone:
 Outside there lurk'd the waiting maid,
 And heard his every tone.

31 She came and stole the Prince's arms,
 Both sword and mail away,
 And hasten'd off to th' upper room,
 To where King Siward lay.

32 "Wake up, my King, wake, Siward, wake!
 "Your slumber is all to deep;
 "Your daughter lies this very night
 "In Habor's arms asleep."

33 Up from his bed King Siward rose,
 And loud was heard to call;
 "Wake up, my faithful troopers, wake;
 "And d'on your armour all.

34 "Wake up, wake up, my gallant men,
 "Arm ye with sword and shield,
 "For here is come Prince Habor's self,
 "And will not feebly yield."

35 They pounded hard his chamber door
      With sword and eke with spear,
   "Up Habor, hie thee to the yard,
      "And lie no longer here."

36 But when he grasp'd behind his head,
      Gone was his trusty brand;
   "Up now, my gentle Sinnelille,
      "Stern business is on hand.

37 "But let me, gentle Sinnelille,
      "One proof of friendship claim;
   "As soon as you shall see me dead,
      "Your chamber set on flame."

38 And out stepp'd Habor, royal prince,
      And manfully he fought,
   Nor while a bedpost yet was left,
      To yield could he be brought.

39 In vain with slender cords of flax
      They tightly bound his hands;
   At once, with ease, the royal prince,
      Asunder snapp'd their bands.

40 Then spake that old and crafty maid,
      Ill rede so prompt to find;
   "Take but one hair from Sinnelille
      "His hands therewith to bind:

41 "Take from her head to bind his hands
      "Only a single hair,
   "And Habor, for his tender love,
      "That band will never tear."

42 From Sinnelille his hands to bind
    But one hair did they take,
  And captive he must yield himself,
    The band he could not break.

43 They carried Habor, royal prince,
    Outside the castle pale,
  And hang'd him on the gallows tree,
    The theme of many a tale.

44 There Habor spake, the royal prince,
    With sad and sullen look;
  "Hang up my scarlet mantle first,
  "And let me on it look.

45 "My mantle on the gallows hang,
    "And let me only see,
  "Whether my gentle Sinnelille
  "Will glad or sorry be."

46 Then spake the lady Sinnelille
    With firm and haughty mind;
  "This day I'll die, and Habor yet
  "In Paradise shall find.

47 "There's many a trooper here at court
    "Of Habor's death is glad;
  "I'll on their brides my vengeance take
  "And make them all as sad."

48 With that at once in every nook
    The fiery brands she threw,
  And kill'd herself, the haughty maid,
    Among the bolsters blue.

49 There came and spake the little page,
   Clad in his red attire;
"Fair Sinnelille with all her maids
"Is in her bower on fire."

50 "Then take my scarlet mantle down,
   "On th' earth it well may lie;
"Had I a hundred thousand lives,
   "Not one redeem would I."

51 King Siward out of his window look'd,
   Sad sight there met his gaze!
Blue flames burst from his daughter's bower,
   And she was in the blaze.

52 "My Sinnelille haste ye to save,
   "Off, off to the smoking pile!
"And ye to the Prince, and him too save
   "From dying death so vile."

53 But when they to the gallows came,
   Hung Habor on the tree;
And when they reach'd the ladies' bower,
   To cinders burnt was she.

54 "O had I e'er before this day
   "The strength of loveties known,
"For all my goodly Danish realm
   "This deed had I not done."

55 Him they had hung, and she was dead,
   Fate sad as e'er was told;
That traitress maid, they buried her
   Alive beneath the mould.

NOTE.

St. 20. l. 4. **word and blow.** in the Danish 'Hand giffuer ingenn suar til cnnde.' I am not sure whether the meaning is, that he does not give another time to answer, or will not himself deign to explain himself.

XXII.

THE LOMBARDS.

This ballad, though devoid of all poetic merit, is not without interest as exhibiting the traditional reason for one of those great emigrations that destroyed the power of ancient Rome.

The name 'Lombard' has usually been derived from *long beard*, but at a period, when beards were usually worn long, this would have been a very insufficient character to distinguish a race, and it is more probable that the second syllable means a *spear* or *lance*, as in Helle-barde a halbert, jærn-bard &c. The name is in meaning but little different from 'German,' which means a *Geer* or *spear*-man. The Teutonic nations seem very generally to have taken their names from the weapons they wore; e. g. Saxons from 'seax' a *curved sword*, Frank from 'franka' a *lance*. Saxo relates that in king Snio's time there was so great a failure of the harvest, and such a famine in Denmark, that the land could not possibly maintain the people. It was therefore determined at the Thing or National Assembly to kill all the children, old people, and cripples. This proposal was made by the brothers Ebbe and Aage; but when they came home and told their mother Gambaruk of it, she shamed them for their inhuman suggestion, and gave them better advice

— namely that a portion of the young people, to be decided by lot, should emigrate and try their fortune in foreign lands. This advice was adopted by the Assembly, and those upon whom the lot fell, left their homes, starting from Bleking, and passing on by way of Gulland and Rygon, till they crossed the Alps, and founded the kingdom of Lombardy.

Saxo seems to have made up the story from two different sources. — The one, an ancient tradition that in the time of Snio or Snede there was a great famine and emigration; and the other, the statement of Paul Warnefrid (Paulus Diaconus) that his forefathers had come to Lombardy from a peninsula in the North, called Scandinavia, where there was at the time a great famine, and whence a portion of the people, as decided by lot, had emigrated under the guidance of Ibor and Agio, whose mother Gambara, a very wise woman, had accompanied them. He says nothing of King Snio, nor of a design to murder the helpless, a cruelty, to which, as P. E. Müller observes, there are several parallels in northern history.

There are similar traditions respecting two other great emigrations as well as that to Lombardy — the one from the island Gothland, and the Swiss one. In an ancient Gothland law it is said that in old times the population had increased to that degree, that the land could not support it, and that a third of the people had been fixed on by lot to emigrate, and had marched to Greece. The other, the Swiss tradition, says that the inhabitants of the canton Uri had been compelled by hunger to leave their homes in Friesland and in Sweden, and the emigrants been decided by casting lots. This is embodied in a ballad of more recent date, which is singularly like the Danish one. In Layamon's Brut l. 13853 the same reason for the emigration of the Angles is put into the mouth of Hengist. After every fifteen years, he says, one in six is obliged to leave his country, lest their number should be too great.

The Lombards.

Grundtv. I. 321 C.

1 There ruled a King the Danish isles,
  King Sneed the name he bare,
 And famine spread through all his land,
  And death, and grim despair.

2 He call'd his wisest men to court,
  And publish'd this decree;
 That each third man throughout the realm
  At once should slaughter'd be.

3 In Seeland dwelt an aged dame;
  These tidings when she knew,
 "Forbid," said she, "the God above,
  "That you such deed should do!

4 "Ne'er heard I yet of loyal men
  "So foully put to death;
 "Beware how those you dare to kill,
  "Whom God has given breath.

5 "'Tis I will give you better rede,
    "Although a poor weak wife;
    "Ye let these people sail abroad,
    "And fight to save their life."

6 The King he muster'd all his men,
    As bade that aged dame;
    And sooth it was a gallant host,
    That at his summons came.

7 The Seeland wife hight Ingeborg,
    As tells the ancient tale;
    And got them built so vast a ship,
    That all therein could sail.

8 Her two bold sons were captains made,
    Two proper men and keen,
    And dauntless each his duty did,
    Wherecever they were seen.

9 At Bleking went those troops on board,
    Indeed a mighty crew;
    The King and council stood on shore,
    And bade them all adieu.

10 Soon as they plough'd the wide deep sea,
    Their joy-song they begun,
    And great the glory wealth and fame,
    They on that voyage won.

11 They reached a port in Lombardy,
    That off in Walland lies,
    And there they slaughter'd all the men,
    And made the women prize.

THE SWISS BALLAD.

Die Theurung hat gewährt so lang,
Dass man in Schweden kein Nahrung fand,
Und in dem Land Ost-Friesen.
Da hand sie g'lidten grosse Noth;
Mancher starb durch Hungersnoth;
Das konnten sie nicht kiesen.

Der König besammelt seinen Rath,
Er sagt den Weisen von der Sach,
Denn er ging um mit Listen.
Es ward gemehret mit der Hand:
Der zehend musst vom Vaterland,
Den andern 's Leben zu fristen.

In Swede this want so long they bore,
Till gone was all their scanty store,
　　And in East Friesland too;
Famine was stalking far and wide,
Many of very hunger died,
　　They knew not what to do.

The King his thanes to council bade,
Before them all the matter laid,
　　Such course he thought the best;
'Twas carried there by show of hand,
'The tenth must leave his native land,
　　'From death to save the rest.'

XXIII.

REGNAR AND KRAGELILLE.

In the ballad of Siward and Brynhild, No. 3, we have had the story of the death of these two personages, who play so great a part in the poetry of the middle-ages throughout all the German and Scandinavian nations. We are to suppose that Brynhild previous to her marriage with Gunther or his brother Hagen, for the names are mismatched in different poems, had had a daughter by her first lover, Sigurd, or Siward the hasty, an extremely beautiful child, named Aslauga, the Kragelille of the present ballad, and who according to the custom of her age and country, a custom still preserved in the Western Isles of Scotland, had been entrusted to Heimir to bring up in his own family.

Regnar, the hero of this piece, is the famous Regnar Lodbrok, the pirate king, who was made captive in Northumberland and perished in a snake-pen. The name *Lodbrok* is derived from his dress, a deer's skin with the hair worn outside, and means 'hairy-breeches.' The ballad-story is inconsistent with history, and no doubt referred originally to some other hero. In another text of it, Grundtvig's letter B. the names are different and that of the knight is Wildemor.

REGNAR AND KRAGELILLE.   247

The following account is taken from the Volsunga
Saga c. 43 as quoted in A. Raszmann's excellent work
Die deutsche Heldensage I. p. 289.

'Heimir heard in Hlyndale the news of Sigurd and
'Brynhild's death. Their daughter Aslaug (the Kra-
'gelille of the ballads) was then three years old, and
'he knew very well that they would endeavour to de-
'stroy her and all her race, and was so anxious about
'her, that he disregarded his realm and his property.
'Seeing that it was impossible to conceal the little girl
'there, he had a harp made, so large that he could
'put her into it, and many jewels of gold and silver,
'and went away with her far from his own country,
'and came at last to Norway. His harp was so in-
'geniously made that he could take it apart and put
'it together again at pleasure, and he used at times
'when he came to water-falls, but never in the vicin-
'ity of buildings, to open it and wash her. He had
'also a soporific leek, which he gave her to eat, and
'which had the property, that a person might live
'long upon it without taking any other food. When-
'ever she cried, he played the harp, and quieted her,
'for Heimir was accomplished in all the arts that were
'then in fashion. He kept also many costly pieces of
'clothing in the harp, and much gold.

'He travelled on till he arrived in Norway, and went
'to a small farmhouse at Spangar-heide, where there
'lived a peasant named Aki, with a wife named Grima,
'and no one else with them. The peasant was that
'day gone into the forest, but his wife was at home,
'and greeted Heimir, and asked him who and what he
'was. He answered that he was a pilgrim, and asked

'the woman for shelter, which she consented to give
'him, and he begged her to light a fire and take him
'to the place where he should sleep. When the old
'woman had lit the fire, he set down the harp at his
'side. She was an unceasing talker, and often looked
'at the harp observing the corner of a costly dress
'hanging out of it, and as the fire blazed up, she
'saw a valuable gold ring under his rags; for he was
'very poorly clothed. When he had warmed himself
'and eaten his supper, he asked her to take him where
'he was to sleep. The old woman told him that he
'would be more comfortable in an outhouse than within,
'for that her husband and she were often very talka-
'tive when he came home. He left that to her, and
'went out with her, and took his harp with him. She
'led him to a barley-barn, and told him she thought
'he would sleep soundly there, and left him.

"The peasant came home late in the evening, and
'found that his wife had done nothing that she ought
'to have done, and was very much displeased. He
'said that he worked every day beyond his strength,
'but that she did nothing to get a penny. "Do not
'be angry, my old man," said she, "for perhaps you
'may win in a short time enough to make us happy
'for life." "What is that?" said he. "Here is a man
'come here for shelter," said she, "and I suspect that
'he carries great wealth with him. He is already in
'advanced age, but must have been a very great war-
'rior, I think I have never seen his equal, but he is
'very tired and sleepy." "It seems to me," said the
'peasant, "very unadvisable to rob the few guests who
'come here." She urged him to murder their visitor,

'threatening him that she would otherwise make the
'stranger her husband, and turn himself, the peasant,
'out of doors. She at last persuaded him to the deed,
'and he sharpened his axe, and went with her to the
'barn, where Heimir was sleeping. She took the harp
'and carried it off, while the peasant crept up to
'Heimir and struck him a deep wound, but the axe
'slipp'd out of his hand, and he ran away. Heimir
'woke, and cried with pain so loud that the pillars
'of the house gave way, and the building fell in.
'And so he died.

'They then kindled a fire, and the woman broke
'open the harp, and found a maiden in it so beautiful
'as she had never seen any before: and much wealth
'beside. She asked her what family she belonged to,
'but the child gave her no answer, as tho' she had not
'learnt to talk. "This business will turn out ill," said
'the peasant, "How shall we provide for the child?"
'"That is easy enough," said Grima, "We will give
'her my mother's name Kraka (a crow), and say she
'is our own daughter and bring her up." "Nobody
'will believe that," said he, "for we are two very
'ugly people, and nobody will think it likely that we
'should have such a beautiful child." "I will manage
'that," said she, "I will cut off her hair, and smear
'her head with tar to prevent its growing again very
'soon, and give her a slouching hat to wear, and
'shabby clothes. And for that matter — people may
'think perhaps that I was very beautiful, when I was
'young, and she shall do all the drudgery."

'They did as they planned, and gave her the hardest
'and dirtiest work to do, and imagined that she could

'not speak because she did not answer. In this way
'she grew up in very great poverty.'

The story is continued in the Regnar Lodbrog Saga, an extract from which is given in Suhm's Historie af Danemark, from which the following is translated.

'It happened one night that Regnar Lodbrok lay
'with his ships in a harbour at Spanger Eide which
'is not far from the southernmost promontory of Norway,
'east from Lindesness. At this place was being brought
'up the Princess Aslaug, Sigurd Svend's daughter,
'under the name of Kraka. Ake, the proprietor of
'the place, and his wife Grima had murdered her fos-
'terfather Heimar, got possession of his treasure, and
'passed off Aslaug as their own daughter under the
'above name; and were employing her to look after
'the cattle. She, knowing very well who she was,
'and longing for her freedom, was glad when she
'saw the numerous beautiful ships; as she thought the
'wished-for opportunity to escape was arrived. With
'that view she washed herself clean, and combed her
'hair, which was long and beautiful, although the
'old woman, her pretended mother, forbad it. In the
'meantime the men, whom Regnar sent ashore to
'bake bread, came to the house. They were imme-
'diately struck with the beautiful girl, and would not
'be convinced that Grima was her mother. They bade
'her to knead the dough, while they baked it, but as
'their eyes were constantly turned towards her, the
'bread was very badly baked, and some of it burnt.
'Regnar was displeased at this, and asked how it had
'happened. They told him every thing, and insisted
'that she was no less beautiful than his first wife,

'Thora. Regnar sent for her to come to him. She
'was to come attended and unattended, clothed and
'unclothed, fasting and having eaten. This was to
'try her understanding. So she took a dog with her,
'wrapp'd herself in a fishing net, and let her hair hang
'over her, and bit into a leek so as to smell of having
'eaten. When she approached the ship, she begged
'for a safe conduct for herself and escort, which was
'given her, but soon violated, for the dog bit Reg-
'nar's hand, and was killed for it. He was much
'taken with the beautiful girl, and prayed Odin to
'dispose her to accede to his wishes. She appealed
'to the safe conduct and desired to return home; re-
'fusing all his handsome presents, including a magni-
'ficent mantle of his Queen Thora; as unbecoming a
'girl in her humble station, and persisted that her
'name was Kraka, and gave not the slightest hint of
'her high birth.

'After a time Regnar returned to the same harbour,
'and sent for Kraka. She told the old people, she
'knew well they had killed her fosterfather, but would
'not revenge it, as she had lived so long with them.
'With that she went to the ship, but refused to pass
'the night there, and Regnar took her home and ho-
'nourably married her.'

In Lyngbye's Færoiske Quæder, Faroese Ballads,
p. 348 there is one of no poetical merit evidently taken from the above story. In the notes we are told
her previous history as given in the Volsunga Saga.
It is sung as a tune for ancient quick dances.

P. E. Müller in his Saga Bibliothek II p. 96 shows
that the story cannot be of very ancient date, and

that the historical Regnar Lodbrok lived many centuries after the time of Sigurd. In this, as in so many other cases, the peasantry, who have composed, or at least preserved, the ballads, have mixed up dates and personages in an inextricable confusion, which it would be more loss of time to attempt to unravel.

Regnar and Kragelille.
Grundt. I. 331. Grimm p. 35.

1 A strange report spreads far and wide,
 Spreads over all the land;
'King Sigurd has his daughter lost,
'Borne off by robber hand.'

2 King Sigurd takes his purple cloak,
 And wraps his head withal,
And mounts, to where his knights and squires
 Sit in the castle hall.

3 On checquer'd board the dice were cast,
 And roll'd about so wide;
Till on Prince Regnar fell the lot
 In search of her to ride.

4 He sought her all the winter long,
 Sought her five winters round;
But nowhere could the stolen maid
 In all these years be found.

5 On through the forest Regnar rode,
   Till, where he cross'd a lawn,
There met him a little serving boy
   About the morning dawn.

6 "Now hark, my little serving boy,
   "What I would say to thee!
"The fairest maiden thou dost know,
   "The same point out to me."

7 "Then list, young knight so brave and fair,
   "Nor be your anger stirr'd;
"The best and fairest maid I know,
   "Is keeping Habor's herd.

8 "Her cloak is made of coarse grey wool,
   "Her gown the skin of goats,
"But like spun gold the yellow hair,
   "That on her shoulder floats."

9 He rode accross the grassy mead,
   And through the tangled thorn,
And found her where she watch'd the goats,
   To keep them off the corn.

10 He drew her kindly within his arm,
   And tapp'd her fair white cheek;
"Now tell me who thy father is,
   "And truth, I prithee, speak."

11 "My father, now an aged man,
   "Herds goats along the coast;
"Myself, they call me Kragelill;
   "My birth I cannot boast."

12 Prince Regnar sternly eyed the maid,
    And drew his glittering knife;
  "Tell me thy father's name and thine,
  "Or it shall cost thy life."

13 "King Sigurd and his Queen were once
  "The parents I could claim.
  "As child they call'd me Swanelille,
  "And that is my proper name."

14 Prince Regnar stay'd to hear no more,
    But wrapp'd in purple weed
  He gently rais'd the maiden up,
    And set her on his steed.

15 And over grassy plain he rode,
    And over furrow'd hill;
  That old man running after them,
    And calling 'Kragelill.'

16 He gave him gold and silver too,
    And sent him pleas'd away;
  But safely back to her father's house
    He brought that lovely may.

17 And now may Regnar, royal prince,
    Lay all his cares aside,
  And sleep in peace and wedded bliss
    Beside his youthful bride.

18 And she the gentle Swanelille
    No longer sighs or weeps,
  But calls a royal prince her own,
    And happy with him sleeps.

NOTES.

St. 4. The ancient inhabitants of the North reckoned time by winters and nights instead of summers and days. Our words *se'n-night* and *fortnight* follow that ancient mode. In accordance with this greater importance attached to the night the Moon was masculine and the Sun feminine.

St. 8.   **like spun gold the yellow hair**

The Scandinavians seem to have thought more of their ladies' hair than of any other feature. See 'Ellen Ove's daughter' No. 68. But yellow hair was as much admired in the south

> 'el cabello de oro fino.'
>
> Belerma. Depping II. 126.

and no less so in own early ballads

> 'Her hair like gold did glister'
>
> Ritson Anct. Engl. Sbngs p. 207.

> 'Her crisped locks like threads of gold'
>
> Ibid. p. XXIV. Perc. II. 161.

> The very hair of my love's head
> Were like the threads of gold.
>
> James Herries. Buch. I. 218.

And in the old translation of Marie's Lanval

> Her here schon as gold wyre.

In the poems and romances of the Middle Ages, and perhaps we may say in their pictures also, the only beauties are fair ones. If one of a darker complexion is mentioned, it is with some such remark as

> Brunette elle est, mais *pourtant* elle est belle.

Their beau ideal was such as Moriana when she knelt to be beheaded.

> Los cabellos de oro puro
> que al suelo quieren llegan,
> y los pechos descubiertos,
> mas blancos que non cristal.

> Hair of pure gold hangs from her head
> To sweep the ground below,
> And bared to view a bosom heaves
> White as the crystal snow.
> Wolf & Hofm. II. p 27.

XXIV.

KARL AND KRAGELILLE.

The following ballad is evidently only a different form of the foregoing. The name of the maiden, Kragelille, is the same in all the versions of the story. The other names differ, as well those of the places as of the persons. In Grundtvig's manuscript B she says her mother was Kremolt, that is Chriemhild or Gudrun, the rival of Brynhilde, and the wife of Sigurd, while in this she says that Brynhilde was her mother. Had we nothing but the ballad, we might suppose the ancient swain had imposed upon his pretentious master, by tutoring a handsome peasant girl to play her part like the gipsy in Peregrine Pickle.

Karl and Kragelille.

Dan. Vis. IV. 231. Grundt. I. 335. A.

1 Sir Carl at his banquet table sat,
   "Swains, hear me every one!
   "Go search me out the fairest maid,
   "That breathes beneath the sun.

2 "Go search her out through all the land
    "And northern kingdoms three,
  "A maid of equal rank with mine,
    "And bring her home to me.

3 "Is she but good and gently bred,
    "For wealth I little care;
  "Ye find and bring me home a maid,
    "Is fit my bed to share."

4 Away they rode, those faithful swains,
    O'er land and realm so wide,
  But nowhere could they find a maid,
    Was fit to be his bride.

5 The faithful swains were riding on
    O'er grassy field and wood,
  And came where tending a farmer's herd
    A fair young maiden stood.

6 Then turn'd and spake the elder swain,
    In scarlet cloak array'd;
  "I see beneath yon wooded cliff
    "A fair and lovely maid."

7 He spurr'd his steed, that ancient swain,
    And rode him down below,
  And spake, and ask'd the fair young maid,
    If with them she would go.

8 "And kindly tell me, gentle maid,
    "The secret truth declare,
  "Of what so noble race you 're born,
    "To be so passing fair?"

9 "My father, he is a simple herd,
"Keeps goats upon the moor;
"Myself—my name is Kragelille,
"Of humble race and poor."

10 Her clothes were fluttering in the wind,
So tatter'd, worn and old;
Her hair about her shoulders hung
Like glittering threads of gold.

11 Her cheek was like the rosebud red,
Her neck like ermine white;
Much wonder'd all those Danish men
To see her in such a plight.

12 But he, that good and ancient swain,
Wrapp'd her in scarlet weed,
And gently rais'd the maiden up,
And placed her on his steed.

13 "But in such haste I must away,
"So far with you to roam?
"Nay, let me here in the meadow stay
"To drive my cattle home."

14 "Fair maid, no sorrow shall you taste,
"No tear shall ever shed;
"We take you hence to a better land,
"A rich young knight to wed."

15 In silken gown of finest hue
And scarlet cloak array'd,
Up to the bower, to young Sir Carl,
They led the lovely maid.

16 With graceful mien the young Sir Carl
    Welcom'd his beauteous bride;
    "Seat thee, fair maid, on cushion blue,
    "Repose thee at my side.

17 "And while we're sitting here alone,
    "The truth, sweet maid, declare,
    "Of what so noble race you 're born,
    "To be so passing fair?"

18 "My father he was call'd Sir Carl,
    "In snake-pen he was kill'd;
    "Myself—my name is Adelrun,
    "My mother's name Bryn-hilde.

19 "While I was yet a tender babe,
    "The boors my father slew,
    "Down into a snake-pen dark and deep
    "My noble father threw.

20 "They drave my mother from out the land,
    "I know not if she 's dead;
    "But me since then, an orphan child,
    "They 've kindly nurs'd and fed."

21 Sir Carl he tapp'd her fair white cheek,
    "Sweet maid, your grief forego,
    "For now my bride, you never more
    "Shall pain or sorrow know.

22 "And if please God, I have the power,
    "As good is my desire,
    "I'll venge you on those wicked boors,
    "Who slew your gallant sire."

23 "If venge me on the boors you will,
"That shall I gladly see,
"But spare, I pray, the farmer's wife,
"For she was good to me."

24 Bravo, Sir Carl! a loyal knight
Will true to his word abide:
That day month was his wedding day,
And Adelrun his bride.

NOTES.

St. 8. This idea of high birth being betrayed by the beauty of the individual often occurs in the romances of the period, as for instance in the German ballad, Die wiedergefundene Königstochter. App. H. d.

Ist das euer Töchterlein.
Dass es so wunderschön mag sein?
But say is that your daughter there.
That she should be so wondrous fair?

St. 9. **My name is Kragelille** — that is *a little crow*.
St. 18. **Snake-pen** Ormegaard.
This was an enclosure filled with thorns and venomous reptiles, into which criminals, and especially pirates were thrown. Such was the fate of the celebrated Regnar Lodbrog, who in the preceding ballad No. 23 is represented as Kragelille's husband: but in popular songs the events are continually assigned to different persons. (See notes to that ballad.) It is probable that Ezekiel alludes to this form of punishment in ch. II v. 6 "Be not afraid of their words, though briers and thorns be with thee, and thou dost dwell among scorpions." It is repeatedly alluded to in Spanish romances, and Rodrigo is represented as having consigned himself to such a snake-pen by way of penance. Wolf & Hofm. I. 21. Depping I. 25. Lockhart No. 2.

In the very beautiful German ballad 'Der unschuldige Tod des jungen Knaben.' Kn. Wun. I. p. 200 the punishment is thus described

> Darinnen liegt ein junger Knab
> Auf seinen Hals gefangen
> Wol vierzig Klafter unter der Erd
> Bei Ottern und bei Schlangen.
>
> In it there lies a poor young man
>   In iron collar bound,
> With snakes and adders fathoms deep
>   Full forty under ground.

In our own writers I do not find any notice of it in ballads of an early period, for that upon Regnar Lodbrok in Evans's collection is evidently modern, and the passage in the Duke of Perth's daughters Kinl. p. 216

> 'Ye shall be hangit on a tree,
> Or thrown into a poison'd lake,
> To feed the toads and rattlesnake,'

has no reference to the ancient snake-pen, and by the mention of rattlesnakes betrays its modern origin.

XXV.

THE FIGHT WITH THE WORM.

The Icelandic tale upon which this is founded, is as follows. Grundtv. Vol. I. p. 343.

'Earl Herrod in West Gothland had a fair daughter 'named Thora, and built a bower for her not far from 'his house, and used every day to send her some small 'present. So he one day sent her a little snake, which 'she was very much pleased with, and put it into a 'box with some gold under it. The snake grew larger 'and larger, till his box was too small, and at last the 'head and tail met round the room, and the gold 'grew too. The snake was so fierce that no one could 'come near the bower except the man who fed it, and 'it ate up an ox a day. The Earl then promised his 'daughter and all the gold that it lay upon to the 'man who should kill it. Regner, the son of Sigurd 'Ring, king of Denmark, was then 15 years old, and 'got himself a cloak and a pair of trowsers made of 'a hairy hide, and sailed to West Gothland. There 'he smeared his clothes with tar, and rolled himself 'in the sand, and went up to the lady's bower, while 'they were all asleep early in the morning, and stabbed 'the snake. A stream of venomous blood reached him, 'but did not penetrate through his clothes. The head

'of the spear broke off, but he carried away the shaft,
'leaving the serpent dead. The king proclaimed that
'whoever could bring the shaft and prove the spear-
'head to be his, might claim the promised reward.
'Regner presented himself and obtained the princess.
'It was from the dress he wore on this occasion that
'he got the name of Lodbrog, 'Hairy breeches.' Saxo's
'history agrees with the Saga except that he re-
'presents Regner as jumping into water with a lamb-
'skin dress on and letting it freeze on him to guard
'him from the venom.'

There is a Faroese ballad that only differs from this tale in representing Regner as being so chivalrous as to wake the serpent before he wounds him, and the serpent as answering him: — one among many cases, that indicate that under the myth of a serpent, a lion, or an eagle was often meant a man called by that name. In the Norwegian the tale occurs mixed up with another one.

There is in Moore's Pictorial book of Ballads and some other collections, one called The Worm of Lambton, in which occur several features of the Danish tale. The heir of Lambton goes out to fish on an Easter morning and has no success, makes a last throw and brings up a little worm an inch and a half in length, and throws it into a clear well.

> He threw it in, and when next he came,
>   He saw, to his surprize,
> It was a foot and a half in length;
>   It had grown so much in size.
> And its wings were long, far stretched and strong,
>   And redder were its eyes.

He goes upon a Crusade, and returning finds that his worm has grown to a huge dragon and is desolating the land. He puts on an armour with razor blades all over it, fights the dragon, and kills it. The legend is said to be an old one, but the ballad is evidently modern.

This growth of a small creature to a frightful monster is common to the tales of all countries. There is a Swedish one that represents a princess as finding a louse in her father's head, which she fed till it grew as large as an ox. It was then killed and skinned, and the king promised his daughter to whoever should guess rightly to what kind of animal the hide belonged. It is probably a burlesque upon stories of this kind.

There is also an East Indian story of a fish which king Manus found and placed first in a tub, and then, as it grew too large for its dwelling, in a lake, and eventually in the sea, where it proved to be Brahma himself, who foretold the flood, and bade Manus build a large ship and save himself and the seven sages.

The Fight with the Worm.

Grundtv. I. 347.

1 As I was a little shepherd boy,
    And sat on a mountain side,
  I caught a playful and spotted snake
    I saw in the rushes glide.

2 I wrapp'd it up in a mantle blue,
      That snake so spotted and barr'd,
   And off to Sir Helsing's daughter fair
      I took it to Lundengard.

3 "O thanks, many thanks, little shepherd boy,
      "My thanks for a gift so brave;
   "And well I will pay thee, if e'er from me
      "A boon thou comest to crave."

4 She cherish'd the snake the winter through,
      She cherish'd it winters three;
   It grew to as foul and fierce a worm,
      As one in the world may see.

5 Sir Helsing he and his wife so fair
      Were daily in tears and woe,
   For now no more for the lothely worm
      Could they to their daughter go.

6 Sir Helsing at court he made it known,
      And over the land so wide;
   Whoever should slay the lothely worm,
      His daughter should have for bride.

7 Out spake Child Sivord Ingorson,
      And bounded across the board;
   "'Tis I will fight with the lothely worm,
      "Sir Helsing, you keep your word."

8 They fought together the livelong day,
      Till sun sank under the hill;
   And then fell Sivord Ingorson,
      And breathless he lay and still.

9 The message was brought to the ladies' bower,
  That Sivord was slain and dead;
 And bitterly wept that gentle maid
  All under the scarlet red.

10 Right bitterly matrons wept and maids
   All under their scarlet red,
  As lay in the cloister at Grimerslew
   The gallant young Sivord dead.

11 So went that whole long winter by,
   And after it winters two,
  The while she sat in her lonely bower,
   And none to her dared to go.

12 Sir Helsing he sent to the royal court,
   His envoys he bade to say;
  'He gives his daughter and all his wealth
   'To him, who the worm will slay.'

13 That heard young Peter Rimboldson,
   And boldly he rose and spake;
  '"Tis I will combat the lothely worm,
   "And all for the maiden's sake."

14 A shirt, that was woven of finest silk,
   He over his shoulders drew,
  And buckled upon it a coat of mail,
   That glitter'd with steel so blue.

15 His velvet jacket he then put on,
   The gold on it gleam'd afar;
  And then the hide of a grisly beast,
   All dabbled in pitch and tar.

16 Eight trenches he dug, so broad and deep,
    And full were they all with blood;
But he in the ninth, young Rimboldson,
    Secure from the venom stood.

17 They strove till sank the evening sun,
    Had striven the livelong day,
And then was beaten the lothely worm,
    And dead on the grass it lay.

18 But great was the joy in Lundengard
    To hear of the victory won;
Sir Helsing he gave his daughter's hand
    To gallant young Rimboldson.

19 And so has young Peter Rimboldson
    Got over his toil and pain,
That fair and noble young lady won,
    That lotheliest monster slain.

XXVI.

THE SWORD OF VENGEANCE.

Grundtvig has given this most remarkable ballad from a single manuscript copy, which seems to be an imperfect one. It bears strong intrinsic evidence of being of Low-German origin, as for instance in the definite article preceding its noun, 'den suoll' for 'Solen,' and in a peculiarity of rhythm, which is such that the accent always falls on the antepenultimate syllable, as is usual in Flemish and Nether-Rhenish ballads, and not on the last syllable of the verse, as in Danish ones. Grundtvig considers it to be a very ancient ballad, but finds no trace of the story in the Sagas. There is one of corresponding import in the Norwegian collection of Landstad p. 235, but differing from it in details. Swords seem to have been gifted with feelings in those old times. That which Freyr gave Skirnir killed men of its own accord, and Tyrfing tasted blood as often as it was unsheathed. Hrolf Krake's sword, Sköfnung, would cry in its sheathe, and of itself leap out to battle; the Berserk Hröngvid's sword, Brynthwari, would do the same. Heroes are often represented as talking to their swords. Such a conversation occurs in a Swedish ballad Arw. II. 77. where the hero, under the influence of a maddening draught given to him by a discarded mistress, slaughters his bride and all her family.

> Sir Salmon rose and left the board,
> And call'd to rede his trusty sword.
> "My sword, wilt thou be staunch and good?
> "Say, hast thou lust to drink of blood?"
> "The blood of man I gladly drink,
> "But thou must not from slaughter shrink."

The same impersonation is met with beyond the range of the Germanic languages in a fine passage from a Finnic poem quoted by Grundtvig from its Swedish version.

> Kulervo Kalervo's son
> Draws from sheath the whetted sword,
> Turns it round and round, and views it,
> Keenly searches out its will,
> Asks if "lusteth now its blade,
> "If it eager longing feels
> "Sinners' guilty flesh to eat,
> "Blood of sinful men to quaff."
> Well his meaning scans the sword,
> Well it grasps the hero's question,
> Answer gives, and these the words:
> "Wherefore should I not, and gladly,
> "Rend and eat of guilty flesh,
> "Quaff with joy the blood of sinners,
> "I who guiltless flesh have eaten,
> "Drunk of blood unsoil'd with sin?"

The most beautiful of this class of poems is Körner's celebrated Schwertlied

> "Du Schwert an meiner Linken,
> "Was soll dein heitres Blinken? &c."

The Sword of vengeance.

Grundtv. I. p. 350. R. Warr. p. 192.

1 Sir Peter came to a castle gate,
   As e'en there sat the king in state.

2 "Welcome, Sir Peter! friend well met!
   "What! not avenged thy father yet?"

3 "I've gone to th' utmost bounds of South,
   "Where scalds the sun a land of drouth;

4 "I've gone to th' utmost bounds of West,
   "Where sinks the sun to nightly rest;

5 "I've gone to th' utmost bounds of North,
   "Where frost unceasing chills the earth;

6 "And here in th' East my course I stay,
   "Where kindles up the light of day;

7 "Yet none, though wide and far I go,
   "Can me my father's murderer show."

8 "And what wilt thou on him bestow,
   "Who doth thy father's murderer show?"

9 "I'll give him silver, give him gold,
   "And merchant coin I'll not withold;

10 "I'll give him these, I'll give him more,
   "The boat that lies on yonder shore."

11 Then said the king with scornful leer,
"Thy father's murderer seest thou here.

12 "Aye" said the king with scornful leer,
"Thy father's murderer seest thou here.

13 "The Lord my God to me be true,
"As I for thee a father slew."

14 Sir Peter smote his heaving breast,
"Lie still, my heart, be thou at rest.

15 "Lie still my heart, not too much haste;
"Our vengeance, trust me, we will taste."

16 Sir Peter walk'd the castle yard,
And with his faithful sword conferr'd.

17 "Hark thee, my sword, so staunch and good,
"Canst thou bestir thyself in blood?

18 "My sword, say, wilt thou stand by me?
"No friend on earth have I but thee."

19 "But how can I then lend thee aid,
"Wrench'd from its hilt my trusty blade?"

20 Sir Peter a famous smithy knew,
And got his sword-blade fix'd anew.

21 They forged the hilt of silver white,
The pommel made of gold so bright.

22 "My sword, now wilt thou stand by me?
"No friend on earth have I but thee."

23 "O be but thou as keen of mood,
"As thou shalt find my temper good.

24 "Be thou as firm and staunch in fight,
"As I shall in my hilt be tight."

25 Sir Peter went to a grassy bank,
Where fast and hard the champions drank.

26 Sir Peter would his sword essay,
And slain at once eight champions lay.

27 Sir Peter's sword so wildly flared,
It neither maid nor mother spared.

28 Sir Peter hew'd with deadly swing,
And spared not, he, or prince or king.

29 Up spake the child in cradle lain,
"So vengest thou a father slain?

30 "The vengeance, thou hast wreak'd for thine,
"Grant God I live to take for mine!"

31 "I've well avenged a father dead,
"To vengeance thou shalt not be bred."

32 With that the threatening brat he slew,
With one blow cut him through and through.

33 "Still thee, my pretty sword so brown;
"For God's sake keep thy choler down."

34 Then spake the sword in sullen mood,
"Thee would I slay and taste thy blood.

35 "Hadst thou by name not call'd on me,
"I would at once have slaughter'd thee."

36 Back to the smith Sir Peter paced,
And got himself in iron cased.

37 He bade them case him foot and hand,
   For he would march and leave the land.

38 He came where lay the buried king,
   And off fell band and iron ring.

NOTES.

c. 1. Daner-kongen, as in many other passages, means here little else than 'King,' and not 'King of the Danes,' as interpreted in the dictionaries, for in the 6th couplet Sir Peter says that he is in the extreme east.

c. 3. 'allt som den snoll hun nieeder seg.' It is not easy to put any interpretation upon this word 'nieeder,' which would seem to mean *sinks*, but as the sun when in the south is at its highest, there must be some mistake in the word, unless we suppose the ancient author to have thought of a map with the north uppermost. I have therefore changed the meaning of the verse altogether.

c. 21. The sword is supposed to have felt not only a human appetite for revenge and bloodshed, but a human cupidity for gold and silver, and is bribed by its master with those precious metals.

c. 28. 'Her Pedder hnog op medd tiender.' The last word is very obscure. Miss Warrens translates it 'Getöne', *clang*.

c. 29. This incident of a child in the cradle threatening vengeance occurs in 'Sir Loumor,' but it is its own mother there who kills it. See No. IV c. 63.

c. 35. This *naming* seems to have been dreaded by combatants above all things, as an omen of death, and even the sword feels disarmed by it. See 'Hildebrand and Hillelille.' No. 94.

c. 37. The meaning of this is obscure, whether he got himself fettered, that he might do no more slaughter, but burst his bonds at the king's grave; or whether it was a coat of mail that he got made, or whether it was a penance that he imposed upon himself. The same incident occurs in the Swedish ballad of Pehr Tyrson Svens. Folkv. III. p. 196.

Per Tyrson går sig åt smedjan
Han lät smida sig jern om medjan.
"Hvad ska' vi nu göra för syndamehn?
"Vi ska' bygga upp en kyrka af kalk och sten."

Peter Tyrson goes to the smithy
He gets himself iron smithed about his middle.
"What shall we now do for my sin?
"We shall build up a church of lime and stone."

He had killed his own sons, not knowing who they were. The passage would favour the idea of its being a penance.

XXVII.

GRIMMER AND HELMER KAMP.

This is a ballad of the same class as Olger the Dane, No. 29. and has been taken from the Rime of Carl and Grym in the Nordske Kämpe Dater, an artificially constructed poem with rimes and alliterations, of no great poetic value or antiquity, and which Suhm considers to be of a date not more ancient than the 15th century. With this our ballad agrees. Carl, king of Sweden, has a beautiful daughter named Ingegerda. Grymur, son of Jarl Eyrik demands her in marriage, but the king makes it the condition of his assent, that Grymur shall first conquer Hialmar, son of Harek, the king of Biarmaland. Grymur receives from the maiden the sword Trausta. As soon as he arrives at Gautaland, Hialmar endeavours to conciliate him and offers him his sister; but Grymur turns a deaf ear to him, and kills him in combat. He then marches home and marries Ingegerda. So far goes the ballad.

The poem relates further that Harek revenges his son's death, kills Carl in battle, and makes peace with Grymur.

Biörner in the preface to the Kämpe Dater mentions

an ancient Swedish ballad of Carl and Grimur now no
longer existing.

The first of the two following translations, A, is from
Mrs. Karen Brahe's manuscript; the second, letter B,
is from the copy published by Vedel, and translated
by Grimm, and republished in the Danske Viser. It
is given as an example of how a ballad varies in two
different copies, when both have been taken from the
same original.

Grimmer. A.
Grundtv. I. p. 353.

1 Brave sons Sir Erick Grimmer had
  And keen for battle fray;
  They never went, but sword in hand,
  To either feast or play.

2 They never went to ladies' dance,
  But with their naked sword;
  Nor ever, but in coat of mail,
  Would sit at banquet board.

3 Young Grimmer built and rigg'd a boat,
  And launch'd it off the strand,
  And swore to sail to the heathen king,
  And win his daughter's hand.

4 So kindly blew the gentle breeze,
  So well they plied the oar,
  They reach'd the isle, and foremost there
  Young Grimmer trod the shore.

5 Off to the heathen king he strode,
    And, wrapp'd in scarlet cloak,
  Up to the presence chamber went,
    And thus the king bespoke.

6 "And here you're sitting, heathen king,
    "Over your festive board!
  "I come to crave your daughter's hand,
    "And wait your gracious word."

7 "My daughter think not thou to win,
    "Nor woo the gentle may,
  "Till first thou hast striven with Helmer Kamp,
    "And fairly gain'd the day."

8 In kinder tone the Princess spoke,
    A lovely maid and fair;
  "None ever came from Bermer-eye
    "Who went to combat there.

9 "There never yet came champion back
    "From fight on Bermer-eye;
  "How small your chance my father knows,
    "And means you there to die."

10 "Sweet maid," young Grimmer so replied
    In scarlet cloak array'd,
  "For coward loon I hold a swain,
    "If he is of death afraid."

11 "Then I shall give you a sword of gold
    "To gird upon your side,
  "And with it freely take the field,
    "Where listeth you to ride.

12 "The sword is of the ruddy gold,
    "Of silver every pin,
  "With this, young Grimmer, trust my word,
    "The victory you shall win."

13 They wound aloft their silken sail,
    They let their pennon fly,
  And kindly breezes bare them on
    Away to Berner-eye.

14 The bold young Grimmer, he it was,
    Who steer'd his boat to land,
  Where Helmer Kamp, the brawny chief,
    Was waiting on the strand.

15 Said Helmer Kamp, for a scornful jest
    Restain he could no more,
  "And who then is this little mouse,
    "Comes shipwreck'd here ashore?"

16 "Thou callest me a little mouse,
    "From thee I shall not run,
  "And dear, I trow, thy joke shall cost,
    "Ere yet the day is done."

17 Young Grimmer met his bulky foe,
    And drew his lady's blade,
  And Helmer Kamp he cut to shreds,
    And well his vaunting paid.

18 His silver and gold they took away,
    As much as they could pile,
  And home, in wealth and glory rich,
    They sail'd from Bermer isle.

19 The maiden stands in her lofty bower,
    Stands looking far and wide;
  "Dear father, make the wedding feast,
    "His ship I 've e'en descry'd."

20 The maiden stands in her lofty bower,
    Stands looking o'er the strand;
  "Dear father, make the wedding feast,
    "My knight is come to land."

21 Young Grimmer left his boat ashore,
    Drew on his scarlet cloak,
  And up to the royal chamber went,
    And thus the king bespoke.

22 "And here you're sitting, heathen king,
    "Over your festive board!
  "I come to crave your daughter's hand,
    "And wait your gracious word."

23 And then arose the heathen king
    In all his pomp and pride,
  And gave his daughter, lovely maid,
    To be young Grimmer's bride.

NOTE.

St. 11. **Sword of gold.** This expression occurs also in the Welch tales in Lady Guest's Mabinogion. From the inefficiency of gold as a weapon we might be tempted to think that they were unacquainted with that metal and called bronze or brass gold, but that we find numerous ornaments in their graves, which prove their use of the more precious metal.

This is not the only place where it is said of a very valuable sword

    T thett suerd thett er aff röde guld.
    The sword it is of red Gold.

Grimmer. B.
Grundtv. I. p. 355. Dan. Vis. I. 104. Grimm p. 298.

1 Childe Grimmer paces the chamber floor,
    And deftly a sword can wield;
    "Now give us the maiden Ingeborg,
    "Before we take the field."

2 "Methinks thou 'rt much too small a man
    "To strike a vigorous blow,
    "Nor couldest, feeble as thou art,
    "Withstand a full-grown foe."

3 "As small and feeble as I may be,
    "My weapon I can wield,
    "And meet me foes, whoever may,
    "I'll make them quit the field."

4 "A champion dwells in Birtingsland,
    "A swordsman stout and brave,
    "Him meet and slay, and then for bride
    "My daughter thou shalt have."

5 Childe Grimmer left the royal hall
    Heaving with smother'd ire;
    "And now" ask'd maiden Ingeborg,
    "What said the king, my sire?"

6 "A champion dwells in Birtingsland,
"A swordsman stout and brave,
"That champion if I meet and slay,
"Your hand then I may have."

7 "Then," spake the maiden Ingeborg,
"The king would you betray;
"In such unequal fight as that
"He knew what danger lay.

8 "But I will lend you a coat of mail,
"Which sword will never bite;
"And helm, whereon the heaviest hand
"No dint shall ever smite.

9 "And with a sword I'll arm you too,
"A finely temper'd glaive,
"That cuts as well through hardest steel,
"As through the liquid wave."

10 The champion stands on Birtingsborg,
Looks out to sea so wide;
"What patch'd and paltry boat is that,
"At anchor seems to ride?"

11 Childe Grimmer little wight it was,
Who steer'd his boat to land,
And he of Birtingsland the lord,
Who held him out his hand.

12 "Welcome, Childe Grimmer, little wight!
"Here thou shalt dwell in peace;
"The half my land I'll share with thee,
"And give thee too my niece."

13 "Nay! that to the maiden Ingeborg
   "Shall ne'er be told or penn'd,
   "That I have taken thy niece to wife,
   "Or made of thee a friend.

14 "But go will we to Vimming's hill,
   "And settle there our strife,
   "Nor either from the ring return,
   "Till one has lost his life."

15 Spake thus that haughty champion,
   So prompt was he of hand,
   "The first blow I may claim as mine
   "In this my proper land."

16 With scornful taunt he then advanced,
   His heavy sword swung round,
   And with one blow Childe Grimmer fell'd,
   And stretch'd him on the ground.

17 But undismay'd Childe Grimmer rose,
   Eager his strength to test;
   "Thou too shalt stand as hard a blow,
   "Ere sinks the sun to rest."

18 His sword in turn Childe Grimmer heav'd,
   And well it did its part;
   It cut the champion's helmet through,
   And clave him to the heart.

19 These last few words the champion spake,
   As down he fell and died;
   "Oh that my brother Rodengard,
   "Were standing near my side!"

20 And well was little Grimmer pleas'd
   Had ended so the fight;
   And booty took to his lady's land,
   Both gold and silver bright.

21 The champion now on battle field
   Lies weltering deep in gore,
   But hale and sound Childe Grimmer lives
   To rob his treasur'd store.

22 He stay'd not long in Birtingsland,
   But sail'd with victory crown'd;
   And joyful sail'd his comrades too
   To share the spoil they found.

23 The maiden stands in her bower aloft,
   Is gazing o'er the strand;
   "And there I see my trulove knight
   "His vessel steer to land."

24 Childe Grimmer, like a gallant man,
   He made no long delay,
   But kept his troth, and that day month
   Was held his wedding day.

NOTES.

St. 1. l. 4. This in Vedel's edition is 'Udi Vor Herres Ferd' 'In our Lord's expedition,' 'Alt i Vor Herris ære' 'All to our Lord's honour,' and in the ancient manuscript from which he copied, as though a Crusade were meant. There is most likely some error in the transcript. The word must originally have been Herrefærd an *expedition*.

St. 15. This striking in turn, which seems to have been champion law, must have been absolutely necessary if a duel was ever to terminate, for the armour was made so strong, that they had to use both hands to the sword, and get a fair blow, to make any impression on it. So we find in No. XI. that the king of Brattens Vendel stands up nobly to receive what he knows will be his deathblow, and in the Hervarar saga eleven champions stand up one after the other to be cut down in their turn by Orvar-odd, whose impenetrable shirt of silk protected him from their blows.

XXVIII.

CHILDE RANILD.

This appears to be one of those ballads which were partly sung and partly told in prose, for we find several such abrupt leaps in it, as to render the sense obscure. The short sayings after each stanza have their parallel in the humourous ballad of Sir John No. 143.

There are few instances of finer impersonation than that of the ship breaking her cables to return to her master at the sound of his horn in St. 27. In the ballad of Sir Olave's Voyage No. 33 intelligence and obedience are ascribed to his ship, but the affection of Ranild's is a still bolder stroke of poetry. There is a fine passage of a similar character in the Scotch ballad of Young Allan, Buch. II. 14.

'If ye will sail, my bonny ship,
  Till we come to dry land,
For ilka iron nail in you
  Of goud there shall be ten.'

The ship she listened all the while,
  And hearing of her hire,
She flew as swift through the salt sea,
  As sparks do frae the fire.

There is another trait worthy of remarking in the following ballad — the king's daughter cutting out the clothes for the troopers at her father's court. We find the same in the Sixth Adventure of the Niebelung Lay. l. 1393 — 1400.

The subject has been taken from the ancient Saga of Hromund Gripson. See Müller's Sagabibl. II. p. 545. There is a very similar Norwegian ballad in Landstad's book, and there is a Swedish one called Ramundur, which finishes the story with his marrying the Princess, after having slain her father, who from fear of him had closed his gates against him.

Childe Ranild.

Grundt. I. p. 372. Landstad p. 189. Arw. I. 114.
R. Warr. p. 216.

1 The King he has a daughter fair,
   And young and shrewd is she,
Knows all that in the world is wrought,
   And all that e'er shall be.
"Were I as wise!" childe Ranild said.

2 The troopers joust in castle yard,
   All clad in coat of mail;
Ranild strikes in, and hits them hard;
   Not apt is he to quail.
"Not very apt," childe Ranild said.

3 Up to her bower Childe Ranild went,
   And pray'd his mother dear;
"O mother, give me better clothes,
   "At mine the troopers jeer.
"Which vexes me," childe Ranild said.

4 She found a cloth of coarse blue yarn,
    And gave him more or less;
"Take that, and beg the royal maid
   "To cut thee out a dress."
"That will I do," childe Ranild said.

5 He took the piece of coarse blue yarn,
    And threw it on her knee;
"Fair maid, will you such kindness show,
   "And garments cut for me?
"And cut them well," childe Ranild said.

6 Long silent sat the maid so sage,
    Sat musing in her mind;
"Childe Ranild, little weenest thou,
   "To what thou art design'd."
"Some good, I trust," childe Ranild said.

7 She took a piece of velvet cloth,
    His clothes of it to make;
"Go, enter thou my father's court.
   "And service in it take."
"That will I do," childe Ranild said.

8 With joy they bare to the ocean strand
    Anchor and slender oars;
So glad was all the royal troop
    To sail to foreign shores.
And joyous too childe Ranild was.

9 Childe Ranild, looking out afar,
    Stood forward on the prow;
"Here comes a man in iron clad,
   "And well his boat can row.
"Hither he comes," childe Ranild said.

10 "Thou sailest like a gallant man,"
   He thus to the steersman spake,
"Here roars in faith a boisterous sea,
   "Might make a coward quake;
"Quite at thine ease," childe Ranild said.

11 Childe Ranild drew and swung his sword,
   As on the prow he stood;
He struck down fifteen champions dead,
   And toss'd them on the flood.
"And there you lie," childe Ranild said.

12 Then up and spake the youthful kemp
   In shirt of ringed mail;
"Childe Ranild, stay, that I the blood
   "From out the hold may bale."
"So bale it out," childe Ranild said.

13 "And once an uncle too I had,
   "King Saxe the name he bare,
"And gallant men were his three sons,
   "Their fate I fain would hear."
"Thou 'st found them then," childe Ranild said.

14 "The eldest son was Adam hight,
   "The second one was Kore,
"The third son he Childe Ranild hight,
   "Like steel the heart he bore."
"And such have I," childe Ranild said.

15 "And art thou then my uncle's son?
   "And true what thou hast told?
"Then come with me to yonder isle,
   "To Thrude's robber hold."
"Come thou with me," childe Ranild said.

16 "He took my treasured gold from me,
 "The horse from out my stall;
"He took my good and faithful sword,
 "My greatest grief of all."
"Why hold not fast?" childe Ranild said.

17 "Took he thy treasur'd gold from thee,
 "Thy horse from out the stall?
"Took he thy good and faithful sword,
 "Thy greatest grief of all?
"Had I that sword!" childe Ranild said.

18 "And art thou then my uncle's son?
 "I'll stand thee in good stead;
"Follow thou me to yonder land,
 "Or else I strike thee dead."
"Then come with me," childe Ranild said.

19 Thrude he stands on Happy isle,
 And looks around so wide,
And sees so many a ship of war
 Over the billows stride.
""Tis even he, childe Ranild, comes."

20 Thrude he stood on Happy isle,
 And wroth of mood he grew;
Up by its roots an oak he tore,
 And 'fore the vessel threw.
"How to get in?" childe Ranild said.

21 Childe Ranild he with anger fill'd
 So fiercely steer'd his boat,
In pieces seven he burst the trunk,
 And sent them all afloat.
"I'll get in yet," childe Ranild said.

22 Into the cavern Ranild went
       On floor so brightly gilt,
    And finding there that famous sword
       With both hands grasp'd the hilt.
    "I've got thee now," childe Ranild said.

23 Thrude, the king of Happy isle,
       His bar of iron hent;
    And fearful sight it was to see,
       How he at Ranild went.
    "I bide thy blow," childe Ranild said.

24 As Thrude smote, so Ranild hew'd,
       Nor one from th' other shrunk;
    He hack'd from Thrude hand and foot,
       And then he fell'd the trunk.
    "There liest thou," childe Ranild said.

25 He took the dripping gory head,
       And cast it in the sound;
    And after it the body threw
       To join it on the ground.
    "They'll meet again," childe Ranild said.

26 Childe Ranild went, this battle done,
       To walk along the strand,
    But gone were all the ships of war,
       That lay before at land.
    "How to get off!" childe Ranild said.

27 His gilded horn childe Ranild took,
       And blew a blast so loud,
    A crack was heard from shore to shore,
       For snapp'd was every shroud.
    "Come ye not back?" childe Ranild said.

28 That good and faithful gilded ship,
 So well his blast she knew,
Asunder sailed her cables nine,
 And back to Ranild flew.
"Right welcome thou!" childe Ranild said.

29 The heap of treasured gold he seized,
 And on his war-ship stored,
And thankful reach'd his port and home
 With all he had on board.
"Here sails the wealthy Ranild in."

30 The King on castle turret stands,
 The Queen upon the wall;
"These heaps of gold, that Ranild brings,
 "Where shall we store them all?
"Touch not what's mine," child Ranild said.

NOTES.

St. 1. We have many examples in these ballads confirmatory of the statement of Tacitus that the Germanic nations ascribed superior wisdom to women. "Inesse feminis sanctum aliquid et providum putant, nec aut consilia earum adspernantur, aut responsa negligunt."

St. 7. The stuff which she used is called 'iffuist,' and in the Notes 'ivist,' words not explained in the dictionaries, but in the Swedish ballad we learn that she used silk and velvet, and this latter is probably the meaning of 'ivist.'

St. 18. This is characteristic. In the 2d line of the stanza his cousin tells him 'jeg giör imod dig well' 'I will do thee a good turn' and in the last line 'eller jeg slaar dig ihiell' 'or I smite thee dead.' This is quite as in the Irish song 'He met with his friend and for love knock'd him down, with a sprig of shillelah' &c.

St. 25. This power of joining on the floor of the sea is common to all Trolds or supernatural monsters, and would imply that Ranild's antagonist was such.

XXIX.

OLGER THE DANE.

The following ballad is founded upon the French romance of Ogier le Danois composed in the 13th century, and translated into Danish in the 16th. This tale, as it flattered the national vanity, became extremely popular, and Christian Pedersen, taking it for truth, incorporated it into his history of Denmark.

In this French romance Charlemagne is besieging Rome, which has been captured by the heathen sultan Cæsubal. Olger is at Charlemagne's court as a hostage, and fights a duel with Carvel, an ally of Cæsubal's and to whom his daughter Gloriant is betrothed. Olger wins the victory, but is treacherously seized by a force lying in ambush, and brought prisoner to the sultan, and entrusted to the care of his daughter Gloriant. Carvel, indignant at this treachery, forsakes the sultan, and goes over to Charlemagne. Then comes Burmann, sultan of Egypt, as suitor to Gloriant, and calumniates her as planning to fly with Olger and abjure her faith. She offers to procure a champion to prove his falsehood and her innocence, and brings Olger to the Sultan, who requires a hostage for his security. This the highminded Carvel offers to be, and comes back from Charlemagne's camp, and gives Olger his horse, his armour, and his sword, 'Kartone.'

Burmann rides the horse 'Belfort,' which springs 30 feet at a step, but is defeated and slain by Olger. Grundtvig shows the probability that this French romance has been originally derived from a northern source, and enters into many interesting particulars, which would here be out of place. Be that as it may, there is no doubt that the ballad, as we have it now, has been derived from the French. A great deal has been written on the subject by German as well as Danish critics.

In the translation I have followed Vedel for the first twenty stanzas, but taken the latter part from Karen Brahe's copy, in which the story is more complete, and the interesting stanzas occur describing the reception given to the hero by the king and his daughter after the battle, the only passage of the kind in the whole collection. The first portion of the ballad in Mrs Brahe's copy is very coarse, and very awkwardly told. Vedel's is as usual made up from several manuscripts with additions of his own. In the 13th and 14th stanzas, with his singular preference for the extravagant, he has adopted the reading which represents Olger as having lain fifteen years in prison, but that is nothing to what he makes Vidrick Verlandson say in No. 11, namely that for a hundred years he had not felt such rage within him. In Mrs Brahe's manuscript Olger says

  Jeg haffuer her lioett ett aar om-kring.
  I have lain here about a year.

Swaning's manuscript gives eight years, Rentzel's fifteen.

This silly and incredible feature of the story has

its counterpart in the Spanish Romance 'Mala la visteis Franceses.' Wolf & Hofm. II p. 321. Rodd II p. 308. Depping II p. 90. Duran IV p. 139. In this the hero Guarinos, refusing to turn Mahometan, lies seven years in jail, where he is loaded with seven hundred weight of iron, and scourged thrice a year, and his horse employed in hauling lime. On a certain festival the Moorish king Marlotes orders that no mother shall suckle a child, or man eat bread, till a certain feat at arms shall be accomplished. When all the Moors have done their utmost and failed, Guarinos begs his jailer to be allowed to mount his horse and try it.

>Marlotes que aquesto oyera,
>De allí lo mandó sacar,
>Solo por ver si en caballo
>El podria passear.
>
>Mandó que so lo buscassen,
>Y allá lo fueron á hallar,
>Que siete años havia,
>Que andaba tirando cal.
>
>Armáronle de sus armas,
>Que bien mohosas están;
>Marlotes, desque lo vido,
>Casi á modo de burlar,
>Dice, que vaya al tablado
>Y lo quiera derribar.
>Guarinos con grande furia
>Un encuentro le fue á dar,
>Que mas de la mitad dél
>En el suelo fuera á echar.

>Marlotes bade them, hearing this,
> The captive knight to bring;
>He would but see, how one so cramp'd
> Could ride in tourney ring.

They sought and found his own good horse,
   Unmounted all this time,
For he seven weary years had toil'd
   In dragging loads of lime.

The knight in his ancient arms they dress'd,
   So rusty all and brown,
And half in joke they bade him ride
   And beat the trophy down.

Stung with their ribald taunts he charg'd,
   And dealt so fierce a blow,
That the gay trophy, more than half,
   Came rattling down below.

The story ends with a general attack made upon him by the Moors, and his gallantly fighting his way through them back to France.

As a singular instance of the spread of ballad poetry, this very Spanish romance was found by Erman to be a popular song in the far regions of Siberia, where the peasantry having, many of them, been themselves the slaves of Mahometan Kirgises, could sympathize with the highminded and indomitable Guarinos.

               See Erman's Reise Vol. I. p. 514.

Olger the Dane.

Grundt. I. p. 391. Dan. Vis. I. 49.

1 King Burman in Iceland camp'd his troops,
   A glittering shield display'd,
Would know what daughters had Iceland's king,
   And whether a handsome maid.

2 "Listen and ponder, Iceland's king,
   "What now I would say to thee;
   "Thy daughter give me, the one so fair,
   "Thy kingdom divide with me.

3 "Either give me the maid to wife,
   "And share with me all thy land,
   "Or else a champion find, so bold,
   "As dares me in fight withstand."

4 "No daughter have I but only one,
   "Maid Gloriant she is hight;
   "I've her to Carvel the king betroth'd,
   "And will not his friendship slight.

5 "I've long to another pledg'd her hand,
   "King Carvel her trulove's name;
   "But if he cannot his bride defend,
   "The maid thou art free to claim."

6 "O hark to me, dearest daughter mine,
   "Here's sudden and baleful news;
   "King Burman has all his troops afield,
   "And e'en for thy favour sues.

7 "A dauntless foe King Burman is,
   "No trifler in battle he;
   "A champion to meet him find we must,
   "Or hither he comes for thee."

8 No longer silence the maiden kept,
   But thus to her father spake;
   "In dungeon yonder a captive lies,
   "A spear with him he might break."

9 She cloak'd her, the maiden Gloriant,
    And thither she took her way,
  To where in a dungeon deep and dark
    The captives around her lay.

10 The maiden Gloriant cried aloud;
    "O listen, ye captives all,
  "Let Olger Dane, if he still is here,
    "Come forward to meet my call.

11 "And art thou living, good Olger Dane?
    "Mine errand is quickly told,
  "King Burman is come, and me demands,
    "King Burman, the swarthy Trold.

12 "My father to him my hand will give,
    "And not to a Christian man;
  "If thou wilt save me, and beat the Trold,
    "I'll help thee in all I can."

13 "A whole long twelvemonth a captive here
    "I've linger'd in iron band;
  "All blessings on you, fair Gloriant,
    "To lend me a helping hand!

14 "A whole long twelvemonth a captive here
    "In hunger and pain and thirst,
  "Too weak am I now to face the Trold,
    "And battle with him the first."

15 "O lend me thine aid, good Olger Dane,
    "My honour and life to save;
  "For rather than take that lothely Trold
    "I would I were in my grave.

16 "The man is so grim, his horse so fierce,
  "I speak but a noted truth,
  "Many have seen it, and all declare,
  "He bites with a wolfish tooth.

17 "They naught for their daily food will eat,
  "But flesh from a Christian rent,
  "And nothing will drink to quench their thirst,
  "But blood with a poison blent."

18 "Your father he gave you a gallant man,
  "King Carvel your trulove's name,
  "And if no match for the Trold is he,
  "King Burman your hand will claim.

19 "But give me again my own good horse,
  "And give me my coat of mail,
  "For your sake, Lady, I'll do my best,
  "At Burman I shall not quail.

20 "King Carvel was long my comrade dear,
  "O would that the truth he knew,
  "That rather I went to certain death,
  "Than Burman should seize on you!"

21 "Then hark! I'll give thee thy own good horse,
  "Thy coat of the steel so bright,
  "And sword-blade, that urged by hero's hand
  "Through hardest of mail can bite."

22 She led from the dungeon Olger Dane,
  And had him so richly drest,
  And set him at table in highest place,
  And pour'd him of wine the best.

23 King Burman into the courtyard rode,
   To seize on the maid he thought,
   But mounted and arm'd met Olger Dane,
   Who set his designs at naught.

24 They fought for an hour, they fought for twain,
   A third too, — and fought their best,
   And then on a stone they took their seat,
   Their limbs for a while to rest.

25 And there as they sat, the heathen king
   Thus Olger the Dane bespake;
   "Believe my God, and I spare thy life,
   "And thee as a captive take."

26 Him answer'd as proudly Olger Dane,
   For mercy did he not care;
   "Go tell them in Hell, thy next abode,
   "'Twas Olger who sent thee there."

27 Again those champions rose to fight,
   And neither his ground would yield,
   Till swords, and helmets, and all was smash'd
   And scatter'd about the field.

28 They fought so manfully, fought so long,
   Till bleeding were both and tired,
   And sank King Burman at Olger's feet,
   And there on the field expired.

29 Olger gave to the gentle maid
   The horse and the rider both,
   "And now, instead of yon heathen hound,
   "King Carvel may claim your troth."

30 The King her father so pleas'd was he,
      He rose from his royal place,
    And welcom'd from battle Olger Dane
      With honour and kindly grace.

31 "Now rise, my daughter, my Gloriant,
      "Thy gratefullest thanks to show,
    "Thyself go welcome good Olger Dane,
      "Who saved thee from all thy woe."

32 Then rising, the maiden Gloriant,
      As slender as any wand,
    She stripp'd him of sword and coat of mail
      And all with her own white hand.

33 She drew him kindly within her arm,
      And warmly his lips she kiss'd;
    "How sound and hale from the fight return'd!
    "Our Father in Heaven be bless'd!"

34 Then spake to his daughter Iceland's king,
      And just were his words and kind;
    "But Olger now to the chamber take,
    "And haste thee his wounds to bind."

NOTES.

St. 1. **Iceland.** It puzzles the commentators to make out what Iceland this could be that had a king, but the venerable Vedel, the first editor, very justly remarks "It is neither necessary nor possible to search out every thing to a tittle, particularly in a poetical trifle, which is merely composed for an honest and agreeable pastime." In Swaning's manuscript the land is Hungary.

St. 11. By the term **Trold** was meant not only a supernatural being, but often a sorcerer, a Berserk, and in some cases, as here, a heathen or Mahometan.

St. 25. This conversation between the bouts was not unusual in old romances. In the French original Olger gives his antagonist a summary of the Christian faith in a long discourse.

The sitting down to rest under the same circumstances occurs in the Spanish romance Don Urgel (Olger) and Bernaldo del Carpio.

> De los escudos y mallas
> todo el campo está sembrado;
> mas un punto de flaqueza
> ninguno ha demostrado.
> Sin conocerse ventaja
> tres horas han peleado.
> Para recebir aliento
> un poco se han apartado.
>
> *Wolf & Hofmann.* 1. p. 46.

> With broken shields and links of mail
>   The battle field was strown,
> And still no sign of weakness yet
>   Had either champion shown.
>
> Three hours with varying equal luck
>   They fought for life and death,
> And parted then for some short space
>   To fetch a little breath.

The Spanish and the Danish ballad are certainly derived from the same tale, as different as are both the persons and the details introduced.

XXX.

SWAIN FELDING.

The event here described resembles closely the achievement of Olger the Dane, and of St. George and the Dragon. Felding and Olger are confounded together in popular tradition. The great broth-pot on the staircase of the Museum at Copenhagen, and the breakfast pot at Aakiœr, and the one at Lyngballegaard in Jylland, are assigned the first to Olger, and the two latter to Felding. Great heroes as in the days of Homer have been regarded by romancers as great eaters also, and both these worthies are therefore supposed to have been accomplished gluttons. There is a traditional legend about Felding in Aarhuus diocese, which may have given rise to the beautiful ballad of Elfinhill No. 136. "I once was an innocent poor young swain." Felding was serving as page at Siellev-Skovgaard, and was sent one day with a message to Ristrup. As he was returning home in the evening, he passed near the barrow or tumulus called 'Borum Es barrow,' and saw on it a great multitude of Elves dancing. One of the Elfgirls came forward and offered him a draught from a superb drinking horn. He took it, but threw the liquor behind him, and where this fell on his horse, it took all the hair clean off. He kept the horn however, set spurs to his horse, and galloped over the brook near Trigebrand's Mill. She had just overtaken him as he got there, but could not cross the water.

> He had won the key-stane o the brig,
> A running stream they dare na cross.

She stood on the bank and implored him to give her back the horn, promising to do for him in return whatever he asked her. He thereupon demanded the strength of 12 men. This he received, and gave her back the horn, but he found that with the strength he had also got the appetite of 12 men, and could eat for twelve.

There is another story about him current in West Jutland. According to this Felding was the son of a servant girl near Ribe, and bondsman of a knight of that neighbourhood. His master sent him one night in December just before Christmas to fetch him a silver mounted horsewhip. The distance was very great, about 30 English miles, and lay over a heath. On the road he was overtaken by a snow-storm, and lost his way, but at last saw a light, which he made for, and reached a cavern in the limestone hill, Daugberg-Doss. There stood a powerful dwarf at the entrance, who asked him in three words Whence? Whither? Wherefore? to which he answered civilly. "Good!" said the dwarf. "It was a pretty errand to send a man upon such a night as this across a desolate heath. You must be tired and hungry. Come in, and sit down, and take something to eat." Felding went in and ate heartily. The dwarf then put a pitcher before him, telling him "Drink once, and move your seat." He drank, and tried to move the seat, but it was of stone, and more than sixteen men could have moved with levers. The dwarf told him to drink once more, and then he could rock the stone. When he had drunk a third time, he could move it from its place. He would have taken another draught at the pitcher, but "No," said the dwarf, "that is enough. You need not be a servant any longer than you choose." He then gave Felding his walking stick to get it mounted with silver at Viborg. It was a large heavy bar of steel. This he took to Viborg, and laid it at the Goldsmith's door, and had a good laugh at the vain attempts his servants made to bring it into the workshop, while he himself could twirl it about with his fingers. When the stick was done, he carried it back to the dwarf, who bade him to come back to him, whenever he found himself in difficulty. At Christmas he had to bring the ale from the cellar, and astonished the guests by bringing in four barrels at once, two of them under his arms, and hanging the other two from his fingers by the bungholes. He broke things and played such pranks, that his master once raised his hand to box his ears, but Felding caught up an enormous stone, that eight men could have hardly moved, and threatened to smash his head with it. His master thereupon set him at liberty. He went to his friend, the dwarf, and consulted him what he had best do. The dwarf advised him to go to the East and take service. He did so, but, wherever he went, he played such extraordinary pranks, that they were glad to be rid of him. While at a priest's he caught up a horse that had strayed into the churchyard, and tossed him over the wall, and killed him.

He was sent to fetch in a calf from the field, and brought the cow instead; in short he went on in such a mad way, that nobody would have any thing more to do with him, and he went back to the dwarf for advice. "Strength" said the dwarf "I could give you, but good sense to use it well, that none but God can give. Go now to the king: he wants strong men, and take my walking stick. It will never miss its blow in an honest cause." Felding did so, and achieved the different feats told of him in the ballads.

This hero seems to have been as popular in Norway as in Denmark. Some time in the 17th century there was a priest to be chosen for a place called Skaanevig near Bergen, and three Candidates presented themselves, and were desired to preach and sing on trial. They preached equally well, but when it came to the singing, and two of them had each sung a psalm, the third, who knew the taste of his peasant arbiters, struck up

> Svend Felding han sidder paa Helsingborg,
> Og roser sig af sin Færd.
>> Swain Felding he sits at Helsingborg
>> And boasts of his mighty deeds.

He was chosen by general acclamation to be their priest.

Who Felding really was, and where he lived, it is impossible to ascertain. There is no doubt much of ancient mythology mixed up with the tales concerning him. Grimm observes a peculiar trait of mythical heroes, namely, that they had horses endowed with human understanding. So in these ballads we find Siward in No. II talking to Grayman, and Vidrick in

No. VII talking to Skimming, and this trait of antiquity occurs in Felding. The old charger working in a mill till he is saddled for the tournament, and then recovering his ancient fire and vigour, is another very general incident in such romances, as remarked upon No. XXIX. The giant, who will eat nothing but maids and ladies, replaces the Dragon of St. George, the Minotaur of Theseus, and the monster of Perseus. Perhaps some of the latter fables may have originated with a tribute of women to be sent to a foreign prince, a very common exaction in Eastern countries, both in ancient and modern times. To take the case of Theseus, for instance — the discovery of the sculptured Minotaurs in the position of tutelary deities amid the ruins of Assyria renders it almost certain that Crete was a province of that empire at the time that the Athenians paid it the tribute of youths and maidens to be devoured by the Minotaur, from which the valour of Theseus relieved them.

There are local traditions about Felding in many places, but it is characteristic of common people in all ages and countries to connect the monuments they find with the stories they know. Price in his Preface to Warton's History of English poetry (page 22 Ed. 1840) gives many curious instances of this. 'We need' says he 'only to refer to the local traditions of distant 'countries which profess to record the history of some 'unusual appearance on the surface of the soil, the 'peculiar character of a vegetable production, or the 'structure of a public monument. Whether in ancient 'Greece or modern Europe, every object of this kind, 'that meets the traveller's eye, is found to have a

'chronicle of its origin; the causes assigned for its
'existence, or its natural and artificial attributes, wear
'a common mythic garb; while in either country, these
'narratives are so strikingly allied to the fictions of
'popular song, that it is sometimes difficult to decide
'whether the muse has supplied their substance, or
'been herself indebted to them for some of her most
'attractive incidents. A mound of earth becomes a
'sepulchre of a favorite hero; a pile of enormous
'stones the easy labour of some gigantic craftsmen; a
'single one the stupendous instrument of daily exer-
'cise to a fabulous king; the conformation of a rock,
'or a mark upon its surface attests the anger or the
'presence of some deity; and the emblems and de-
'corations of a monumental effigy must be either ex-
'plained from the events of popular history, or perverted
'from their original character to give some passage in
'it a locality. Volcanic eruptions have been attributed
'to a Typhon; the tints on certain flowers to the death
'of an Ajax or a Hyacinthus.'

To return to our hero Felding — beside the two
great soup-pots before mentioned — there is a sword
3 ells long treasured at Aakiœr as having belonged to
him. At Siellev-Skovgaard there is another. Vedel
says 'It is known to every body that he was born and
'resident in the beautiful country between Aarhuus and
'Hothernæs. In the wood near the former is seen the
'ruin of his stable, where he used to fasten his horses
'to iron links, and which was so contrived that the
'brook could be turned through it. There was found
'near this spot the great kettle before mentioned and
'a coat of mail, and a sword, which used to be kept

'in the castle hall. In the churchbook at Selufsborg
'are entries of the deaths of himself and family on
'certain holy days, but the dates are not given. The
'letters on the tombstone are obliterated.' The holy-
days to which Vedel refers, are probably those on
which mass was offered for their souls. Anne Krabbe,
whose valuable manuscript has served for the text of
so many of these ballads, visited the spot on 16th
July 1608 and saw there the pot and the stable, from
which she brought away a stone as a keepsake; and
saw the brook which the ancient owner used to turn
through it. After all, we may say, perhaps, of Felding and Olger what Don Quixote said of two other
heroes. "That there lived such a man as the Cid
there is no doubt, or that there was such a man as
Bernardo del Carpio; but, that they achieved all the
great deeds attributed to them, I will not venture to
affirm."

Swain Felding.
Grundt. I. 404 A. Dan. Vis. I. 150. Ochl. p. 44. Arw. I. 129.

1 The gallant Swain Felding he mounted horse,
 To Rome-ward his way he bent,
And thankful may Danish pilgrims be,
 That thither he ever went.

2 The gallant Swain Felding he mounted horse,
 From Denmark he rode away,
And lodged one night with a lady fair,
 A kind and a gentle may.

3 It was with a lady he found his home,
  And peerless she was, so fair;
  And him she seated the first at board
  'Bove all the knights who were there.

4 Swain Felding she seated the first at board
  'Bove knights of the highest fame,
  And then she pray'd him himself to say
  The country from which he came.

5 She look'd at his fine-wrought linen shirt
  All broider'd with gold so bright;
  "No needy poor pilgrim man is this,
  "We're sheltering here to-night.

6 "'Tis surely no needy pilgrim man,
  "Is here for the night our guest;
  "'Tis either the king of Denmark's self,
  "Or 'tis of his knights the best."

7 "No king of Denmark am I, fair maid,
  "Nor make me so high a boast;
  "I'm but a needy poor pilgrim man
  "From Denmark's sandy coast.

8 "And, gentle my lady, let me say,
  "And take not my words amiss,
  "In Denmark too there are children born
  "To want, and to wealth and bliss."

9 "I've heard it said, and I've heard it sung,
  "That Danish men are so brave,
  "And now I thank God that one is come
  "This harried poor realm to save.

10 "O list to my grief, my noble Sir,
    "O list to a moving tale;
    "There dwells in my land a lothely Trold
    "Has brought on us death and bale.

11 "There 's come to my land a lothely Trold
    "This realm to harry and waste,
    "And saving of maids' and ladies' flesh
    "No food will he deign to taste."

12 "Had I but a horse and coat of mail,
    "Right welcome were now the chance
    "For maiden so fair and nobly born
    "To break with the Trold a lance."

13 They led from the stall fine Spanish steeds
    So white and so gaily drest;
    Like dogs they crouch'd on the ground with fear,
    So soon as their heads he press'd.

14 "I gladly would give a hundred marks,
    "And all of the gold so red,
    "Could I but borrow a Danish horse
    "On Danish island bred."

15 Just then was passing a miller man,
    "And I have a horse," he cried,
    "As stout and as gallant a Danish horse,
    "As knight could desire to ride.

16 "My horse is sprung of the Danish race,
    "And nurtur'd in Seaby wood,
    "And every time that he goes to mill,
    "Bears fifteen hundred good."

17 "Now hark thee, mine honest millerman,
   "Bring hither thy horse to me;
   "And if we are Danes, — we two — my troth! —
   "We'll match of the Southrons three."

18 With haunches high and a broad strong chest,
   And all as the miller said,
   Came forward the horse, and Felding's self
   The saddle upon him laid.

19 He saddled and rein'd him, as seem'd him good,
   And tight did he draw the girth,
   Till burst was the band, and down the horse
   Fell knuckling upon the earth.

20 "These fifteen rings of the massive gold,
   "That I have from Denmark brought,
   "I'll give them to pay for a saddlegirth,
   "Can one for the gold be bought."

21 In making a girth for Felding's horse
   Both matrons and maidens strove;
   An ell in breadth, and a quarter thick,
   So stout was the girth they wove.

22 He drew from his hands the gauntlets small,
   From hands as a lady's white,
   And saddled himself that noble horse,
   Nor trusted to menial wight.

23 He girded so hard the brave good horse,
   It could not endure the strain,
   But fell before him on bended knee,
   As tho' it would tell its pain.

24 "And now that I see, good gallant steed,
    "That thou hast a human wit,
  "I'll slacken thy girth a hole or two,
  "Before upon thee I sit."

25 The first assault that the heroes rode,
    Their charge was so fierce and hard,
  Swain Felding's lance was broken in two
  And shield roll'd on the sward.

26 'Twas then so subtle an artifice
    Came into Swain Felding's mind;
  "Return to-morrow to meet me here,
  "And me thou wilt surely find."

27 And off to the church Swain Felding went,
    By priest was duly sped,
  And craftily fast on his spear-pole bound
  A wafer of holy bread.

28 "Away with that crown-hilt useless sword!
  "No such will I longer wear,
  "And fetch me hither a cutter mast
  "To serve me to-day for spear."

29 The second tilt that the heroes rode,
    So boiling with wrath were they,
  The neck of the Trold was broken in two,
  His head roll'd far away;

30 In three were his legs, in five his head,
    His back was in pieces nine; —
  Swain Felding then to the lady rode,
  Would drink her a bowl of wine.

31 Nine knights she had sent, who off his horse
    Should help her champion down;
  "If you will our lily fair maiden wed,
    "Then your's is our land and crown."

32 "Ah no! a maiden I've long betroth'd,
    "Her father a lord at Rome,
  "And if I should break my plighted vows,
    "Awaits me a painful doom.

33 "A maiden, my friends, I've long betroth'd
    "Away on the Eastern shore,
  "And would not for tons of the ruddy gold
    "Be false to the vows I swore.

34 "But build and with every comfort fill
    "A house beside the way,
  "And shelter beneath its friendly roof
    "The pilgrims that hither stray.

35 "And chiefly our Danish pilgrims lodge,
    "Nor spare of the wine and bread,
  "And bid them to pray for Felding's soul,
    "When he shall himself be dead."

NOTES.

St. 26. This looks like taking an unfair advantage of his adversary, but it is to be understood that Felding supposed his lance to be bewitched by the Trold, and only put himself on even terms with him by the artifice he adopted.

St. 32. **doom.** He is going to Rome for absolution and fears that a severe penance would be imposed upon him, if he offended a Roman lord; no very chivalrous motive for his fidelity to the lady. But Felding is always the Dane of the lower class, the bondswoman's son, and in the following ballad displays his ill-breeding more conspicuously.

XXXI.
SWAIN FELDING AND QUEEN JUDITH.

In the whole range of Scandinavian ballads, and it is a very extensive one, there is none more characteristic than this, or more strangely contrasting with the chivalrous spirit that breathes in those of Southern Europe, the Spanish for instance, where the ladies are always treated with courtesy, as rough as may be the language occasionaly adressed to the men by such Hotspurs as the Cid or Roldan. Felding is the impersonation of a Dane, the national hero, the John Bull of his country. We have occasion to see in several other ballads that the peasantry, by or for whom they were composed, had in the old times no notion of gallantry towards women. But here is an envoy sent by his king to fetch home a princess to be the royal bride, bandying the coarsest insults with her; and it must be confessed that the young lady seems to have been as little either delicate or dignified as the envoy was polite. It is altogether a most curious picture of the period according to peasant notions. In all collections of this kind it must be borne in mind that ballads were never intended for the drawing room, but the entertainment of the middle classes and the peasantry, and it would be unjust to the

Danes to suppose this a real picture of the manners of their court.

It is supposed to refer to King Erick Plough-penny, so called from a tax he imposed, and his Queen Judith, whom he married in 1293. The different copies of the ballad vary very much, and are probably all of them much altered from the original one.

It is not quite clear what is meant in the 12th and 13th stanzas; probably that the lady was Moorish and of a swarthy complexion, as in manuscript A, in which Felding proposes to dip her in the sea during the voyage, and christen her 'Juliana.' Her country is called Beder-land, which would imply that she was of a more alien race than the German. The repugnance to German manners of a later period will have led to the alteration.

Swain Felding and Queen Judith.

Grundtv. I. 416. B. Dan. Vis. I. 150. Grimm p. 316.

1 There swarm to visit Denmark's realm
    So many men of fame;
Aye, thither come more German knights,
    Than I have the power to name.

2 The stately Danish king it was,
    Two swains was heard to call;
"Go, knaves, the Swain Sir Felding bid
"Come to the council hall."

3 And in the Swain, Sir Felding came,
   And stood before the board;
   "What will you with me, Danish king?
   "And wherefore send me word?"

4 "Hark thee, Sir Felding, faithful Swain,
   "Mine errand thou shalt do;
   "Embark, and off to Germany,
   "And fetch my bride so true."

5 "If I to Germany shall go
   "To fetch you home the fair,
   "Alone, you well know Danish king,
   "I cannot journey there.

6 "A hundred knights in iron clad
   "These you for me must find;
   "And let my coat, as fits my rank,
   "With martin fur be lined."

7 Their silken sail with gold so bright
   On gilded mast they spread,
   In two months time the gallant ship
   To Germany had sped.

8 They furl'd their sail, and anchor cast
   Out on the glittering sand;
   And there swain Felding's self it was,
   Who first debark'd on land.

9 In passing through the royal court
   They donn'd each man his cloak,
   And up to the presence chamber went,
   And thus the king bespoke.

10 "Hail, highborn king of Germany!
   "Here at your festive board!
   "The king who rules the Danish realm,
   "By me has sent you word."

11 "At table set these gentlemen,
   "And bowl and towel bring."
   Long ere the hour of rest was come,
   His answer made the king.

12 But up Swain Felding rose and spake,
   Soon as fair Judith came;
   "Shame on the hands, should wash thine eyes!
   "On both those hands be shame!

13 "Shame and disgrace befall the hands,
   "That ought to wash thine eyes!
   "And shame on her, should water bring,
   "And at thy bidding plies!"

14 "Hark thee, Swain Felding, stay thy sneers,
   "Nor me presume to slight;
   "For thou art—that I 've learnt for truth—
   'Thyself a baseborn wight."

15 "Let me be ne'er so basely born,
   "I've kinsmen firm and tried,
   "And daily clothe in scarlet cloth,
   "And own the horse I ride."

16 "The vilest rogue, can he but find
   "A pair of crimson hose,
   "Comes bragging here to Germany,
   "And calls himself a rose."

17 "The vilest wench, if red and white
   "She wears her mottled face,
   "Will come to our honest Danish land,
   "And claim a Lady's place."

18 Swain Felding up in his brawny arms
   The bride, fair Judith, took,
   And down in his ship so roughly set,
   That all the vessel shook.

19 Their sails of silk they hoisted up
   High on the gilded mast,
   In two weeks' time to Denmark's coast
   The briny seas had pass'd.

20 Swain Felding he the rudder held,
   And steer'd the ship to land,
   As e'en his lord, the Danish king,
   Was riding along the strand.

21 Swain Felding waved his hat on high
   To greet the Danish king;
   "Urge not your steed so fast, my lord;
   " 'Tis no great prize we bring."

22 So soon as maiden Judtelille
   Her bridal chamber view'd;
   "Shame," said she, "on the carpenters,
   "Who here the timber hew'd!

23 "Shame on the bungling carpenters,
   "Who shared the meat and beer!
   "And on the Swain Sir Felding shame,
   "The slothful overseer!"

24 "The posts are all of poplar wood,
    "Of oak is every pin;
    "Nor ought with Denmark's king to sleep
    "A Judtelille therein."

25 Then up Sir Peter Kempe spake,
    A hero stout and stark;
    "I'll stake in joust with thee to day
    "A horse and a hundred mark."

26 "Not much have I of gold and coin,
    "Or aught that gold will buy;
    "Our ladies' honour be the stake,
    "A fall with thee I'll try."

27 The first assault those heroes rode,
    They both spurr'd on so bold,
    Swain Felding's lance was snapp'd in two,
    And far his buckler roll'd.

28 Beneath her cloak smiled Judtelille
    Her champion's feat to see;
    "And such as this are all the men,
    "I've hither brought with me."

29 In haste away to the bridal house
    The Swain Sir Felding ran;
    "My liege, lend me your horse to-day
    "To ride and meet my man."

30 "Out from his stall my Grayleg lead
    "With eagle-plumage hide;
    "Him to the Swain Sir Felding give,
    "Such horses he can ride.

31 "Out from his stall my Grayleg lead,
    "Gold saddle on him lay;
    "More than eight winters will have past,
    "Since last he saw the day."

32 The second bout those heroes rode,
    They charged with might and main;
    Sir Peter's horse fell on his knee,
    His head roll'd on the plain.

33 She wrung her hands, fair Judtelille,
    And sorely seem'd distrest;
    "O! that to Denmark I should bring
    "My bravest knights and best!"

34 But gaily laugh'd the Danish king
    Beneath his mantle red;
    "Such are the Danish troopers all,
    "By me are clothed and fed."

35 Fair Judith ask'd her morning gift,
    As day began to break;
    "Give me thy Swain Sir Felding's head,
    "There's nothing else I take."

36 "Castles and forts I freely give,
    "And wealth in ruddy gold;
    "But give thee not the gallant men,
    "Through whom my land I hold."

37 Then up the Swain Sir Felding spake;
    As there he stood alone;
    "If I to Judith bent a knee,
    "I' faith 'twould break the bone."

NOTES.

St. 2. **The Swain Sir Felding.** 'Her Suend Felding' I am unable to discover from these ballads or other sources, what was the rank and position of a Svend. In general he seems to be the paid retainer of a knight, but here we see him placed above the knights of his escort. He was the son of a bondswoman, and thence may have retained the lower rank of Svend.

St. 11. Offering the guests a napkin and water each was the general fashion, and a necessary one while forks were unknown. So in Layamon's Brut l. 22878. at Arthur's banquet

elc þer feng water and clæd

every one there received water and cloth.

St. 36. This is a solitary instance in these ballads of a Morning-gift being refused to a bride.

Appendix A.

THE ELDER HILDEBRAND AND THE YOUNGER.

In the ballads belonging to the Diderick cycle, and in the Niebelung lay one of the most prominent characters is the Master Hildebrand, and in the oldest poem extant in the German language, 'Hildebrand and Hadubrand', he is the hero. I have thought therefore, that it would not be uninteresting to the reader to insert a translation of a very fine ballad written in the 15th century, and founded upon that ancient piece. The name of *Master*, so constantly given to the Elder Hildebrand, seems to have been due to his station as Master of the Wolfings or Ylfinger. This accounts for the offer he makes his son in the 13th stanza. The following has been translated from the Flemish, which has the appearance of being a much older, and it is certainly a much better composition, than any of the German copies of it.

A Danish version of this was admitted by Syv into his collection, but being clearly of foreign origin has been very properly rejected by the editors of the Dansko Viser. The incidents are different, but the story much the same as in the Niflunga Saga ch. 375.

In the first line I have followed Thijm's not very trustworthy authority in rendering 'te lande' *homewards*. In general it means 'by land' like the German 'zu lande.' This first stanza is of extremely difficult construction in the Flemish and the German copies alike. The three German ones all differ from one another and from the Flemish, and are all equally ungrammatical.

The German version will be found in the Knab. Wund. I. 137 and again IV. 295, and in Raszmann's Heldensage V. II. p. 646.

A very similar story is contained in the Lai de Milon one of the Poésies de Marie de France. V. I. p. 328.

In the fragmentary ancient German poem the younger champion is called Hadubrand. For the story as told in the Niflunga Saga see Hagen's Helden Sagen V. II. p. 417. and Raszmann V. II. p. 640.

The Elder Hildebrand and the Younger.

Fallersleben p. 1. Willems p. 129. Thijm I. p. 169.

Ik wil te lande rijden,
Sprac meester Hildebrant.

1 "I mean to journey homewards,"
 Said Master Hildebrand,
 "If one the way will show me
 "To Berne in yonder land.
 "For many days and weary
 "My home I've never seen,
 "Nor fully two and thirty years
 "My wife Dame Goodeline."

2 "And if you journey homewards,"
    Duke Amelung replied,
  "You 'll find upon the border
    "A youth your thrust will bide.
  "You 'll find upon the border
    "The younger Hildebrand;
  "And tho' you came with twelve men,
    "He 'll meet you hand to hand."

3 "And should he charge against me,
    "And show me hostile mood,
  "I'll hew his shield in sunder,
    "I'll do him little good;
  "I'll slash him through his buckler
    "With one back-handed blow,
  "Will send him home to his mother
    "A year to wail his woe."

4 "Ah! do not so, good Master,"
    Young Diderick replied,
  "I've found in that young Hildebrand
    "A faithful friend and tried.
  "Nay rather greet him kindly,
    "And surely for my sake,
  "So dearly as he loves me,
    "Your road he 'll let you take."

5 But 'midst their very parley
    He gallop'd towards the wood,
  And on the border moorland
    Old Hildebrand he stood;

And on the border moorland
   That stalwart youth was found;
"What want you then, old Graybeard,
   "Here on my father's ground?"

6 "You wear as rich a harness,
   "As were a king your sire;
"Your glittering blinds mine eyesight,
   "And wakes my heart's desire.
"But back return to comfort,
   "And shelter'd chimney-side."
Loud laugh'd the veteran hero,
   And gaily thus replied.

7 "What! I return to comfort,
   "And live at home in peace!
"To pant for fields and fighting
   "My heart will never cease,
"For battle-fields and fighting,
   "Until my dying day:
"'Tis that, my brave young hero,
   "Has turn'd my hair so gray."

8 "Your beard I'll pull by handfuls,
   "I'll buffet you beside,
"Till both your cheeks so wrinkled
   "With crimson blood are dyed.
"Your shield and glittering harness
   "Yield without further strife,
"And hold yourself my captive,
   "If you will save your life."

9 "My shield and glittering harness!
    "With them for food I've toil'd,
  "And never was nor will be
    "By any man despoil'd."
  Thereon they left their parley,
    And swords began to clink:
  How two such heroes battle waged,
    Yourselves you well may think.

10 The young man on the elder
    A blow so heavy dealt;
  As he in all his lifetime
    Before had never felt.
  His noble horse it stagger'd
    Full twenty fathoms back;
  "You 've surely learnt from ladies
    "Such blows as that to hack."

11 "'Twere shame if I from ladies
    "Had learnt to wield my brand,
  "For knights and highbred gentlemen
    "Are in my father's land.
  "Aye! knights and squires so worthy
    "Still at my father's dwell,
  "And much as they have taught me,
    "I teach myself as well."

12 With skill contrived the old man
    To sink his shield so low,
  That when the younger struck him,
    He caught the coming blow:

Then seized him round the middle,
 Just where the waist is small,
And down he threw him backwards
 On grassy turf to sprawl.

13 "Who rubs against a kettle,
 "Will soil him with its dirt;
"And that you 've done, young hero,
 "And done it to your hurt.
"I'll now be your Confessor,
 "So make your shrift to me:
"Say, are your kinsmen Wolfings?
 "For then I'll set you free."

14 "If Wolfings? — Those are Wolfings,
 "That in the forest roam:
"Nay, I'm a knighted soldier,
 "And Greece my native home.
"A duchess is my mother,
 "Dame Goodeline her name,
"Old Hildebrand my father,
 "And such the race I claim."

15 "A duchess is your mother,
 "And Goodeline her name!
"Old Hildebrand your father!
 "Then you for son I claim."
He lifted up his helmet,
 He kiss'd him on the cheek;
"He 's safe, thank God Almighty!
 "The very son I seek."

16 "O father, dearest father,
 "The wounds I've even dealt,
"Those wounds will all my lifelong.
 "Here in my heart be felt."
"Be silent, son, be silent,
 "For wounds I know a cure;
"And we will live together,
 "God make our purpose sure!

17 "Now bind and lead me captive,
 "As men with captives do,
"And if the people ask you,
 "What man you have with you,
"So shall you tell the people,
 "It is the vilest knave,
"Whom life upon this earthball
 "A mother ever gave."

18 It was upon a Saturday
 At th' hour of eventide,
Was seen the younger Hildebrand
 From out the wood to ride;
He wore upon his helmet
 A little wreath of gold,
And at his side his father
 In bondage seem'd to hold.

19 With manner frank and hearty
 His captive in he led,
And sat him by his mother,
 And at the table's head,

"My son, my son, bethink you,
"This is a little free
"To set a captive stranger
"In higher place than me."

20 "O mother, said he, mother,
"I can no more refrain;
"On yonder grassy moorland
"He me had nearly slain.
"'Tis Hildebrand the elder,
"My father 'tis so dear;
"Now fold him to your bosom,
"And bid him welcome here."

21 She clasp'd him to her bosom,
His dear old lips she kiss'd:
"He 's safe, thank God Almighty!
"Whom I so long have miss'd.
"Now let us leave the country,
"And thither all return,
"To where our friends and kindred dwell,
"The happy town of Bern."

NOTES.

St. 1, l. 4. Bern is Verona, the capital of Diderick's kingdom.

St. 2, l. 2. In the Niflunga Saga Amelung-land is the name of the country, but the Duke is called Conrad. He there tells Hildebrand how his son might be recognised, and the old man attacks him knowing that he is his own son, rather than incur the disgrace, as it was then considered, of tell-. ing his name first.

St. 8, l. 8. Fallersleben gives a different reading of this stanza, making the last line

If God preserves my life.

St. 10, l. 7. The meaning of this expression, that a woman must have taught him such a blow, would seem to be a mere bravado, as much as to say that he, the Elder, had hardly felt it. But in the Niflunga Saga the son pretends to yield up his sword to his father, and chops at his arm, as he thinks to take it. Upon this the old man says "Thy wife but not thy father must have taught thee this." Erlach speculates who the lady was, who taught him, and decides upon Chriemhild. It is obviously a mere taunt, taken in either sense.

St. 14, l. 1. The old man asks him if he is of the party of the Wölfings. This the son pretends to misunderstand, as though his father had asked him if he were a Werwolf or outlaw, roaming the forest.

St. 17, l. 1. The same trick we find played by Siward and his nephew in No. VIII St. 20.

Appendix B.

RIDDLE RIMES.

The contest in riddles that we find in Childe Norman may be well illustrated by a Faroese ballad describing such a trial of wit between King Heidrik and the God Odin disguised as the blind man Gestur. The Edda poem called Wafthrudnismal exhibits a very similar contest between Odin and the giant Wafthrudnir, in which they mutually staked their heads, and which also terminates by Odin asking the giant what Balder said at the funeral pyre. In this Faroese ballad the riddles are put to the king, and we are to understand that the blind Gestur is to puzzle the king with such as he cannot answer, or to lose his life. The beginning of it may remind us of the 'Abbot of Canterbury,' Percy II. 343. The story is found in the Hervararsaga.

'A thane (Herse) of the name of Gestur or Gest in 'Rithgothland had deeply offended Heidrek. This king 'had appointed twelve men who should judge all great 'crimes, and whoever had been found guilty, was either 'to be sentenced by the twelve, or must propound 'riddles to him which he could not answer. Gestur 'was as fearful of the one as of the other, and made

'sacrifices to Odin, to get help from him. Odin pre-
'sented himself to him, and promised to go in his stead
'before the king; which he did, and gave him a number
'of riddling descriptions of natural objects, which Hei-
'drek was able to answer, but at last he ask'd him
'what Odin whispered into Baldur's ear, before he was
'laid on the pyre. Upon this Heidrek discovered that
'it was Odin himself, reproached him, and drew his
'sword, Tyrfing, upon him. But Odin changed himself
'to a falcon, and flew away so quickly, that he only
'lost his tail, and that is the reason that falcons have
'so short a tail to this day. In his flight Odin told
'him that, as a penalty for having broken his safe-con-
'duct, he should die by the hands of the vilest bonds-
'men. A little while afterwards he was murdered in
'his sleep by some Scotch bondsmen.' He had been
a most blood-thirsty ruffian all his life. Müller, Saga-
bibliothek p. 561.

The conclusion of the ballad it will be seen does
not exactly tally with the Saga, but it is a most remarkable thing that the peasants and fishermen of
those lonely islands should have preserved so much
of the tale in its purity for so many centuries by the
aid of memory only.

Riddle rimes.

Gátu rima.

Hammershaimb. II. 26.

1 Gestur leaves the judgment hall
    Blind and sad and full of care;
  'Till an aged man* he meets with,
    All so gray his flowing hair.

2 'Tis an aged man he meets with,
    All so gray his flowing hair;
  "Why, blind Gestur, why so silent?
  "Why so sad and full of care?"

3 "That is not so very strange,
  "That 'tween my teeth I keep my tongue;
  "Riddles — they are too much for me,
  "And I to-morrow must be hung.

4 "'That is not so very strange,
  "That I should mope alone and cry:
  "Riddles — they are too much for me,
  "And I must e'en to-morrow die."

5 "How much then of gold so ruddy
  "Wilt thou swear to give to me,
  "If I now to Heidrik go,
  "And riddles put the king for thee?"

* See Note.

6 "Twelve good marks I swear to pay thee,
   "All of gold so ruddy red,
   "If thou wilt to Heidrik go,
   "And if thou savest me my head."

7 "Go then, thou, go tend thy meadow,
   "Go in peace thy farm to dress;
   "I shall off to Heidrik's hall,
   "And riddles give the king to guess."

8 "Three and ten the riddles are,
   "Now guess me one, and say the word,
   "How you name the ruddy drum,
   "That over all the world is heard."

9 "All thy riddles I shall scan,
   "And guess thee this the first of all;
   "Thunder is the ruddy drum,
   "Whose strokes so loud and heavy fall."

10 "Hear me, Heidrik, hear me, king,
   "And say, what neighbours you can show,
   "Enter both the selfsame door,
   "And yet do not each other know?"

11 "Thoughts of mine and thoughts of thine,
   "No neighbours are, but come and go;
   "Enter both the selfsame door,
   "And yet do not each other know."

12 "Hear me Heidrik, hear me, king,
   "Can you tell me any brothers
   "Lie at sea beyond the rocks,
   "And yet no fathers have nor mothers?"

13 "Eastern stream and Western stream,
 "And surely we may call them brothers,
 "Lie at sea beyond the rocks,
 "And yet no fathers have nor mothers."

14 "Hear me, Heidrik, hear me, king,
 "And what is that, say, do you know,
 "Hard as horn and soft as down,
 "And white as is the drifted snow?"

15 "All thy riddles, blindman Gestur,
 "Ply thy best, shall all be scann'd;
 "Ocean 'tis, is soft and hard,
 "And drifts it's snowy foam on land."

16 "Hear me, tell me, Heidrik king,
 "Tell me, where the tree doth grow,
 "Upward turns its root to heaven,
 "Downward turns its top below?"

17 "Icicle on house's eave,
 "For there such tree is wont to grow, .
 "Upward turns its root to heaven,
 "Downward turns its top below."

18 "Hear me, Heidrik, hear me, king,
 "And tell me do you know the wood,
 "Hewn away each Sabbath morn,
 "And yet as full as e'er it stood?"

19 "Beard it is on chin of man,
 "Tho' truly 'tis no sort of wood,
 "Down is hewn each Sabbath morn,
 "And yet as full as e'er it stood."

20 "Hear me, Heidrik, tell me, king,
   "Who are they, the twin-born brothers,
   "Both in one great hall were bred,
   "And yet no fathers had nor mothers?"

21 "Cakes of Turf and brimstone blocks,
   "And surely we may call them brothers,
   "Both in one great hall were bred,
   "And yet no fathers had nor mothers."

Here there follow four stanzas, which are answers without the respective questions. These and the 30th and 31th stanzas are here inserted conjecturally.

[22 "Hear me, Heidrik, tell me, king,
   "Known is such a guest to you,
   "Grumbles when to feast it goes,
   "And all its followers grumble too?"]

23 "Sow that back to sty returns,
   "Grumbles o'er the grassy mead;
   "Grunting hogs and squeaking pigs,
   "Grumble when they go to feed."

[24 "Hear me, Heidrik, hear me, king,
   "Guess and tell me what is that,
   "Ceaseless goes, and while it goes,
   "Is ever falling down as flat?"]

25 "All thy riddles I shall guess,
   "And well enough can answer that;
   "Hammer that in smithy goes,
   "Is ever falling down as flat."

[26 "Hear me, Heidrik, hear me, king,
"Guess and say who that will be,
"Rides his course uncheck'd, unalter'd,
"Over land and over sea?"]

27 "All thy riddles I shall guess,
"Little glory that to me,
"Odin he can ride on Sleipner
"Over land and over sea."

[28 "Hear me, Heidrik, tell me, king,
"Who can see without the light?
"Who can ride, and find his way,
"Alike by day or darkest night?"]

29 "All thy riddles, see, I guess,
"But boast not I, tho' boast I might;
"Odin he can ride in darkness,
"Find his way by day or night."

[30 "Hear me, Heidrik, tell me, king,
"What was that, that Balder good
"Whisper'd into Odin's ear,
"Before he climb'd the blazing wood?"

31 "Thou, old man, thyself art Odin,
"None but Odin that could know."
Up the king, and Tyrfing brandish'd,
Blade that never miss'd a blow.]

32 Odin shaped to a wild wood-falcon,
O'er the hall of Heidrik flew;
He the king was burnt to cinder,
Burnt were all his troopers too.

33 Odin shaped to a wild wood-falcon
Flew away across the sea;
Burnt was Heidrik, burnt to cinder,
Burnt was all his company.

NOTES.

St. 1. **an aged man.** This is Odin in disguise. He usually presented himself as an old man with long white hair.

St. 21. **Cakes of turf and brimstone blocks.** In the Faroese the word is 'brennistein,' which means litterally 'burn-stone.' We might rather have expected coal to be named as the brother of peat, and etymologically 'brennistein' would convey that meaning, but it seems to be used exclusively in the sense given to it in the text.

As a further instance of this riddling in another and alien race the following Esthian poem may deserve a place here. I cannot refrain from remarking as a rather curious fact, that we find exactly the same trochaic metre in verses of four feet used to the exclusion of almost every other metre, in Finn, Esthian, Faroese and Spanish ballads, and as a friend profoundly acquainted with popular song, Dr. Rob. Dickson, informs me, in the poetry of all the barbarous nations round the North pole, dipping down in America among the red Indians. It is probably a metre that comes naturally to the human ear where the language allows it. As such it is used in several popular hymns of the Roman church.

The following is from the Swedish, in the Fosterlandskt Album, Helsingfors 1845. Part 1. p. 13.

Riddle, riddle, men of mettle,
Guess me, guess me, gentle maidens,
Say what rises blue from billows,

Blue from billows, red from meadow,
Climbs so round from top of forest,
Rises heavenward mild and lovely?

Clean I guess and tell thy riddle;
Blue the moon goes up from billow,
Blue from billow, red from meadow,
Climbs so round from top of forest,
Rises heavenward mild and lovely.

Riddle, riddle, men of mettle,
Guess me, guess me, gentle maidens,
Say what laps the foam of ocean,
Say what drinks of river's eddy,
Say what sips of fountain water?

Clean I guess and tell thy riddle;
'Tis the bow, the heavenly rainbow,
'Tis the bow laps foam from ocean,
'Tis the bow drinks river eddies,
'Tis the bow sips fountain water.

What can walk on top of grasshalm,
Safe from point to point can wander,
Ligthly rock on water-rushes,
Live tho' milk it never feeds on,
Thrive tho' never tasting butter.

'Tis the honey bird so gentle,
'Tis the bee so light and airy,
Tender fly, the house's godsend,
She can walk on top of grass-halm,
Safe from point to point can wander,
Lightly rock on water rushes,
Live tho' milk she never feeds on,
Thrive tho' never tasting butter.

The last two verses are characteristic enough of a purely pastoral race like some of the Finn tribes.

PART II.

LEGENDARY BALLADS.

XXXII.
LITTLE KATEY.

This was originally a legend of Saint Catharine, but has since the Reformation become a popular ballad, having thrown off its cloister weeds and put on a secular dress, as Grundtvig expresses it. For the very beautiful and interesting legend, upon which the tale is founded, see Mrs. Jamieson's Poetry of Sacred Art p. 277.

Catharine was the daughter of Sabinella, queen of Egypt, and was niece of Constantine. At the age of fourteen she became by the death of her parents herself the queen of the country, but being devoted to philosophical studies, shut herself up in the palace, and withdrew herself from the cares and the pageantry of her station. In vain her people urged her to marry. She refused to do so, until she should have found a man of noblest birth, and beyond all other men rich, beautiful, and benign. There seemed to qe no hope of discovering any such, but two days journey into the desert there dwelt a hermit, to whom the Virgin Mary revealed herself, and told him that her Son was such a husband as the young queen desired. The hermit thereupon carried her a picture representing the Virgin and her Son, and when Catharine beheld the heavenly face of the Redeemer, her heart was filled with love of his beauty and innocence, and she abandoned her books and her philosophers to contemplate it. In a dream that night she was conveyed up a high mountain to a sanctuary, where she was received by a company of angels clothed |in white and wearing chaplets of white lilies on their heads, and was led by them to an inner court, where there was another company of angels clothed in purple and wearing chaplets of red roses on their heads. They led her on to an inner chamber, and there she saw a queen standing in her state, whose beauty and majesty no heart might think, nor pen of man describe, and around her a glorious company of angels, saints, and martyrs. This queen received her graciously, and led her to our Lord, who turned his head from her, and said. "She is not fair nor beautiful enough for me." At these words the maiden awoke in a passion of grief, and wept till it was morning. The hermit, to whom she told her vision, instructed her in the Christian faith and baptised her, and on the following night the Virgin Mary again appeared to her in a vision, and presented her to her Son, who placed a ring upon her finger, and plighted his troth to her. When she awoke, she found the ring there, and henceforward abandoned all the pomp of earthly sovereignty.

At this time the Emperor Maximin persecuted the Church, and coming to Alexandria commanded all the Christians to worship the heathen gods on pain of the severest torments. Catharine met him on the steps of the temple, and argued the truths of her religion with such eloquence, that Maximin was confounded. He summoned together fifty the most learned philosophers of his realm, but Catharine silenced them all, and in the end they all became converted to the faith of Christ. Maximin then ordered her to be dragged to his palace, and being inflamed by her beauty endeavoured to corrupt her, but she rejected his offers with scorn. He had her thrown into a dungeon to starve, but angels descended and ministered to her. At the end of twelve days the gaoler Porphyry and the Empress entered her cell, and found it filled with fragrance and light. Thereupon they also, and two hundred of their attendants fell at her feet and declared themselves Christians. Maximin upon his return was seized with fury, and had his wife and Porphyry and all the other converts put to a cruel death, and being more than ever inflamed by the beauty and wisdom of Catharine, he offered to make her his empress and the mistress of the whole world, if she would repudiate the name of Christ. But she rejected all his offers with scorn. He then commanded four wheels to be made armed with sharp points and blades, two revolving in one direction and two in the other, and Catharine to be placed between them. But at the moment when the executioners would have begun to turn them, an angel of God descended and broke them to pieces, and killed three thousand of the people. Nevertheless the emperor Maximin ordered her to be carried outside the town, and scourged with rods, and beheaded, which was done. And when she was dead, angels carried her body over the desert to Mount Sinai, but Maximin was defeated in battle, and his body devoured by birds and beasts.

The legend will be found at much greater length in Mrs Jamieson's work. It has been confounded with that of another female saint, Eulalia, a Spanish martyr, whose story is related in a hymn by Prudentius. This lady is represented as having confronted Dacian a prefect of the Emperor Maximinian at twelve years of age, and as having been tortured to death by his orders for having spat in his face and trampled on the offerings designed for his gods. A dove issued from her mouth as she expired, and winged its way towards heaven. [See below.] She is now the tutelary saint of Merida, where this is supposed to have happened.

The ballad which has been founded upon these two tales is very popular in every part of Sweden as well as Denmark, and varies extremely, so much so that, as the Swedish editors observe, it is seldom sung in two places alike; an evidence perhaps of its great antiquity. The most perfect copy of it is that given in the Svenska Folkvisor, and from this I have borrowed the two introductory and the two concluding stanzas. The rest of the Swedish ballad will be found in the For. Quart. V. XXVI. p. 44. The versification of the Danish original is singularly fluent and beautiful.

> Og hör, du liden Karin, og vil du vare min,
> Syv silkestukne Særker dem vil jeg give dig.

The legend has furnished the subject of many exquisite paintings, more especially those of B. Luini at Milan.

Little Katey.

Grundtv. II. 549 D. Svensk. Folkv. I. 11. Dan. Vis. III. 397.

1 Among the lovely maidens
   Who serv'd the Prince's hall,
   Was shining little Katey
   A star above them all.

2 She like a star was shining
   Beyond them all so fair,
   As thus to little Katey
   The Prince began his prayer.

3 "But hear me, Little Katey,
   "And say thou wilt be mine,
   "Seven silk-embroider'd dresses
   "I'll give thee to be thine."

4 "I'll take no broider'd dresses,
   "None such on me bestow;
   "Those dresses give your Princess,
   "Let me with honour go."

5 "But hear me, little Katey,
   "And say thou wilt be mine,
   "A fort and moated castle
   "I'll give thee to be thine."

6 "I'll take no fort or castle,
   "None such on me bestow;
   "Those castles give your Princess,
   "Let me with honour go."

7   "But hear me, little Katey,
     "And say thou wilt be mine,
     "A crown of gold I'll give thee;
     "The brightest shall be thine."

8   "I'll take no crown or jewels,
     "None such on me bestow;
     "But give them to your Princess,
     "Let me with honour go."

9   Aloft went little Katey,
     And 'fore her lady stood;
     "So said my lord, your husband,
     "And urged me all he cou'd."

10   "Should he repeat the offers
     "He made to thee to-day,
     "Think thou on God Almighty,
     "And firmly say him nay."

11   "But hear me, little Katey,
     "If mine thou wilt not be,
     "I'll make the gloomiest dungeon
     "A dwelling place for thee."

12   In dark and noisome dungeon
     The gentle maid he cast;
     Himself the door he bolted,
     And lock'd her in it fast.

13   "But hear me, Little Katey,
     "If mine thou wilt not be,
     "There yawns a spikeset barrel,
     "Is ready now for thee."

14   Within that spikeset barrel
     The gentle maid was bound,
     And came himself the tyrant,
     And roll'd it round and round.

15   But tho' her tongue was voiceless,
     At heart the prince she bless'd,
     And pray'd her heavenly father
     To give him peace and rest.

16   And then two snowy pigeons
     Came down from out the sky;
     With them the gentle Katey
     To heaven was seen to fly.

17   And two black frightful ravens
     Came up from out of hell,
     And off to a place of torment
     They took the prince to dwell.

NOTES.

St. 11. This punishment of the spikeset barrel we find again in the fine ballad of Folker Lowmanson No. 65. It occurs also in the Scotch one 'The Laird of Wariestoun.' Kinloch p. 49.

   Word 's gane to her father, the great Duniepace,
   And an angry man was he,
   Cries "Fy! gar mak a barrel o spikes,
   And row her doun some brae."

We have it also in the Dutch ballad of Count Floris and Gerard van Velzen. See Appendix E.

According to the Legend the wheel to which St. Catharine was bound, was broken by an angel. [See above.]

The soul flying up to heaven in the shape of a snow-white pigeon was a favourite idea with both painters and poets in the middle ages. It is found in the hymn of Prudentius to St. Catharine's counterpart, St. Eulalia. Περιστεφανων Hymn. III l. 160 written probably about A. D. 400. The following is the account of her life as given by Adonis, Archbishop of Vienne.

'Eulalia cum esset annorum 13, jussu Daciani præ-
'sidis plurima tormenta perpessa, novissime in equuleo
'suspensa, et exungulata, faculis ardentibus ex utroque
'latere appositis, hausto igne spiritum reddidit, et cer-
'nentibus Christianis in specie columbæ niveæ cœlum
'petiit. Cujus beatum corpus per triduum jussu Præ-
'sidis pependit in ligno. Sed cui humana fuerant
'obsequia denegata, cœlestia fuerunt munera concessa:
nam nix desuper corpus puellæ aspersit.'

'Eulalia, when she was 13 years of age, was seized by order of Dacian the prefect, and subjected to many tortures and at last was racked, and torn with hooks. Burning torches were then applied to her on both sides, and she swallowed the fire 'and expired, and in the sight of the Christians was changed into the shape of a snowy pigeon and soared up to heaven. Her blessed body by order of the prefect was left three days hanging on the stake. But although human obsequies were refused her, heavenly favours were conceded to her: for a coating of snow fell and covered her.'

The rising of the pigeon from her dying body is thus described by Prudentius. 1. c.

>Emicat inde columba repens
>Martyris os nive candidior
>Visa relinquere, et astra sequi.
>Spiritus hic erat Eulaliæ
>Lacteolus, celer, innocuus.

'Then suddenly darts out a pigeon whiter than snow, seeming to leave the martyr's mouth, and to rise to the stars. This was the soul of Eulalia, milk-white, swift, innocent.'

The very long and circumstantial account of her martyrdom given by Prudentius is curious, as having been written at so early a period. It is amplified by Florez in his España Sagrada Vol. XIII. into a long homily.

We have this legend in the oldest French poem extant, one supposed to have been written in the 9th century, and as it has considerable beauty, and is unquestionably related to our Danish ballad, I am tempted to subjoin a translation from the copy of it in F. Wolf's Lais und Sequenzen p. 468.

>Buona pulcella fut Eulalia,
>Bel auret corps, bellezour anima.

1 A virtuous maid Eulalia was,
   Of person fair, and purer soul,
   And her would force the foes of God
   To serve and worship Beelzeboul.

2 But she to all they said was deaf,
   The God of heaven would not forswear,
   Their silver, gold, or dresses take,
   Or yield to either threats or prayer.

3   So when no other means avail'd
      To lead this gentle maid to sin,
    They dragg'd her up before the king,
      The pagans' ruler, Maximin.

4   With fruitless zeal he urged her long
      To disavow the Christian name;
    She from her duty would not swerve,
      Would rather bear the torturing flame.

5   Her virgin honour safe to keep
      A blessed martyr's death she died;
    But fire, the hottest could be made,
      Shrunk from her guiltless limbs aside.

6   The king believ'd not what they told,
      But bade at once behead the maid;
    And meek, without one bitter word,
      She bowed her neck beneath the blade.

7   She gladly left a sinful world,
      Since Jesus such command had given,
    And rising like a snow-white dove,
      She soar'd an angel up to heaven.

8   Let us this holy maid beseech
      To deign to pray for us below;
    That after death Christ save our souls,
      And us poor sinners mercy show.

In this piece we find all the features of our Danish ballad, in another form certainly, but virtually the same; for the worship of the devil appears from the 17th line of the original, the first of the fifth stanza of this translation, to have been a sacrifice of her person, such as was demanded of Little Katey, and her death by decapitation also agrees with the legend of St. Catharine. It is a remarkable instance of the retentive character of the Scandinavian mind that, notwithstanding the Reformation, a legendary tale, which was the subject of a popular song in France a thousand years ago, is popular in Denmark and Sweden to this day.

XXXIII.
SAINT OLAVE'S VOYAGE.

Upon this ballad a writer in the 6th Volume of the Foreign Quarterly remarks p. 59.
'The graceful flow of the verse, and its high poe-
'tical and imaginative beauties, speak for themselves.
'The pictures of the superstition of the times are vivid
'and characteristic — the contrast between the rashness
'of Harald and the calm self-possession of Olave —
'the introduction of supernatural natures subdued by
'the influence of the Christian saint, all are pourtrayed
'with great felicity. What more striking image of
'swiftness than the vessel's passing the arrows shot
'from her deck — what more imaginative display of
'power than the levelling of hills and valleys into one
'great ocean, over which the saint conducts his victori-
'ous ship?'

W. Grimm says that this legend is not to be found in the Norse Chronicles. Harald was only fifteen years old when his halfbrother Olave was killed in 1028. Neither is there any thing in the 'Saint Olave's Saga' of the Heimskringla that agrees with it, although there are other stories of his piety; for instance —
'He was once on a Sunday sitting lost in deep thought,
'and cutting chips from a bit of wood with a knife.
'His servant says to him — "Sir, it is Monday to-

'morrow." The king looks at the servant, remembers 'what he has done, and asks for a light. He then 'collects all the chips together, lays them on his hand, 'kindles them, and lets them burn away on it.' Heimsk. cap. 201. Vedel understood the legend to have arisen from St. Olave having dragged his ships overland from one port to another; an undertaking of no great difficulty except from the quantity of timber to be felled to make a road. This according to W. Herbert was on the occasion of a plundering expedition which the sainted king undertook against Sweden. He had sailed through the Stocksound and plundered the coasts of the Malar lake, but upon his return found the channel blocked up by his enemies. In this dilemma he cut his way in the night through the neck of land called Agnafit, and the waters of the lake being swollen carried his fleet through it. The Swedes the next morning found that he had escaped into the Baltic.

The legend is evidently mixed up with the more ancient myth of the God Thor, and the wars he waged against Trolds and Giants.

Saint Olave's Voyage.
Dan. Vis. II. 8. Grundtv. II. 134. Grimm p. 69. Oehl. p. 138.

1 Olave and Harald disagreed,
  Which should to Norway's rocks succeed.
  At Tronhiem so pleasant it is to rest.

2 "Which of us two the best can sail,
  "Shall rule all Norway, hill and dale.

3 "Which of us first shall reach the strand,
"Shall king be crown'd of all the land."

4 'Twas Harald Hardrade answer made,
"Be it even so, as thou hast said.

5 "But, if I sail today with thee,
"Then thou shalt change thy ship with me;

6 "For with thy Dragon's rapid pace
"How is my drudging Ox to race?

7 "Like wind-borne cloud thy Dragon flies,
"My Ox his way as slowly plies."

8 "Harald, if so it pleases thee,
"I will to these thy terms agree.

9 "If mine is a better one than thine,
"I'll take thy ship, and give thee mine.

10 "The lively Dragon thou shalt take,
"And I with the Ox my voyage make.

11 "But first we both to church will go,
"Before we either sail or row."

12 As Olave through the churchyard strode,
Like golden thread his tresses glow'd.

13 A message came in haste to say,
"Thy brother Harald sails away."

14 "So let them sail, if sail they will,
"To God's word we will listen still.

15 "But while at Mass I hear His word,
"Go ye and water take on board."

16 "We go to table, eat our meal,
   "And hasten then to launch our keel."

17 They took their meal, and sought the strand,
   Where lay the tardy Ox at land;

18 And water, anchor, rope and oar
   They quickly aboard their vessel bore.

19 Saint Olave sat on the ship's prow;
   "Now, Ox, in name of Jesus go."

20 Saint Olave seized his long white horn;
   "Now go, as if in fields of corn."

21 Such strides the Ox began to make,
   That high with billows foam'd the wake.

22 "See, thou who sittest on the mast,
   "If Harald's ship we are catching fast."

23 "For all the world naught else I see,
   "Than just the top of a lofty tree.

24 "And now I see near Norway's land
   "A silken sail with golden band.

25 "And now where Norway's shoals must lie,
   "I see the Dragon's mainsail fly.

26 "I see just under Norway's side,
   "With rapid leaps the Dragon stride."

27 A blow on the Ox's ribs he gave;
   "Put out thy strength and dance the wave."

28 St. Olave struck him across the eye;
   "Now faster still to harbour hie."

29 The Ox began to plunge and leap,
   Their legs the crew no more could keep.

30 He took him cords of flax and bast,
   And bound his sailors to the mast.

31 "How shall we sail?" the steersman cried,
   "And who shall now the vessel guide?"

32 Olave the saint unglov'd his hand,
   Himself went at the helm to stand.

33 "We sail o'er hills and cliffs today,
   "Just where we find the nearest way."

34 Forth forth they go, and hill and dale
   Melt into waves as on they sail.

35 They scud through fell and mountain blue;
   And scare the cavern'd Elfin crew.

36 "Who sails there through my treasur'd heap,
   "To make my aged father weep?"

37 "Turn thee to stone, and stone remain,
   "And wait till I come back again."

38 They sail'd across the hills of Scone,
   And froze the swarthy Elves to stone.

39 There stood a hag with spinning wheel;
   "And why should we thine anger feel?

40 "Saint Olave, thou, with ruddy beard,
   "Thy ship has through my cellar steer'd."

41 The Saint look'd back, "Thou hag of Scone,
   "Stand there and turn to granite stone."

42 Onward without mishap they sped,
    Before them rock and forest fled.

43 So swift they left them all astern,
    No eye could longer aught discern.

44 Saint Olave forward aim'd his bow,
    The shaft fell on the deck below.

45 Down from the prow he shot the shaft,
    It reach'd the frothing sea abaft.

46 Saint Olave, who on God relied,
    Three days the first his home descried.

47 Harald so fierce with anger burn'd,
    He into a lothely dragon turn'd.

48 A pious zeal Saint Olave bore,
    And so the crown of Norway wore.

49 And now to church Saint Olave went
    Humbly his heartfelt thanks to vent:

50 And while he round the churchyard paced,'
    His streaming hair a glory graced.

51 Whom God assists will win their aim,
    Their foes win naught but grief and shame.
    At Tronhiem so pleasant it is to rest.

NOTE.

St. 6. **Dragon**
"Kings of the main, their leaders brave,
Their ships the Dragons of the wave."
Scott. Lay of last Minstrel.

XXXIV.

SAINT OLAVE AT HORNELEN.

Vedel explains the victories of St. Olave over the Trolds and spirits to mean, that by introducing Christianity into Norway he rescued the poor ignorant natives from the power of Satan and his agents. There are several ballads on this subject still preserved in the Faroe islands, more perfect and better than the Danish ones and many legends still in vogue among the peasantry of Norway. Faye in his Norske Saga p. 118 tells us

'When St. Olave in ancient times was going from 'district to district to introduce Christianity and build 'churches, he found great opposition not only from the 'pagan people, but also from Trolds, Jutules, and 'Sprites, who were in great number on the mountains. 'These beings could not endure St. Olave, partly be-'cause he gave them much pain by using the cross, 'and partly because he built so many churches, whose 'bells disturbed their rest. But as much as they tried 'to obstruct him, they effected nothing, and were all 'turned into stone. Such metamorphosed Trolds one 'may see all over the country. When he resolved 'to build a church at Gaarden, a sprite, a Giogr or a 'Gyver, expressed great dissatisfaction at it and told

'him that before he had finished his church, he, the
'sprite, would build a bridge across the Steensfiord.
'Olave accepted the challenge, and before the bridge
'was half ready, his church was completed, and the
'bells pealing merrily. The sprite was so enraged,
'that he threw at it great masses of rock, which he
'had intended for his bridge, and failing to strike it,
'in his fury he tore off his own leg and slung it at
'the church, but aimed too high, and the limb fell in-
'to the morass behind, where it causes a villanous
'stench to this day!'

St. Olave at Hornelen.
Grundtv. II. 140. Dan. Vis. II. 15. Oehl. p. 144.

1 Saint Olave, good king, o'er Norway's land
   So well and so wisely reign'd,
   God's word he made wife and man obey,
   And justice and law maintain'd.

2 Saint Olave down on the ocean strand
   Had built him a gallant Snake,*
   And now on the Trolds at Hornelen,
   His vengeance resolved to take.

3 But answer'd the steersman, as at the stern
   With rudder in hand he stood;
   "So grim are the Trolds at Hornelen,
   "That harbour was never good."

* A Snekke or snake ship, a long row-boat.

4 Up spake King Olave so free and bold,
    And sprang on his Ox's prow;
"Take tackle on board, and now cast off,
"In Jesus' name let go."

5 The Ox he puff'd, and loud he blew,
    And over the billows strode;
So sail'd Saint Olave to Hornelen,
    With woe to the Trold's abode.

6 The giant he stalk'd from out the hill,
    Along the hoary rocks,
And saw there Olave the sainted king,
    And breasting the wave his Ox.

7 His eyes were like two burning pyres,
    And yawning his mouth to shout;
His finger nails were hooked and long,
    Like goat's horns hanging out.

8 A beard he had like a horse's mane,
    That hung to touch his knee;
His body was long, and shagg'd with hair,
    And fearful his claws to see.

9 "There never in older times or since
    "A snake-ship has come to land,
"That off to my cavern I could not drag,
    "With only a single hand."

10 "Then" answer'd him Olave, the sainted king,
    He fear'd not a Troldish foe,
"Throw over the Ox thy cords and chains,
    "And see how that will go."

11 The Ox he seiz'd by his horn and stern,
    And thought to have crush'd with ease,
    But into a cliff he sank himself,
    Till over both his knees.

12 "Though here I must stand a sunken rock,
    "And further I cannot move,
    "A strain of the back and tug of hand
    "With thee I would gladly prove."

13 "Hold thou thy peace, thou baleful sprite,
    "And there as a rock remain;
    "For never till Doomsday hurt shalt thou
    "A Christian man again."

14 Out ran from a cavern an aged hag,
    And yell'd with a voice so shrill,
    And look'd so grim, as she hobbled along,
    He bade the old crone be still.

15 Much wonder'd at this the smaller Trolds,
    Who dwelt on the rocky shore;
    "But what has befallen our aged crone,
    "That now she cries no more?

16 "Then surely this is the Redbeard saint
    "Who long has threaten'd our race;
    "If we with our iron bars come out,
    "We'll give him but little grace."

17 But turn'd were their trunks to shapeless blocks,
    Their necks to their body press'd,
    Their backs all broken to pieces small,
    And heads crush'd into their breast.

18 Such wonder at Hornelen then was wrought,
   As never was wrought before;
 The cave with water was drown'd so deep,
   That no one could find the door.

19 So thanks let all men give to God,
   And thanks to Saint Olave too,
 The sailor to Hornelen now may steer,
   Nor care for what Trolds may do.

XXXV.

THE BURIED MOTHER.

This affecting tale is widely spread. It occurs in ballad form in all the Scandinavian countries, and according to Jamieson North. Antiq. p. 318 was once known in Scotland. In the Slavonian, Lithuanian and Esthonian languages there are ballads corresponding to it, but none of equal beauty with the Danish, if we may credit the opinion expressed by Mrs. Talvj in her Historical view of Slavic Literature.

'The Danes have a beautiful ballad on this subject. 'It is one of the most affecting that we have ever 'met with. The Slavic nations certainly have nothing 'to compare with it in beauty, but the most of them 'possess songs on the same subject.'

There is great variety in the names as they occur in different copies, and many important differences in the text, as might be expected in a piece sung in so many dialects and distant places.

A Polish song of nearly the same general import will be found translated in Talvj's Slavic Literature p. 399. The Norwegian ballad 'Den vonde stiukmodir' seems like an imperfect recollection of the Danish mixed with some other one. Lands. p. 542.

The buried mother.

Dan. Vis. I. 205. Grundtv. II. 480. Grimm p. 147. Oehl. p. 82. Sven. Folkv. III. 33. 36. Arw. II. 94. 97. R. Warr. p. 183.

1 Swain Dyring he journey'd up the land,
   And won a lovely maiden's hand;

2 Seven years she lived his home to share,
   And seven the sweetest children bare;

3 But stalking through the land came death,
   And stopp'd that gentle lady's breath.

4 Swain Dyring rode again up land,
   And gain'd another maiden's hand.

5 He won his bride, and home she came,
   A grim and harsh ill-favour'd dame.

6 When from her gilded wain she stepp'd,
   The seven poor children stood and wept.

7 They stood, those little things, and cried,
   But kick'd them off th' unfeeling bride.

8 She gave them neither bread nor beer,
   "Hunger and hate will be your cheer."

9 She took away their bolsters blue,
   "Bare straw shall be the bed for you."

10 She took away their fire and light,
    "In blind-house ye shall sleep all night."

11 They cried one evening, till the sound
    Their mother heard beneath the ground.

12 She heard it, as in her grave she lay,
   "But go I must their pain to stay."

13 At God's high throne she bent her knee,
   "O let me, Lord, my children see."

14 And such her prayer, and tale of woe,
   That God in mercy let her go.

15 "But there on earth no longer stay,
   "When cock shall crow the dawn of day."

16 Out from their chest she stretch'd her bones,
   And rent her way through earth and stones.

17 As through the street she glided by,
   Loud all the hounds howl'd to the sky.

18 She reach'd her husband's courtyard gate,
   And there her eldest daughter sate.

19 "O daughter mine, why so in tears?
   "How fare my other little dears?"

20 "No mother at all art thou of mine,
   "Thou 'rt not like her, though fair and fine;

21 "My mother's cheeks were white and red,
   "But thine are pale, and like the dead."

22 "And how should I be fine or fair,
   "When death has bleach'd the cheeks I bear?

23 "Or how should I be white and red,
   "So long, my child, as I've been dead?"

24 She found her children's sleeping place,
   And wet with tears each little face.

25 She nurs'd them all with mother's care,
   She comb'd and dress'd their silky hair.

26 The infant babe she took on lap,
   And offer'd him the welcome pap.

27 Her eldest daughter then she sped,
   To fetch Swain Dyring out of bed.

28 And when before her chair he stood,
   She chid him thus in angry mood:

29 "I left thee store of beer and bread,
   "I find my children all unfed.

30 "I left thee bolsters of softest down,
   "And here on straw I find them thrown.

31 "I left thee many a good waxlight,
   "And here they lie in the dark all night.

32 "This warning take, thy duty learn,
   "'Tis ill for you, if I return.

33 "There's crowing now the rooster red,
   "And back to the earth must go the dead;

34 "And now I hear the black cock crow,
   "Heaven's gate is open, and I must go.

35 "Now crows the white return of day,
   "A moment more I dare not stay."

36 Whenever hound was heard to whine,
   They gave the children bread and wine.

37 Whenever hound was heard to bark,
   They thought the dead walk'd in the dark.

38 Whenever hound was heard to howl,
They thought they saw a corpse's cowl.

NOTES.

c. 1. The expression here translated *up the land* is in the original 'under öe'. It is one of those which have come into use to replace obsolete words that were wanted for the rime's sake. 'Under öe' means *under the island* literally, but it usually has no other sense than *away*. It is a corruption of the Old Norse 'ondundr ey' *to the land*.

c. 8. 'Hunger and hate' seems to have been a common alliteration. It occurs over and over again in Layamon's Brut as well as in Danish poems, agreeably to the adage 'where want comes in at the door, love flies out of the window.' In this passage it is probably mutual hate among themselves that the stepmother threatens.

c. 33. The necessity of the dead returning to their graves at cockcrow is an old superstition and very general. See Notes to Sir Ogey and Lady Elsey. No. III.

XXXVI.

SABBATH BREAKING.

This ballad is said to be founded on fact. Two gentlemen, whose names according to Anne Crabbe, the lady whose manuscript has been adopted for the text, were Nilus Hawk and Jenus Maar (Martin), went out to hunt on an Easter morning. The hare, which they were chasing, escaped, and their dogs fell upon each other, which led to a quarrel between the gentlemen, and their death at each other's hands. There is still a monument, she says, in the church of No-dagger, in which they are represented on horseback with spears in their hands, and this she had seen herself in the year 1610. It is doubtful however, says Grundtvig, whether the monument, that the lady saw, had any thing to do with the story. It is probably, like another one usually taken for a representation of Swain Felding, an ancient sculpture of the crucifixion with Roman soldiers round the cross.

There is a very similar English legend in Sheldon's Minstrelsy of the English Borders. A knight named Mordyngton rode out fox-hunting on a Sunday, and suddenly lost sight of the fox which he was chasing. The rest of the company after a long and fruitless search for it rode home, but Mordyngton declared he

would ride till Doomsday rather than not catch it.
Presently up rode Satan in disguise, and offered him
a fresh horse, a black one, in exchange for his own,
which was tired. Mordyngton mounted it, and still
rides it, and will do so till Doomsday. It is he who
is the Wild Huntsman.

The sirnames in this ballad are uniformly the same
in all copies of it, but their Christian names are often
transposed.

There is a Swedish version of it in Arwidsson,
who says that it was formerly very widely spread
over Scandinavia.

Sabbath breaking.

Grundtv. II. 603. Dan. Vis. III. 322. Oehl. p. 271. Grimm
p. 183. Arw. II. 68. R. Warr. p. 170.

1 Sir Jonas Hawk and Sir Nilus Mard
   Two comrades dear were they,
And rode together in chase of game
   The morning of Easter day.

2 They pass'd the cloister, they pass'd the church,
   Nor had they a thought of mass;
But hasten'd away with hawks and hounds
   Off into the wild morass.

3 By church and cloister alike they rode,
   And scorn'd any mass to hear,
And came on the heath, and told their dreams,
   The weary way to cheer.

4 "It seem'd, as over the bridge I rode,
　"My horse with a sudden bound
　"Had started and thrown me off his back,
　"And trod on me on the ground."

5 "And didst thou seem, Sir Nilus Mard,
　　"Across a bridge to ride?
　"'This vision doth surely, trust my words,
　　"Some evil for us betide."

6 Thus all so friendly these comrades rode
　　And came to a wooded hill;
　"'True, true, Sir Jonas, the dream I have dream'd,
　　"Does certainly bode us ill.

7 "My horse so wildly rear'd and plunged,
　　"My boots were full of blood,
　"And senseless he threw me upon the turf,
　　"And ran to the forest stud."

8 But onward they rode, nor gave their dreams
　　One further thought or care,
　For near them a tiny creature ran,
　　They took it to be a hare.

9 The creature spake with a human voice,
　　And utter'd the words so plain;
　"Sir Nilus, hark thee! recall thy dogs,
　　"For me thou wilt chase in vain.

10 "A steak of my body thou wilt not broil,
　　"Though hunting me all the day,
　"But when thou art come on the open field,
　　"A different game wilt play.

11 "Aye tho' thou huntest me all day long,
   "I come not beneath thy knife;
   "But sure as thou dost so, trust my words,
   "Thy comrade will lose his life."

12 "Sir Nilus, aware!" Sir Jonas cried
   With loud and derisive shout,
   "The hare is making for yonder wood;
   "Now what are your dogs about?

13 "Yourself will have train'd those precious hounds,
   "May well of the pack be vain;
   "They run as swiftly on salty sea,
   "As over the grassy plain!"

14 "Ride on," replied Sir Nilus Mard,
   While anger heav'd his breast,
   "Ride whither thou wilt, thou basely born,
   "But make not my hounds thy jest.

15 "Ride whither thou wilt, thou basely born,
   "Nor stop to chide at a hound,
   "Perhaps thou mayest thy father find,
   "Go scour the country round."

16 "No bastard nor fatherless child am I,
   "For father! — I do know mine,
   "He left to me household stuff and land,
   "That never did one of thine."

17 They drew their circle upon the ground
   In midst of the wild black heath,
   And there they closed in an angry fight,
   And struggled for life and death.

18 They fought for a day, they fought for two,
    Alone on the moory plain,
  Nor would they either the circle quit
    Till one had the other slain.

19 And there lay both those gentlemen,
    And slowly they bled to death;
  And off their horses, and hawks and hounds
    Fled wildly across the heath.

20 And they fought too, those noble steeds,
    As were they with fury fill'd;
  And hound beside them was match'd with hound,
    Till each had the other kill'd.

21 Ah! luckless the hounds they bred and train'd,
    The cause of so deadly strife,
  Two comrades for them in combat fell,
    And bootlessly lost their life.

22 The gentle Mettelille, sorely wept,
    Sir Nilus's youthful bride,
  And Sidselille, she, fair lovely maid,
    Sat sorrowing, till she died.

23 And so I counsel you each and all,
    Ride not to the healthful chase,
  Till, late or early, you've been to church,
    And pray'd to your God for grace.

NOTES.

St. 13. As this is evidently said tauntingly, and meant as an insult, I have ventured here to alter the personal pronoun from the first to the second. In the original the speaker says of his own hounds, that they run over the sea.

St. 19. This image of the hawks and hounds going astray on the death or absence of their master is a favourite one. So in Lord Beichan

> My hounds they all go masterless,
> My hawks they flee from tree to tree.

and is very effectively introduced into one of the finest ballads in any language 'The twa corbies' Moth. p. 7.

St. 20. Such a combat among horses deserted by their masters actually took place, when Romano embarked his men to return from Holstein to Spain.

XXXVII.

THE CRUEL SISTER.

In this ballad we have an instance of the wide dispersion of a tale rather singular than pretty. It is essentially the same in the Scottish as in the Danish, and is equally popular in the other Scandinavian countries, Sweden, Norway, Iceland, and the Faroe islands as in Denmark. The Scottish ballad will be found in Scott V. II. p. 79 Jamieson V. I. p. 50 and p. 315. Buchan V. II. p. 128 (but much tampered with) Aytoun V. I. p. 194. Bell p. 206.

The very affecting refusal of the drowning sister in B. to give up her lover is found in all the Norwegian and Icelandic copies, and in one of the Swedish. The Scotch, Faroese and most of the Swedish ones let her resign him.

There is a German story in Grimm's Kindermärchen No. 28, in which a young man murders his brother in order to get the king's daughter. Many years after a herdsman finds the bones, and makes of one of them a mouthpiece to his horn, which, as he sets it to his lips, plays

>Ach du liebes Hirtelein,
>Du bläst auf mein Knöchelein;
>Mein Bruder hat mich erschlagen,
>Unter der Brücke begraben.

But hark, my pretty shepherd boy!
Thou blowest on my bone:
My brother kill'd and buried me
Below the bridge of stone.

All these stories have a great general similarity with such differences as would seem to imply an extremely ancient origin and long period during which they have passed unwritten from one generation to another, and from one country to another, and as this particular ballad is one of those which have been most confidently brought forward to prove by their similarity to English and Scotch ballads on the same subject, that we must have derived them from the same source at a very remote period, when we formed one nation with the continental Germans, the following piece is given here, from the Esthian language, to show that the same argument would include that alien nation in our family circle, and that all such reasoning is fallacious. The translation is from the German of Neus.

THE LYRE.
Grundtv. II. 512.

Along the footpath sang the dames,
Along the footpath through the mead,
On village green there sang the brides.
On churchyard path sang I the while,
Within the church, within the pale —
"My sisters in law they murdered me,
With heavy millstone struck me down,

With whetted bill-hook mangled me."
And whither carried they the corpse?
To yonder moor where berries grow.
But what grew there from out of it?
A graceful birch-tree up I sprang,
A pretty bush I rose to view.
What of that pretty birch was made?
The birch was hewn, and made a lyre,
Was like a viol carved and shaped.
Of what were made the tuneful strings?
Of hair from her, the lovely bride,
Of locks that deck'd the house-chick's head.
But where are now the minstrels all,
Should draw the tones from lyre so sweet?
"My little brother, hark, my dear,
Go carry thou the lyre to hall,
There on the couch's edge recline,
And touch with thumb the sounding strings,
Thy finger-ends among them ply,
And drop the hammer lustily."
But sad the tune her brother play'd,
And full of woe the orphan's lyre,
As when the Wierland maidens wept,
And Harrien's brides were full of woe,
As though she left her father's house,
As though she left her mother's home,
To go to share her husband's house,
To dwell a wife beside her spouse.

In Talvj's Slavonian Literature p. 329 there is a ballad something similar in its general drift. A mother curses her daughter, who thereupon becomes a maple tree, from which two young minstrels make a fiddle, which when it is played before her recalls to her mind her daughter's sad fate. The tree in this tale talks to the minstrels, but not the fiddle to the mother. The idea is not entirely one of modern times, for it

occurs in Ovid's story of Syrinx, of whom it is said
that after she was turned into a cane, she

"Effecisse sonum tenuem similemque querenti.'
Metam. L. 1. 708.

'Sighed a soft note like one who made complaint.'

Unfortunately for the interesting theory of the extreme antiquity of this ballad and its origin in some common home of our ancestors, Mr. E. F. Rimbault has discovered that it was composed in the 17th century by a Doctor in Divinity, James Smith, who was born about 1604, and became canon and chaunter in Exeter Cathedral. A copy of it printed in 1656 is appended to his article in Notes and Queries Vol. V. p. 591. and is the same as that printed in Jamieson Vol. I. p. 315.

The cruel Sister. A.

Grundtv. II. p. 512. A. Sven. Folkv. I. 81.

1 There lived an honest man and true,
   O might I follow thee!
   And daughters had but only two;
   So dupest thou not me!

2 The younger bright as is the sun,
   But black as dirt the elder one.

3 The younger suitors came to woo,
   With th' elder none would have to do.

4 The younger loom and shuttle plied,
   The elder slept at chimney side.

5 The elder took her sister's hand,
"Come, let us go to yonder strand.

6 "To yonder strand let us repair,
"And wash ourselves so clean and fair."

7 As on the younger stepp'd so gay,
The wind would with her ringlets play.

8 The elder follow'd close behind,
And anger fill'd her sullen mind;

9 As on a stone the younger trod,
She thrust her into the rushing flood.

10 "O hear me, sister, let me live,
"And thee my best gold cup I give."

11 "I'll get thy best gold cup, and more,
"But thou shalt never come ashore."

12 "O hear me, sister, let me live,
"And thee my buckle of gold I give."

13 "Thy buckle of gold I'll have, and more,
"But thou shalt never come ashore."

14 "O hear me, sister, let me live,
"And thee my trulove I will give."

15 "Thy trulove I shall get, and more,
"But thou shalt never come ashore."

16 By God's high will a tempest blew,
And on the coast her body threw.

17 Two minstrels walked along the strand,
And saw the maiden float to land.

THE CRUEL SISTER.

18 They took her golden hair so long,
   And therewithal their fiddle strung.

19 "To yon great house we'll now repair,
   "Their merry wedding-feast to share."

20 The first string sang a doleful sound,
   "The bride her younger sister drown'd."

21 The second string, as that they tried,
   "In terror sits the youthful bride."

22 The third string sang beneath their bow,
   "And surely now her tears will flow."

23 The bride stripp'd off her golden band,
   And laid it on the minstrel's hand.

24 Tuesday began her heart to ache,
   And Thursday night smoked at the stake.

NOTE.

There is great variety in the different copies of this ballad. The place at which the father lived is in this one called Orlog, in another Simonsby, in a third Sönderbro, in a fourth Odense By, in others unnamed.

The conclusion varies still more. Ms. F gives the drowning scene thus,

10 "O sister, sister save my life,
   "And take my silver-hilted knife."

11 "Sink, sink, come not again to life,
   "I safely get thy silver'd knife."

12 "O help me out of the stifling ooze,
"And take my silver-buckled shoes."

13 "Sink, sink, come not from out the ooze,
"I safely get thy buckled shoes."

14 "Help, sister, help for mercy's sake!
"And e'en my dearest trulove take."

15 "Sink to the bottom, sister, sink,
"Thy trulove is safely mine, I think."

The cruel Sister. B.
Grundtv. V. II. p. 515 E. See Arw. II. 139.

1 There came a wooing suitors two,
And both the younger maid to woo.
'Tis merry at summertide.

2 To her alone their court they paid,
And much it vex'd the elder maid.

3 "Dear little sister, take my hand,
"And go with me to yonder strand."

4 "But why then go to the water-side,
"When all our clothes are wash'd and dried?"

5 "We 'll wash ourselves as white as snow,
"And be more like two sisters so."

6 With flowing hair the younger went,
On ill designs the elder bent.

7 The younger maid stepp'd on a stone,
   And by the elder down was thrown.

8 "O dearest sister, let me live,
   "And thee my gilded shrine I'll give."

9 "What profits me thy gilded shrine,
   "Unless thy trulove too is mine?"

10 "Him give I not my life to save,
   "Nay, rather sink beneath the wave."

11 "Float on then, float away to sea;
   "Thy trulove safely falls to me."

12 A storm from th' east began to blow,
   And drive the body to and fro.

13 The sea roll'd in, so hard it blew,
   And on the coast the maiden threw.

14 It chanced two minstrels paced the strand,
   And saw the body float to land.

15 They took her locks of yellow hair,
   With them they strung their bows so fair.

16 They then cut off her fingers small,
   And made their fiddle-screws withal.

17 So to the nearest town they went,
   To share the feast and merriment.

18 A lively tune they fain would play,
   The fiddle sang a piteous lay;

19 And ever, when they drew their bow,
   Counted its wrongs, and told its woe.

20 It said "My sister sits as bride,
"And he is my trulove at her side."

NOTE

c. 10. This as Grundtvig remarks is an incomparably prettier turn than in the other versions, where she offers her lover.

XXXVIII.

SIR MORTEN OF FOGELSONG.

This, Grundtvig observes, is one of the many variations of the Wild huntsman, so popular among all Northern nations. It is based on the idea that the dead man cannot find rest in the grave, till an injustice, which he has committed during life, has been repaired. The blood in the shoes is agreeable to the northern superstition, that in case of any absent relative being murdered, the armour, sword or shoes of the deceased would be covered with blood.

This piece is considered by the Danish and Swedish editors to bear intrinsic evidence of very high antiquity. The locality is uncertain, since there are many places that bear the name of Fugl-sang, or Birdsong.

Sir Morten of Fogelsong.
Grundtv. II. 501. Dan. Vis. I. 215. Arwids II. 106.
R. Warr. p. 179.

1 Sir Morten, lord of Fogelsong,
   Rode over the greenwood lawn,
And there he breath'd a poison blast,
   About the morning dawn.
Dead rides Sir Morten of Fogelsong.

2   He gave the cloister his good grey horse,
      The church a sum of gold,
    And died, and with a solemn dirge
      Was laid beneath the mould.

3   All heap'd with earth, as best they could,
      They left his buried corse,
    But ere the toll of midnight bell
      He rose and mounted horse.

4   A knight there was, Sir Folmer Skot,
      Rode over hill and dale,
    And after him Sir Morten rode,
      And pray'd him hear his tale.

5   "O stay, thou good Sir Folmer Skot,
      "And kindly lend a ear,
    "And by my holy Christian faith
      "No harm hast thou to fear."

6   "But first, Sir Morten, tell me how
      "Thou ridest here to day,
    "And only yesternight a corse
      "We laid thee in the clay?"

7   "It's not for doom I am riding here,
      "It's not at court to sue,
    "But only for a plot of ground
      "To two small orphans due.

8   It's not because of buried gold,
      It's not to venge a wrong;

But for those orphans' little field
Forsworn to Fogelsong.

9 "Now haste to Lady Mettelille,
"And tell her my request,
"She give those orphans back the field,
"And let my soul have rest.

10 "And tell the Lady Mettelille,
"If doubt should cross her mind,
"That close beside my chamber door
"My slippers she may find.

11 "Those two nightslippers, where they stand
"Beside the chamber door,
"Tonight ere toll of midnight bell
"Shall both be full of gore."

12 "Go then, go rest thy weary bones,
Sir Morten, noble knight,
"For on my Christian faith I swear,
"Those orphans get their right."

13 And all in black Sir Morten went
Down to his dark abode,
And black were both his hawk and hound,
And troop that with him rode.

14 The noble Lady Mettelille
Obey'd her lord's request,
And gave the children back their field,
And so his soul had rest.

NOTE.

St. 13. The black hound seems to be a necessary figure in these apparitions. So in the Spanish Romance of Don Pedro the spectre that warns him on the hunting field. Wolf & Hofm. I. 212

"a su lado de trailla
traia un perro negro."

'at his side in a leash he led a black hound.'

XXXIX.

MARIBO WELL.

The scene of this legend is the island Laaland. The Algrave according to Syv was a count from Aaleholm. Grimm p. 507. remarks that the German story of the Machandel tree rests on the same superstition about collecting the limbs of the deceased. The Abbey at Maribo was built in 1416, and if the ballad was made by its monks, it must be admitted that they understood how to advertise a watering place. One is tempted to think that this superstition of holy water restoring the dead may have originated with an ill understood notion of the power of baptism to give a new life. The cauldron of Medea, and the fountain of health in Florida will occur to the reader as other instances of a somewhat similar credulity. The horrid barbarity of serving up the limbs of a slaughtered person at the table of a friend may be derived from the Greek story of Thyestes, of whom it is said that, when he discovered that he had been feasting upon one of his own children at the table of his brother Atreus, the sun went backwards in its course with horror. The same mode of vengeance is found in other ballads as for instance in a fine old Flemish one in Uhland's Alte Deutsche Balladen called Brunenþergh p. 161. Willems p. 135. Fallersleben p. 34.

> Si leiden hem op eenen disch,
> Si sneden hem uut sijn herte frisch,
> Si gavent der liefste t'eten
> Tot eender morghen-beten.
>
> They laid him down on a table board,
> They cut his heart from out his breast.
> They gave it to her he once adored,
> A dainty bit for her dinner drest.

This also was a husband's vengeance upon the lover of his wife. It ended more tragically than in our Danish ballad, for the lady ate of the dish, and died upon hearing what it was. There is a similar tale in Boccacio's Decameron, the 9th novel of the 4th day, in which the lady is represented as throwing herself from the window when she learns the truth. It is said to be founded upon fact, such vengeance having really been taken upon the troubadour William de Cabetaing by his lord, Raymond de Segliano. A similar story is told of Fayel and De Coucy.

In the story of the Machandel, or almond tree, to which Grimm alludes, the father eats all the flesh from the bones of his little son, who had been killed and cooked by the mother in law. The bones are buried beneath the tree, and a bird rises from the boughs, which sings the tale of the murder, and is eventually restored to his own shape, as a little boy. This does not appear to me to have any thing to do with the Danish ballad, which I am satisfied was an Allegory in the first place, or a misunderstood dogma of Christianity; as seems to be Grundtvig's opinion from his

titling it 'Livsvandet,' Water of Life, and placing
it among the Legendary ones.

Maribo Well.

Grundtv. II. 505. Dan. Vis. I. 316 Grimm p. 81.

1 The Algrave loud on his cornet blew,
    The long and weary night
  The Queen in her bower his signal knew.
    Of love I feel the might.

2 She call'd to her page "Run, boy, with speed,
  And hither to me the Algrave lead."

3 The Algrave he stood before her board;
  "What wish you, my Queen? why send me word?"

4 "Dear Algrave, if once the king were dead,
  I'd make thee lord of my gold so red."

5 "O softly! my Queen, hush! say not so;
  "There may be listeners; who can know?"

6 They thought full surely none else was near,
  The King had listened with heedful ear.

7 The king two servants was heard to call;
  "Go bid the Queen to the audience hall."

8 "Now tell me, my fair and graceful Queen,
  "What was it you told the Count yestre'en?"

9 "I told him no other than this, I vow,
  "Than just how great and how good wert thou."

10 The King two servants was heard to call;
"Go bid the Count to the audience hall."

11 "Now tell me, Sir Count, and tell me right,
"What told you the Queen of me last night?"

12 "I told her, and nothing else, I vow,
"How good and noble a king wast thou."

13 He bade his page boy "The cooks go call,
"And bid them come to the audience hall.

14 "Go, chop yon Algrave to pieces fine,
"And serve him up to the Queen to dine.

15 "Go, chop him to pieces as small as fish,
"And serve him up on the Queen's own dish."

16 The Queen saw what on the table came,
"Now that is surely no kind of game."

17 She look'd again, and she rightly guess'd,
"The count it must be, the cooks have dress'd."

18 To save him she knew was not too late,
And cull'd each morsel, the small and great.

19 She wrapp'd them up in an ermine fine,
And laid them all in a gilded shrine.

20 Those morsels she took, so chopp'd and rent,
And straight to the Maribo fountain went.

21 She dipp'd them where clearest the water ran,
"Stand up, stand up, thou Christian man!"

22 And up on his feet did the Algrave stand,
Thank God for his mercy, and leave the land.

XL.

ST. STEPHEN, AND HEROD.

This rather ridiculous legend was taken down by Erik Pontoppidan from the lips of an old beggar woman at the beginning of the last century, as a specimen of the remains of papistry among the Danish people. The old woman was singing it at his door, and upon being asked by him whether she believed it, "God forbid," said she, "that I should doubt it." It had already been alluded to by Syv in 1695.

It exists in a more extended form in the Faroe islands, but without the first five verses. This version improves upon the miracle by representing the cock as having been not only roasted but cut in two.

In English we find it in Ritson's 'Ancient English Songs' page 83. as a 'Carol for St. Stephen's day.' In this English ballad Stephen is represented as a kitchen boy or waiter in the hall, but in Denmark and Sweden as a stable boy. As patron of horses he was acknowledged by all German and Scandinavian races, and in England therefore as well as elsewhere.

The story of the cock was originally applied to other saints as St. James, St. Peter, or the Virgin.

The oldest account of it is in Vinc. Bellovacensis from an author who lived about 1200. Two friends sat down to dinner in Bologna, and one bade the other to carve the cock, which he did, so that, as he said, not St. Peter or our Lord himself could put it together again. The cock sprang up, clapped his wings and crowed, scattering the sauce over the two friends, and rendering them lepers till the day of their death. The same miracle is related as having occurred to prove the innocence of persons falsely accused, and is found in the legends of Spain, Britany, Italy and Sclavonian countries. How it came to be appropriated to St. Stephen does not appear. The boar's head, which he brings in, was the established Yule-tide dish of the North in old heathen times, as well as afterwards. This English ballad is of the beginning of the 15th century, and is much older than any other on the subject.

CAROL FOR SAINT STEPHEN'S DAY.

1 Saint Stephen was a clerk in king Herodes hall,
 And served him of bread and cloth, as ever king befalle.

2 Stephen out of kitchen came with boar's head on honde,
 He saw a star was fair and bright, over Bethlem stonde.

3 He cast adown the boar's head, and went into the hall;
 I forsake thee, king Herodes, and thine werkes all.

4 I forsake thee, king Herodes, and thine werkes all,
 There is a child in Bethlem born, is better than we all.

5 What aileth thee, Stephen, what is thee befalle?
 Lacketh thee either meat or drink in king Herodes hall?

⁶ Lacketh me neither meat nor drink in king Herodes hall,
There is a child in Bethlem born, is better than we all.

⁷ What aileth thee, Stephen, art thou wode? or thou ginnest
    to brede?
Lacketh thee either gold or fee, or any rich weede?

⁸ Lacketh me neither gold nor fee, ne none rich weede,
There is a child in Bethlem born, shall help us at our need.

⁹ That is all so sooth, Stephen, all so sooth, I wiss,
As this capon crow shall, that lyth here in my dish.

¹⁰ That word was not so soon said, that word in that hall,
The capon crew: 'Christus natus est' among the lordes all.

¹¹ Riseth up my tormentors, by two, and all by one,
And leadeth Stephen out of town, and stoneth him with
    stone.

¹² Token they Stephen, and stoned him in the way,
And therefore is his even on Christes owen day.

befalle happen'd. viz as well as ever happen'd to a king.
wode mad.
brede upbraid. Dan. bebreide. In Chaucer the line 'For veray wo out of his wit he braide' is explained 'he went or ran out of his wits.'
weed dress.

As to Saint Stephen's connexion with horses — this seems to have originated from the accident that his holiday fell on the day that in old heathen times was dedicated to Freya, in honour of whom horse-races were held, with other amusements, which the people upon the introduction of Christianity were unwilling to forego, and which they transferred to Stephen, when they no longer dared to worship Freya.

It is a curious instance of the tenacity with which nations preserve old customs, that so many centuries after heathen gods and goddesses had been given up and forgotten, people still unwittingly preserved the rites established in honour of them.

The following Danish ballad, as observed by Grundtvig, from whose valuable annotations most of the above has been taken, is a testimony to the old Christian legend of Stephen and Herod, and to the heathen superstition respecting horses at Yule-tide.

St. Stephen and Herod.

Grundtv. II. 525.

1 A virgin pure was risen on earth,
  The rose of womankind,
 The fairest maid in all this world,
  For Queen of heaven design'd.

2 Her cheeks were like the roses red,
  Her neck as ermine fair;
 Because so sweet a maid she was,
  Our Lord was she to bear.

3 In glory th' angel Gabriel came,
  To Mary sent was he;
 "'Tis from the Lord of hosts I come,
 "Christ's mother you shall be."

4 Answer the pious Mary made,
   As God put in her mind;
   "His holy will be done: in me
   "His handmaid he shall find."

5 For two score weeks with child she went
   Without or pain or care;
   On Yule-night, by His own high will,
   Her blessed Lord she bare.

6 Saint Stephen saw the star's bright shine,
   As he his horses drave;
   "Of truth is now the Prophet born,
   "Who all the world shall save."

7 "On Stephen's tale," King Herod said,
   "No faith will I bestow,
   "Unless this roasted cock stand up,
   "And clap his wings and crow."

8 Straight clapp'd his wings the cock, and crow'd,
   "*Our Lord is born to-night.*"
   From off his throne King Herod fell,
   And swoon'd away for fright.

9 Uprose the King and mounted horse,
   To Bethlehem town to ride;
   He fain that little child would kill,
   Which all his power defied.

10 But Mary took in arms her babe,
    Joseph his ass's rein,
    And so through Jewish land they rode
    To Egypt's sandy plain.

11 Full fourteen thousand babies small
   The tyrant caused to slay;
   Jesus, ere sank the sun to rest,
   Was thirty miles away.

END OF THE FIRST VOLUME.

www.ingramcontent.com/pod-product-compliance
Lightning Source LLC
Chambersburg PA
CBHW022116300426
44117CB00007B/740